Dogs of Meadowbrook

William Schwenn

PublishAmerica
Baltimore

© 2008 by William Schwenn.
All rights reserved. No part of this book may be reproduced, stored in a retrieval system or transmitted in any form or by any means without the prior written permission of the publishers, except by a reviewer who may quote brief passages in a review to be printed in a newspaper, magazine or journal.

First printing

ISBN: 1-60672-366-9
PUBLISHED BY PUBLISHAMERICA, LLLP
www.publishamerica.com
Baltimore

Printed in the United States of America

There are some simple truths…

and the dogs know what they are.

—Joseph Duemer

Table of Contents

Foreword 7
Acknowledgments 9
Prologue 11

Part One: Assembling the Pack 15
    Chapter 1: The Legend 17
    Chapter 2: The Borders 29
    Chapter 3: Chelsea 38
    Chapter 4: Ruffy 41
    Chapter 5: Freckles 52
    Chapter 6: Scamp 60

Part Two: Meadowbrook Life and Times 67
    Chapter 7: Boss Tag 69
    Chapter 8: Windi-Woo 79
    Chapter 9: Ball Games 82
    Chapter 10: Border Patrol 88
    Chapter 11: It's a Jungle out There 91
    Chapter 12: Seasonal Stuff 100
    Chapter 13: Magical Field 120
    Chapter 14: Characters 129
    Chapter 15: Home 140
    Chapter 16: At Day's End 147

Part Three: Beyond the Boundaries 151
    Chapter 17: Going to Town 153
    Chapter 18: Field Visitors 157

Chapter 19: Refuge 162
Chapter 20: Chance Encounter 168
Chapter 21: Missing 174

Part Four: Partings 181
Chapter 22: The Breed's the Thing 183
Chapter 23: Tag's to the Last 188
Chapter 24: Travelin' On 192
Chapter 25: Tag's Last Job 196
Chapter 26: Chelsea Stays Home... 207
Chapter 27: Farewell, Meadowbrook 212

Epilogue 215

Foreword

People who write about their dogs—and their lives with their dogs—always *mean* well. Their dogs are heroes, special friends, confidants, substitutes for human companionship, buddies. People have written truthfully that dogs in their lives gave them understanding, comfort, fun, and hope when none was available elsewhere, and in ways no one else could provide. People want to tell the world that their furry pals are bigger than words can describe, and should be recognized as the most magical, most worthy, most wonderful beings on the planet. But if that was all I was after in recounting the tales of Meadowbrook, I wouldn't do it, for as much as I loved the characters in this book, adoration of pet-partners has been written by more capable writers, some of whom lived more astounding stories than I have experienced.

Meadowbrook was always a special place, offering mysteries and wonders of its own that my wife Mary and I simply and gratefully accepted during our fourteen years there. Our dogs—living lives sometimes known only to them, sometimes shared with us—added their own magic to make Meadowbrook what it ultimately became. And what it became was a place so uniquely blended with them that my wife and I could not live there without them. The richness of their spirits, the uniquely doggy way they invented fun as they explored the wonders of their habitat, and their weaving of their daily lives into ours, wrote in time a story whose ending had to move us away from there if we were to continue anywhere. Such is the mystical nature of some happenings in a world that often ignores—if it ever notices—feelings and events that are outside the numbing chores and daily routines of human existence.

My purpose in accurately telling the lives we shared with our dogs of Meadowbrook is to confirm that the really important stuff of life is ridiculously simple, and some of it cannot be rationally explained. Dogs teach us that—if we listen.

Acknowledgments

These are easy.

Ratches—our first. The legend. The standard by which all others have been, and will always be measured. The one, who, like I've heard it said of firstborn, bore the brunt of my inadequate efforts to be a better human being; I wish I had the chance to start over with him. He deserves that.

Tag and Windi—the brains of the Meadowbrook outfit (human element included). They found jobs to do and did them exceedingly well—so well, in fact, that my wife and I aspire to be a fraction as capable of doing "our" appointed work in this life as they were. Tag showed all of us what it was to be a genuine pack leader; Windi showed us courage—and most amazingly, a playful nature blended with it. The Meadowbrook story is so much about them, it could not have happened without them.

Chelsea—Miss Sunshine. In every respect, she was the very definition of *happy*. A doggy dog, who took my heart with her when she left us; it is only by remembering moments with her that I have gained any of it back.

Ruffin (Ruffy)—a gentle giant. He was Tag's special charge. His brindle coat and 100-pound stature brought out the "ooh's" and "aah's" from everyone. He was a magnificent sweetheart.

Freckles—ghost dog. A free spirit, a chaser of butterflies—until they caught her. Dizzy, delicate of nature, iron constitution, born to run in the fields. An associate member of the pack, she was always *around*, but never really *with* us. Curiously, hers was the closest to the spirit of Meadowbrook.

Scamper (Scraps)—Cleopatra eyes, willful beyond her size, tough beyond her comfort, loving beyond this world—literally. The final addition to our six-pack, she is with us still—in her assuredly *own* way.

Mary—the love of my life, my editor, the angel in my life who continually reveals to me the wonders of dogs and most everything else good that this planet has to offer, and my partner. William Penn said it best: "She is but half a wife who is not, nor is capable of being, a *friend*."

Prologue

Where to begin telling a story?

"Begin at the beginning" has a nice ring to it...but I wonder how helpful that is, really. I don't think a story ever does have a *true* beginning. Everything that has ever happened started before...*that*.

Two baseball teams ready to go: one positioned out on the field, most of the other one in a dugout, pitcher on the mound holding the ball, batter in his box, catcher in his squat, umpire raises one hand and (finally) says: "Play ball!"

Ask anyone there, "When did the story of this game start?" and what do you think you'll hear in response? This isn't hard stuff—except that the guy on the mound is a surprise starter fresh from the bullpen, courtesy of a temper tantrum by the regular rotation guy, who, two hours earlier, lashed out at nobody there with his throwing hand in a badly timed gesture that found the edge of the door to his locker, which he did while still fuming over a domestic squabble the night before. The story of *this* game started with—*what?*—a stupid locker door? The regular starter's marriage? A bad temper-tantrum habit he picked up during adolescence? A case of bad parenting when he was four? A bad seed?

I could start the story of the Meadowbrook dogs with (think, "Play ball!") the day all of them were actually, finally there at a country home my wife and I called "Meadowbrook." That would be okay, I guess, if we had all come together there at the same time, but it didn't happen that way—not even close. In fact, having dogs at Meadowbrook wouldn't have happened without nearly a dozen years of our learning something about how human life can meaningfully, amazingly, fundamentally interact with a canine companion—especially if that canine is a partner in, and a teacher of, life. Heck, Meadowbrook wouldn't have happened in the first place if it hadn't been for...well, that's the point: everything we do and don't do has consequences. *If I hadn't had such a great game when the scout happened to be in the stands that one day of that one year; if I had taken the regular route instead of the short cut; if I had slept a half-hour longer that morning; if I hadn't gone back to the office to pick up the book I had left there. If, if, if....* Accidents happen. Fate steps in. It's all a roll of the dice, right? No?

Pick any day of your life, and try connecting the dots from sun-up to sundown; and if you manage to do that, alter just *one* of them, and project how the remainder of that day would have gone. Makes you think. Scary stuff. *Nah, not really*: Not when you think about what life *really* is. And what, pray tell, is life? An adventure. A continuous, streaming adventure. Life *happens*. We can try to tie it up in a nice package if we want to, but we'll just as likely find out soon enough that we wrapped the wrong box. Just live it. Everything we do starts right now. 'Course, the story of what we do started with whatever happened before the universe started. Anybody got time to hear *that* version?

A simple question: when does anything start?

The Meadowbrook game began, I suppose, a long time and a long way from there, when a six-week-old pup took us home, and began his journey into our hearts.

****

Staring uncertainly at a run-down, one-car garage standing by itself on an out-of-the-way street in an aging section of Washington, D.C., we wondered whether the Pets ad we called about was such a good idea after all. In the damp, cold, late-winter morning, Mary and I were skinny kids in our mid-20s, recent purchasers of a tiny house in the Northern Virginia suburbs, giddy with happiness: our house was on a corner lot, and was totally fenced. Now, after frustrating months of apartment claustrophobia, we could finally have a dog!

The ad was simple, but alluring: "Lab-mix puppies for sale, $75." Next to those that wanted $150 or more, this one spoke to our poverty-level incomes better. As excited as we were to launch ourselves into a life with our very own dog, we weren't too sure about how this little venture was going. The area we found ourselves in that morning looked rough. Shivering, we glanced around again at the grayness of everything: chipped concrete stoops, behind them crumbling townhouses needing paint, litter everywhere, the neighborhood struggling to come alive and face another insistent day. We looked at each other, then back to the garage where the girl on the phone the day before said we should meet her.

Seeing no signs of life, we were wondering whether to knock on the large garage door, climb the outside stairway to a door on the upper level to look through a window, or leave. Just then, a sleepy young woman appeared, murmured, "Hi," by way of introduction, and led us over to a makeshift box-and-blanket affair beside the garage. I peeked over the top, and found a bunch of lab-mix puppies tumbling all over each other, filling the box with those noisy little tummy-grunt sounds puppies make. The owner of the golden retriever mom and her pups lived in a small apartment above the garage. She seemed sweet, living life simply with her dog, and now her companion had puppies, apparently from a successful date with a black lab. Black labs must be fairly irresistible: there are about twelve gazillion black lab-mix puppies in America at any given time.

We didn't get to chat very long. Mary had just begun to paw around in the tangle of fur and tummies when an all-black member of the gang stepped out of the group, and walked with a purpose toward our car parked at the curb like he knew it was ours. Like he knew *he* was ours. More, like he knew *we* were *his*.

Not much to say after that; it's nice when others or events make decisions for us, and this little fellow had clearly done that. What a remarkably self-assured, almost trot over to our car, leaving all of us behind, speechless. Some stammering, some shrugging of our shoulders at each other, and I found myself fishing into my wallet for $75….big bucks in 1974, especially for newlyweds with a mortgage.

For now, it was time to catch up to our guy—something I would spend his lifetime doing.

Part One

Assembling the Pack

Chapter 1
The Legend

For such a little fella he seemed supremely confident, quietly strong—worthy of a special name. "Jake" wasn't going to get it. It had to be something that suggested more self-confidence than blocky toughness: something *different*—maybe something starting with an "rrr" sound...because...I...*liked* the "rrr" sound. Out of nowhere, "Ratches." I said it aloud to Mary. She was unimpressed. I tried others, but there it was: Ratches—Patches, except with an R instead of a P, I'd later tell everybody. To tell the truth, *I* thought it was a strange name, too, but it felt right. As we all know from listening to songs, you hear them often enough, they sometimes grow on you; anything repeated long enough starts to sound normal. That's my discomforting theory as to why a lot of what we humans do happens.

From the start, we thought he should get used to living his own life since we both worked away from the home. As a part of that, we also figured he would be better off getting acclimated to his own house whenever we weren't there—or awake—to play with him. So at bedtime that first night, we set him inside his dog house, tucked under a huge quince bush off the back corner of our small, starter home. "G'night, Ratches," I called out one last time before closing the back door. "Sleep tight. Stay warm."

"Think he'll be okay out there, Skip?" worried Mary. "It feels a little chilly already. Maybe we should bring him in the first night; he won't feel so alone or lost. What do you think?"

"Nah...he'll be fine. If he's going to be an outside dog at night, he needs to start out that way."

Yeah, well, it isn't your *puppy paws sittin' out there in the cold all night*, she thought.

But she went along with it, if not entirely in spirit. Besides, it was a good plan: train the dog to be comfortable in his own element, because we humans were not going to be around during the work days (except when we were sick—and what fun were we going to be then?) *It's important that we set the tone the first night*, I thought. *Let him be. He'll be fine.* I was as *certain* about our dog's welfare as I was *ignorant—a cross poor Ratches would end up too often having to bear.*

Naturally, that first night turned out to be one of those uncommon, but not completely unheard of weather events in the suburbs of our nation's capital. Even after the earliest flowers had popped out, a random late-winter night there could be bone-chilling, and on this particular one the elements outdid themselves: through the wee hours after midnight, the temperature plunged, dipping to 7 degrees by morning's first light. When I cracked open the back door that morning, icy air seared the inside of my nose. *Yikes!* I called to our new puppy, but got no response (no real surprise, though, that he didn't answer to a name we'd only given him hours before). I looked over at the outside thermometer and…*Good Lord! Seven degrees?* I bolted down the steps and over to the doorway of his little house, leaned down, and called him again: "Ratches—you in there?—You *okay?*" Nothing. Now on my knees on the frozen ground, fearing the worst, I poked my head through his doorway and waited until my eyes grew accustomed to the dark interior. Against the blackness of the back of his house and army surplus wool blankets, I finally saw a pair of eyes peering back at me. I have often wondered what he was thinking at that moment: probably just as well I don't know. He got up, waddled past me into the world-turned-icebox, piddled, and as he padded back toward his house, glanced up and gave me his first, "When's breakfast?" look.

Okaaaay.

Ratches' first bark was a long time coming—a couple of months later, to be exact—long after we had decided he might not ever utter a word. Out behind our 750-square-foot house in our even tinier back yard, right next to our back door, lying on a cheap-o lawn chair on a weekend afternoon, with Ratches on my lap, I was startled when he suddenly sat up, looked me squarely in the eye, and studied me. After a minute, he let out one solid bark! That was all— just one high-pitched puppy-bark. *Hi. Just so you know, I've got a lot of work to do on you, and I intend to do it!* He continued to look at me, sizing me up I guess; then he turned around, and with his back to me, settled down on my stomach for a while—surveying the neighborhood, thinking his thoughts. Finally, he hopped off my lap, and trotted into his dog house to rest and plan.

It was weeks later before we were treated to another bark from this dog of few words.

Early on, we treated Ratches like a *dog*. What I knew about dogs wasn't that much, really. Growing up through grade school and high school, our family had a toy fox terrier, who was a great companion, but I was busy being a growing kid, paying attention to all the things that can consume every waking moment of a growing kid's existence: school, homework, sports, a few friends, dating, music. Not much time left to get to know one's dog. I knew our dog had feelings and moods, but that was about the extent of my doggy awareness. So when Mary and I brought Ratches home, I drew on my experience with dogs third-hand: from TV, watching other dogs in the parks, stuff like that. And one thing I was sure of was that dogs like to play catch with a ball. That had to be a fundamental, universal thing. The human throws a ball, the dog retrieves it.

Wrong. First time out, I tossed the tennis ball a short distance, Ratches' ears went up, he trotted on over, picked it up, and brought it back toward (but definitely not *to*) me, and let it fall to the ground. Then he looked off to the side at whatever else was going on in the world. I tossed it a second time. He looked at it roll along, away from us, with barely a hint of interest.

"Go get it, Ratches!" I excitedly told him. "Bring the ball! Go get the ball! Bring it back! Bring it here, boy!"

Nothing doing. Hardly a wag—just a little one, to be courteous. Looking up at me, like I was goofy. *I brought it to you already ... why'd you just throw it away again?*

I walked to get the ball, glad I hadn't thrown it a country mile. Walked back, to where our strange little dude was still sitting, studying me with the keen attention of a scientist, observing some new phenomenon. Holding the ball close to his muzzle for emphasis, I told him the obvious, in case he missed it the first time: "Go get the ball, Ratches!" as I tossed it thirty feet. This time, I followed it up with a frenzy of encouraging cheers. I think he got tired of listening to that, because he finally sprang from a sit to a jog over to the where the ball lay, picked it up (my heart nearly stopped, I was so pleased), held it, took a step back toward me, and "Ptooey," spit it out to the side, trotted on over *past* me and began exploring things other than me and my dumb ball-toss game.

Mary, having watched all this from a short distance, began to laugh, which really topped off my fun-with-dog session. "He doesn't see the *point* of it, honey," she said, clutching her mid-section, trying to speak while totally tickled.

"You threw the ball, and he brought it back. I think he figures that if you're going to keep throwing the ball away, why bother bringing it back to you?" Hearing her own words, she cracked up, and altogether lost it. *My wife, the comic.*

Well, that was the end of ball-toss with Ratches, the dog. It was, however, the beginning of my awareness of Ratches, the individual. Ratches, the *thinking* individual. Ratches, the personality with an emerging set of values, thoughts, philosophies, who could be a real partner in life. Mary got that early on; it took me longer.

Not giving up on Ratches-the-*dog*, I next tried to teach him a few key phrases that were important in our Carolina Tar Heel household. Rabid basketball fans, Mary and I thought it would be cool if he would learn "Go, Heels!" Getting him to bark even *once* turned out to be tough enough—he just wasn't "into" barking. Looking back on that later, we understood that he actually *thought* about things, and made good judgment calls as to what was needed or appropriate: to him, barking for barking's sake was, well, pointless. So, getting him to double-bark took a while. *We* practiced it a lot more than *he* did. Watching his face was a study in all the right things: so eager to please, he enthusiastically tried to get it, though for the life of him, he couldn't figure out what in the devil we were trying to get him to do, or why. After we were nearly hoarse from doing our best doggy impression of "bark-bark!" he finally mustered up some energy, and muffled a barely audible "Woof." So we bark-barked louder. He shifted his weight back and forth on his front legs, looking pained (like he was embarrassed), and finally gave it another quiet, "Woof."

So it went. The mental messages passed like ships in the night. (Us: *You're a dog! Why don't you just bark?*) (Ratches: *Why all the noise from you people? There's nothing to bark at!*) Eventually, the poor guy looked off to the side with a deep, explosive sigh. *No interpreter needed for that.*

I think as much out of exasperation as anything else, Ratches finally came up with a good, healthy "Bark!" Then, when we still looked so expectantly at him, feeling the desperation of our hope, he followed that one with another, admittedly less-potent, "Bark." *Close enough.* Give him a cookie treat. "Want to try it again, Ratches?" I begged.

Well, yeah—I get it now. Why didn't you show me the cookies before?

It is a testament to his devotion to us (and, yeah, the dog treats didn't hurt) that he went along with this nonsense as much as he did. He ultimately got the hang of it, and we were off and running with a "Go, Heels!" dog. His zeal got the better of him sometimes, though, so three (not two) barks came out, "Bark, bark, bark!"

"Aw, Ratches," I said, disappointed.

"I think he's saying, 'Go, Tar Heels,' Skip," chimed in Mary.

"Yeah—cool!" *Mary—ever the optimist.* We both pretended not to have heard his four-bark episodes. A good heart, eager to please and play along, this dog was a keeper. And, except for basketball game nights on TV, he was a quiet keeper—a dog of few words. A philosopher dog.

One night while I was out of town on business travel, this fellow-of-few-words woke Mary in the middle of the night with a barrage of barks. She tried to shush him from the front door, but with no luck: he kept at it, lunging at the fence, focused at something a ways up the street. Lights came on in one house after another as neighbors stirred to life amid the clamor, followed by the flashing blue lights of a police car. The next day, Ratches was recognized a neighborhood hero. It turns out he had interrupted a break-in. It was more than a little incredible that this "outside dog," who, despite constant late-night comings and goings of teenagers and other folks through the neighborhood, rarely barked at night, would choose this single time to make a ruckus and wake everybody up. Cool dude, this guy.

From glimpses on weekends and in the longer daylight hours of summer, we learned through the next four and a half years that Ratches was living his own individual, full life on that corner lot. Wagging his long, bushy tail, he greeted people of all ages as they walked by the fence—kids playing, adults exercising—and they called him by name. His favorite game (one the area teenagers never grew tired of) was racing cars along the inside of the fence facing the two streets. Over the years, those two straight stretches of ground looked like the track at Churchill Downs. Spotting a car coming down the main drag, and wanting to get a head start on it, Ratches, full of eager anticipation, headed down that stretch of fence on a tear, grinning the whole way, tongue flapping to the side. The more savvy and playful drivers sometimes slowed—even stopped—before getting to our yard, waiting for him to finish his solo run all the way down to the far end of the fence. As soon as he saw that he had made the run by himself, he'd barrel on back to the corner (starting point). Of course, the instant he arrived there, the car's engine roared to life, and the race was on!

Ratches was uprooted to Greensboro, North Carolina, where I pursued a career with a federal court. Unfortunately, the fenced yard there wasn't nearly as interesting for him: the problem wasn't so much that it was a smaller area, but that it was a *back* yard—removed from all the street action. It had its good points: it was nicely shaded by huge sycamore trees, and he could enjoy the sounds of a creek that ran just outside the entire length of the longest portion of the fence. But no longer was he able to participate meaningfully in world events as "up close and personal" as he had on a corner fenced lot. To help make up for that, we tried to provide him with different stimuli: ride-alongs around town, lots of walks on city trails, and some far away travels.

In retrospect, we weren't sure how much fun some of our ideas for him actually were. Once, we stuffed him in the back of a small Dodge hatchback for a ten-hour drive to New Jersey for a Christmas holiday visit with my parents. His nose pressed up against the long, low, slanted back window the whole way, he caught more than a few looks from passing cars on that trip. When we finally arrived, it was a few minutes before he found a way to un-kink his legs to hop/fall out of the car and down onto the ground. Our guilty consciences never let us do that to him again. Santa's bag was full of dog treats that Christmas, if that helped.

Our favorite special event with Ratches was an annual mid-winter trip to Ocracoke on the Outer Banks of the North Carolina seashore. He rode in the back seat of a Fiat Sport Spider, crammed in there with suitcases (not much trunk room in that car). After the motel check-in, we hit the beach, where he roamed and ran to get the kinks out. The three of us took long daily walks on a stretch of beach and sand dunes that forms a four-mile long peninsula on Ocracoke Island, which in those days was virtually deserted in February. Along the way, I skipped seashells on the thin water of an oncoming or receding wave; he eagerly chased, crunched and ate them. (After a bunch of those, the boy worked up a thirst, and with nothing around to satisfy it but salty sea water, he gulped that down, too. It didn't take too many nights of "sharing his pain" before we learned to carry a bottle of fresh water and a small bowl with us.) Midway through those cold and windy walks, Mary and I snuggled under wool blankets among the dunes, while Ratches stood guard at a respectful distance. He interrupted our snooze only once: a national park ranger had left her car to patrol the dunes, and had started walking toward us. Ratches stopped her with a single bark, which also woke us up. We peeked over the dune to show ourselves, and waved sleepily: she nodded and returned to her car under the unwavering, watchful gaze of Ratches.

Back home, Ratches and Mary shared daytime walks on a recreational path that ran 3½ miles alongside a creek through part of the city. That we were protected and safe in his care was never more apparent than during one of those. The path occasionally crossed under streets: although those tunnels were not terribly long, they were fairly dark, and Mary felt more comfortable having a 90-pound dog walking through them with her. One day, as the two of them approached one of the underpasses, Ratches stopped suddenly, growled a sustained, low, "Grrrr," and wouldn't let Mary go forward. Not panicked, just focused, Ratches maintained his posture until Mary decided maybe this time she should detour up to the overhead street and bypass this particular tunnel on this particular day. Good thing she did. When she returned to the path on the other side of the underpass, she glanced back to notice a decidedly unsavory-looking character lurking a couple of yards inside the tunnel staring out at her. Something about that scene gave my otherwise unflappable wife the willies. We began to realize that our dog had quietly fashioned a life that interacted with ours at every level. He thought about things he wanted to do and not do, and things he wanted *us* to do and not do. He protected us in very real ways. And, being a friend, he could also be *silly*.

The three of us "kids" lit out with a sled in the back of our car one weekend morning after a rare snowfall had blanketed Greensboro. A long, sloping hill in the town's Revolutionary War park provided a wonderful place for sledding. Ratches got the hang of having snow fun real quick: Mary had made it not halfway down the hill, picking up speed, when our boy darted over toward her at a full run, reached over, snatched the wool cap off her head, and merrily ran off with his prize, shaking it back and forth for all the world to see. He tossed it up into the air, pounced on it, shook the snow out of it, and ran circles around the still-sledding Mary, careful to stay out of range of me trying to get it back. I was a little perturbed that Mary's new hat was being trashed, but she and Ratches ignored me, lost in the frolics of Happyville!

Mary and Ratches bonded while I threw my energy into the office job. They took their daily walks along the city path; when she felt too tired to go, he lay in the foyer across the room from her, muzzle on the floor, eyes rolled up, not letting her get away with that for long. If that didn't do it, a very audible, measured sigh did.

"It's the only thing he gets to do during the day," she often told me when I got home from work. "I just couldn't say no to that."

Ratches showed us how tuned in to human feelings dogs can be. When I came through the front door after a long workday and gave Mary a hug, she looked over at Ratches to see what kind of day I'd had. No matter what I said upon arriving home, Ratches had the true "read" on my feelings, and knew how the evening was likely to go. I often tried to put on a better "front" for Mary than how I was actually doing, only to see Ratches turn and head downstairs, asking to go outside for a while. "Okay," Mary pressed, "what *really* happened today?"

Tattletale. Couldn't fool him. He was tuned in to us—especially to me.

Mary swears that Ratches was my guardian angel, sent here to show me how to be a better person. Anytime my irritable, irritating self came to the fore, he was quick to walk a short distance away, then turn around and look at me, head and ears down, *clearly disappointed. Geez, dog, gimme a break.* Living with your conscience out there in front of you all the time got old, but...that was Ratches.

Years into our emerging relationship of trust and friendship with him I once asked Mary, "Would you take $3,000 for Ratches if offered?"

"No! Of course not!" was Mary's adamant reply.

"Would we take $10,000?" I needled her again.

"Nope," she said.

"Well, then, I guess we have at least a ten-thousand-dollar dog," I said. That phrase became a slogan around our house. The fact is, we would have turned down ten times that figure, and more. His legendary status with us has endured. In her typically understated manner, Mary has flatly declared through time that Ratches was "pretty great." *So he was.*

In our last year in Greensboro, Ratches revealed to us something more startling than we would have believed about dogs: they can be tuned in to a higher level of existence than humans generally are. A family at the end of the cul-de-sac we lived on had traveled to Canada on vacation. Leaving home with their two daughters, they returned, devastated, with only one. The younger sister fell victim to a freak aneurism just after getting off a Ferris wheel at a local fair, and the cul-de-sac we shared had lost its sunshine. The agony of her father was beyond words, and it reached Ratches. Never before even attempting to escape our fenced backyard, Ratches saw or felt something that persuaded him to somehow free himself from his fenced yard and go out among the neighborhood streets, undoubtedly looking for his special friend. He was later found, watching and waiting, in the yard next door to where she had lived. The young girl whose life ended so abruptly and prematurely had been the one person in the neighborhood who almost daily stopped by our backyard fence to scratch Ratches' ears, and give him some human connection time when Mary and I were at work or otherwise found ourselves busy doing things away from him. I like to think they have found each other in sunshine somewhere; if they have, his ears are being well rubbed.

When Mary returned to the working world after four years of giving us some breathing time while I acclimated to a managerial role for the first time in my life, we decided that the extra income should be invested in land—preferably land affording us privacy, surrounded by nature, and suitable for us to someday build a house on. We had found our dog by looking at ads in the newspaper: why not look for land the same way? Deep down, we thought this was probably a ridiculous way to go about finding property that would meet all our special hopes and needs as a future homeplace. But what would be the harm in looking? (*None, except* that *kind of thinking has emptied a lot of checkbooks and spawned a ton of loans in these United States.*) Our first time through the "Lots and Acreage" section, a short, plain ad declared "41.4 acres" available. The distance from the city was appealing to us: twenty miles straight north of Greensboro. Separated from the city by two major highways running east/west, accessible only by a winding ribbon of an old country road, this location was our best hope to preserve our privacy from urban sprawl for a long time. We called the realtor and agreed to meet her the next Saturday morning.

It was early February. The stubble remains of a corn field in mid-winter offer a kind of charm not everyone appreciates: for me, it is the richness of a place where time slows down, where you can smell the earth and feel its breadth. I went nuts when I saw deer prints all over the place. "Deer!" I exclaimed to the realtor. My wife groaned. *There went negotiating.* Confirming that, the realtor beamed. But there was one thing standing in the way of buying this place: Mary had to agree. Mary does not part with money enthusiastically. I don't think it has anything to do with her Scottish genes: I just think she is part of that portion of humans who become very, *very* uncomfortable at the prospect of parting with money—even for things they really desire. Writer's cramp starts when the pen hits the checkbook. Sooo, we tried to figure out whether this was a place we really, REALLY wanted.

The property had its drawbacks: there was no pathway in to the only level part, a five-acre field, located smack-dab in the middle of the 41.4-acre parcel. Ringing the property were a couple of creeks, creating a sort of moat around—and hundreds of feet below—the field. Leaving the state-maintained gravel road, you faced a daunting hike, first down to the nearest creek, then back up to the field. Building a driveway in that steep terrain would be tough. (Access to electricity turned out to be an even worse problem; neither of us had thought of that, and *of course* it never occurred to the realtor to mention it.) We did the normal "agonizing" thing people do when they're contemplating spending too much money: we decided to take one more walk on that land and see if anything came to us that would help us decide finally whether to move forward with an offer or forget it and look elsewhere. Our decision to walk the property *with our dog* proved to be critical.

The next day, Ratches dutifully trudged down the first incline, then up the next one, padded his way across the field with us, then down the next (even steeper) hill, through heavy woods, until we reached the second creek. In the late Sunday afternoon light, with frigid temperatures fast approaching, Mary and I were just not making any progress in deciding *anything*. That's when Ratches plopped down on a small, relatively flat piece of ground next to the babbling water, snagged a hanging vine with his teeth, and started chewing on it playfully. He seemed at home. Here was a city dog completely relaxed in the deep woods: a happier or more contented a dog there never was.

Mary looked at me and chuckled, "Well, I guess this is the place."

If Ratches picked it out, it had to be okay; that much we had learned in the years of our three-way partnership. The decision made, we walked in silence back the way we had come, the reality of what we were financially contemplating hitting us for the first time. It was unsettling. Second thoughts irritatingly bullied their way into our heads as we climbed the last hillside—out of breath, tired, cold, and a little scared. After the dark woods, a welcome brightness appeared as we approached the road clearing. I stopped, and stared at the last of the sunlight filtering through the roadside branches. "Look!" I whispered to Mary. "It's like gold dust sprinkled in the air." That's how it appeared to me then, and how I have remembered it to this day. It was magical. Ratches had found us Meadowbrook—a field between two streams.

It didn't take long before we figured (Okay, *I*—the family spender—figured) that saving Mary's income would not outpace the rapidly increasing costs of house construction: there was no financial gain to be realized by waiting to build our dream house. If we're going to do this thing, we might as well get on with it, and have that many more years to enjoy living the country life! So we threw all caution to the wind, sold our city house, applied the entire net proceeds of sale to pay for the acreage, stuffed our worldly possessions into a tiny rental house, and began our odyssey to become country folks.

With zero dollars to put down on a home construction project, we relied on the kindness of a local Savings and Loan (and a builder they trusted) to get this show on the road. While those arrangements were beginning, we contracted with a local grader, who, with his trusty, small bulldozer, fought bees and brush to carve out a driveway path down the first steep incline and up the second to reach the future house site at one end of the field. (I had approached a big-time grading company to do the work, but discouraged by the terrain, they declined the job. Later, seeing the path now cleared by the first fellow, that same contractor happily agreed to re-work the path, add a mountain of dirt and a monster culvert, and otherwise finish the driveway, using equipment the size of our first house. We remained especially grateful to that first individual, whose foresight and grit opened the way for our future Meadowbrook home.)

Ratches kept me company as I walked for hours up and down both sides of the half-mile driveway, spreading grass seed, fertilizer, lime and straw. Now an older dog, he wanted to spend more of our time together stretched out on a tarp I had brought along, when I might scratch his ears and snooze with him. Unfortunately, daylight was fading fast, and I had "miles to go before I could sleep," so the work came first—one of the decisions I have regretted in my life.

Ratches was with us all the time that we were freed from our work, but the office schedule took us away from him five days out of every seven, and on those days he was left in a back yard behind a tall wooden fence, walling him off at our rental house from the outside world. One particularly clear, cool morning I turned to see him trying to peer through a slit in that fence as I was getting into my car for another day at the office. There was a growing urgency in his appeal to be with us; I chalked it up to his wanting to get on with living in a place that offered more of a life to a dog accustomed to more contact with the world and stimulating things to do in a happy dog's life. I wish it had been that simple. And I wish I had taken that day off work to run with him on our country land—another regret that never heals.

After a summer of nearly losing our minds haggling with the power company and local landowners, we were eventually awarded power easements so the house builder could start construction. By the following spring we moved to the great unknown. Happy as I was to be in the middle of so much privacy, it also made me a little uneasy to be that far away from town. It was harder on Ratches: he was now removed from any human contact other than ours, plunked down in a fenced yard in a strange setting, with woodsy noises, and smells and sights different from anything he'd ever known. He at least had the familiarity of his dog house (a wonderfully large one, hand-made by my father), with his name carefully painted in an arc over the swinging door entrance. When we were able to be home with him, Mary, as usual, made the difference: she put the "home" touches on everything, calmed me and Ratches, and we began a life in the middle of our very own world.

Unfortunately, it was not meant for Ratches to be a Meadowbrook dog. While at the rented house, he began to lift and hold his head low over the floor, and appeared to be concentrating, but at nothing we could understand. This was new behavior, and it didn't look or feel normal. A quick exam and blood test by the veterinarian suggested liver cancer; Ratches' strange behavior was, in fact, a normal canine response to intense pain. The operation on his liver produced a curious result, however: the lab results came back negative for the invasive cells the doctor had expected to find. Mary and I had literally prayed several evenings after his surgery while we waited days for the lab results. Stroking the fur of our best friend, we were hoping for a miracle: maybe we had one. A few months later, Ratches moved with us to the country, and the cancer that had apparently been there all along made the journey with him. This time, surgery was not going to help, and the only remedy to relieve him of his pain was to take on some of our own. Our tears that horrible afternoon in the back room of the animal hospital stung hard.

"Save us a place, Ratches," I softly asked as we released him.

We spent the rest of that day away from our offices, walking on the same, long path through the city park we had strolled with Ratches so many times, watching him try to sneak up on squirrels, making a life in partnership with him. We squeezed each other's hands as we walked in sometimes faltering steps, through blurred vision. More tears; more pain; it just wouldn't end. I felt like I was literally losing my mind—myself—in grief. This was a loss of family like I had never known, and it was wrenching. Time passed, but nothing helped—*nothing*.

Chapter 2
The Borders

Hard to consider, it was an even tougher thing to suggest. But I began to think that the only way Mary and I would ever resume any sort of life was to at least *look* at another puppy—maybe even find two who would keep each other company while we were miles away for long days at work. Ratches had been left alone too much while we had attended to things demanded of us in the human world; we weren't going to make that mistake again.

One afternoon later that summer in my office, I glanced over the ads in the Pets section of the newspaper, and noted some Border collie litters. When I got home that night and mentioned it to Mary, she reluctantly agreed that it was probably something we should at least consider doing, but neither her heart nor mine was in it. We agreed we'd probably find out in the process that we didn't want any dogs—at least not yet. We didn't know what we thought—we just felt bad, and we didn't know what to do about it. The next day was Friday; we could take a drive and be with some puppies—a nice, friendly thing to do after a long work week. We weren't betraying our Ratches: this was just…something to do.

Lexington—one of the centers of North Carolina's furniture industry—had a furniture factory that loomed over rows of mill houses. Like the thousands of others spread over the Tar Heel State from a bygone era when textile plants and tobacco plots fed North Carolina families from the mountains to the coast, the modest house we drove up to was neat, if unassuming, complete with a small backyard and a young girl playing on the grass. Its special charm came from a whirlwind of black-and-white, six-week-old fluffballs—a back lot in Walt Disney studios. Full of energy, they were a bargain at only $75 each. Trying to single one out, while they all tore around the place running circles around each other, made me dizzy. So I gave that up, and tried instead to take the whole scene in. Puppies let you know what kind of family environment they live in, so we liked the owners even before we met them. The ad for these guys might just as well have said, "Totally healthy, adorable pups, raring to live life in 'fun' mode!" Knowing we wanted to take home a couple from this batch was a no-brainer, but trying to decide which ones was going to be hard. Or—maybe *not*.

Beyond all the mayhem, I spotted an odd-looking female standing off to the rear of everything else with her mother, quietly looking at me. When I returned her look, she continued to study me for a few seconds, then whipped around, ran over to a plastic watering can, grabbed it by the spout, raced with it over to mom, and the two of them engaged in free-spirited play the simplicity and wonder of which I have rarely seen in this world.

"Mary." I motioned toward the pup. "Check out that one way over there."

She was quiet for a few moments, then said, "Her head is shaped funny—like a pan." Mary was referring to the pup's rather flat, triangle-shaped noggin that I, too, had noticed, but figured it was part of a newborn thing that would eventually change and become more proportional to the rest of her body with time and natural growth.

"That'll change with time," I said, "you know," I added without conviction. I got *the look*. Mary wasn't so sure.

Still, the play between mother-dog and daughter-puppy continued with such antics and with such creativity (I mean, how much cool stuff can *people* think of to do with a watering can?) that Mary was becoming intrigued. More chat with the people-mom and people-daughter followed, and finally a somewhat-annoyed husband joined the group (I had the feeling we had interrupted his supper). It was getting dark, and in good old-fashioned body language, hubby was letting us know it was clearly time to "piddle, or get off the puppy farm."

"Okay," Mary said at last, "let's take little 'pan head.'" Not exactly a ringing endorsement, but I ran with it.

Now to choose the other one. Frankly, as is probably the case with all working couples, I was tired. Long work week, and I wanted to go home. Not knowing anything about Border collies except for some snippets of Scottish folklore and a few snapshots from doggy articles, I remembered something about a white line running up the muzzle from nose to forehead being a classic indicator of the breed. I had noticed one male pup there that had a white circle around his nose: this was somewhat unusual, and made him look especially adorable. So I offered him as my next choice, Mary said, "Okay." We paid the good folks $150 for the pair, and I scooped up "Circle Nose" while Mary went to try to extract "Pan Head" from the watering-can game.

Pups in hand, we approached the gate to exit the backyard and head for our truck. I turned back to the people to thank them again, when *bam!*—another male pup banged into me. This guy had seen with alarm that I was about to leave him behind, and he wasn't having it! At a full run, he roared up and tagged me *hard* with both front feet; when I released the other male and leaned down to see this new guy, he tagged me again, this time on my chest with such force that it knocked me off balance, and over on my backside I went. Encouraged by that success, he pounced on me, looked earnestly into my eyes, planted his front paws on my chest, and started licking my chops. Then he did something pretty amazing: pinning me on my back with two front paws squarely on my chest, he looked calmly and pointedly into my eyes again. *Do you get it, now?* he asked. He couldn't have been clearer if he'd whipped out a note pad and pencil, written me that message, and shoved it at my nose.

"Honey," an amused Mary observed from my left, "he seems to have picked *you* out. How can you not pick *him*?"

How could I not, indeed. "Okay, little guy." I laughed. "I guess you're the one."

The ride back that night was long and tough on them. I never had the sense they felt uprooted from their mama or home, but they were not crazy about my driving. We had them in a cardboard box on the floor in the back of the truck cab, where I had hoped they might quietly snooze the hour-and a-half trip home. No such luck. Whether it was the darkness, how I handled the curves, the uncertainty of where they were and where they were going, or a combination of things, the male—then the female—became engaged in bouts of barfing that prompted us to forego the air conditioning and lower the windows for the remainder of our flight.

The next day, sitting on our deck overlooking the field of our new home in the middle of the 41-acre woods, I had no trouble suggesting names to Mary for these guys.

"The little fellow tagged me hard," I reminded her. "Let's call him 'Tag.'"

"And that female runs so fast, like the wind. How about 'Windi.' with an I instead of a y, just to make it, you know, different—special—like she is?"

"Tag and Windi: Windi and Tag," Mary sounded it out, nodding. "That's good. Oh, Skip, I like it!"

Tag and Windi, like their predecessor, would be outdoor dogs, joining us indoors at nights and on weekend days, and for truck forays into town or around the countryside. They never knew Ratches, but I told them about him from time to time, and how they had big paw prints to fill. Tucking them each night into the big house with the legend's name freshly re-painted above its door, I assured them Ratches would be watching over them, and told them to sleep well, and grow strong. The "grow strong" part was important: hawks had come to expect breakfasts and dinners from our five-acre field, and our new pups looked a whole lot like bunnies from a couple hundred feet up. I will forever have the image of Mary clutching one pup under each arm close to her chest, nervously glimpsing skyward as a hawk made steadily lower circles overhead, drawing a bead on those two furry bodies. I started laughing and couldn't stop, but Mary was dead serious: what was going to happen while we were at work during the day, she wondered, leaving these innocents exposed to the ravaging instincts of battle-hardened country hawks? We needn't have worried. It turns out that Border collies are as smart as their rep suggests: they burrowed under the shed and stayed there during the day, protected from predatory skies. Whether it was for that reason, or to escape the intense summer sun building up heat inside their well-insulated doghouses (good in winter—not so great in summer), who knows? All we knew was that when the first of us got home each afternoon from work, Tag and Windi scrambled out from under the shed, intact and happy.

If you haven't seen Border collie greeting behavior, you have not seen life fully enjoyed. Tails wag excitedly in all directions with inexhaustible energy! First thing in the morning, that kind of greeting just boosts your spirit, makes problems disappear, and gives you a jolt of happy that no human being I've ever known can inspire. Late in the afternoon, having just returned home from workplace calamities, getting that kind of a reception is doubly rewarding. *Why can't I have employees like that*, I wondered? *More unsettling*, why can't *I* be more of an employee like that?

Meadowbrook was beginning to take shape: sitting on one end of a long, rectangular field, the back of the house faced west, overlooking the length of the field, while the front was tucked up against dark woods. From our bedroom that ran front to back on the second floor, we could watch through a huge bay window deer—sometimes a dozen or more at a time—grazing on the distant end of the field, or enjoy the antics of birds and squirrels at tree house level through a string of double-hung windows on the opposite wall. Sunny to the west, shady to the east, our bedroom offered two worlds at all times. Through the west-facing bay window, we watched hail storms and tornado winds approaching with awe-inspiring speed and power. A funnel cloud once formed above the trees just beyond the western end of the field, then split into two halves, nearly shearing off the tops of huge oaks and beeches as the separated cells roared down the sides of our field, narrowly missing both ends of the house. We returned home from a beach trip to find small areas of woods near the house that had been trashed by micro-bursts of deadly wind. Despite these close encounters (or maybe *because* of them), we always felt safe in our home snuggled tight against the woods. Just part of the magic of Meadowbrook.

A mere thirty feet from the north end of our house, four hundred feet of fencing anchored by a Leonard shed formed a "dog yard." Our driveway wound its way from the state-maintained gravel road a half-mile away up a long hill from the intervening creek and past the dog yard, splitting off left to the front of the house, and to the right between the house and the dog yard to form a large paved area between human and dog houses. Running out from that central, paved area and down the right side of the field for about a hundred feet was a grassy stretch that we kept mowed short for Frisbee- and ball-tossing games. The pavement between house and dog yard was a hot zone during sunny summer days, so it shouldn't have surprised us that late one Saturday evening, putting the dogs out for the night turned into a calamitous encounter with Mr. Copperhead, still happily soaking up the day's heat on still-warm asphalt (see Chapter 11).

The Borders' most memorable contribution to our Meadowbrook life that first year was to put on a bona fide show for Mary's step-mother who came for a short visit from Florida. She was not a dog person—this was apparent early in the visit. But she was a trooper, so she gave it a good "college try." True to their breed's reputation, Tag and Windi were as sharp at reading people as they would have been spotting predators in a field of sheep. Having already figured out there was nothing to lose in their relationship with step-mom, they set about doing what Border collies do best: they terrorized her—gleefully, totally, inexhaustibly! They accomplished this ridiculously easily.

The first afternoon of her visit, step-mom was seated on our sofa, facing Mary and me a few feet away next to the fireplace. An area rug ran between the sofa and the fireplace; the flooring everywhere else around the sofa was hardwood—*and slick*. We had just begun to chat when out of nowhere flew in the Borders, one chasing the other in a steady blur of speed, racing around and around the sofa in an ever-tightening circle. NASCAR drivers would have applauded with envy the blitzkrieg pace of this whirlwind event. Startled, step-mom jerked her feet and legs up and onto the sofa—impressive, considering her age and the speed with which she accomplished this—then leaned forward, eyes widening at what was happening, cutting herself off from whatever she had started to say. As the circus intensified, step-mom tightened her legs up under her, and pressed farther into the back of the sofa.... Well!—uh, my—uh—my...goodness!" she burbled, as the frenetic pups exploded by in front of her yet again. An added bonus to this hysteria was to hear the bouncing of their heads, butts, whatever, off the legs of small wooden tables placed behind and on each end of the sofa as the ring of fur-blur crashed around and around step-mom at a dizzying pace!

Mary (the one in the family with manners) recognized step-mom's increasing anxiety, and tried to exhort the crazed Border pups, "*Quit it!*" I might have tried to help if I hadn't been laughing so hard. I think I hurt myself. It wasn't clear when she first arrived how long step-mom had intended to stay, but she left that afternoon. I don't blame her: this was a nuthouse. I know our housekeeping has never been the best in the world, but I don't think that was the key player in her decision to bolt from Meadowbrook and return to civilization. She is a delightful woman, and deserved something less frightening than the reception she got from over-enthusiastic pups with sheep-herding instincts coursing through their veins. Unfortunately, she had wandered into youthful BC behavior. We know from attending sheep herding trials that young Border collies are a challenge to teach. Eventually most of them learn the ropes, but oh, those first couple of training years!

For our part, Mary and I settled into a routine of commuting through countryside to our respective cities to work: I to the court in Greensboro (25 minutes), and Mary to a county environmental agency in Winston-Salem (45 minutes). Over the course of our thirteen years at Meadowbrook, my commute lengthened to 40 minutes—Mary's to an hour. We both watched woods and fields give way to the unending sprawl of subdivision housing. Cars and trucks parked where cows once grazed; backyard fences closed young families into boxes packed tightly along paved ribbons sentimentally named after the former occupants of these once idyllic hillsides... "Apple Drive," "Oak Lane,"

"Beech Terrace." Of the emerging titles of the new America along my route to town, my personal favorite? "The Orchard" (Stages I, II, and coming soon—III). *Lots of luck maneuvering a tractor through that conglomerate of asphalt and sheetrock to find an apple ripening in the sun, glistening from morning dew or afternoon thundershower.* As the last of these signs of "progress" receded in my rearview mirror late each afternoon, I eagerly anticipated making that final turn onto our gravel road, then felt the irritating clutter and weight of the work day literally slip away as our driveway appeared and brought me all the way home to the private, nature refuge of Meadowbrook.

Sometime during that first year, the county sheriff (the high sheriff, himself—the elected one) paid us a visit. I like to think he was just being conscientious, keeping an eye on all his constituents, checking in on newcomers and such. 'Course, it might have been that he (like everyone else in that area) had heard we had a "Gucci tub" installed in our master bathroom, and wanted to check that out for himself. It seems that our contractor had met the bathtub delivery truck at the local, old-time country store a mile down the road during our house construction days, which turned out to be a lively event that fed the local news exchange. Apparently not many folks up that way had jets in their tubs: the old-timers around the wood stove in that store looked at us a little differently whenever we stopped in there for a *long* time after that.

Tag and Windi met the high sheriff at the end of the driveway when he pulled up beside the house, but when he stepped out of the car, and they got a look at his uniform, guns and badge, they scattered at Border speed the heck away from him. He turned in their direction just in time to see two fuzzy butts book it through the dog yard fence and dive under their protective shed. With a bemused "hmph," he turned back around toward us, his face all business.

"You need two things to live in the country," he told us calmly, with all the confidence of a life-long country boy, "a shotgun...and a *big* dog." Unoffended, two sets of eyes continued to peer out at him from under the dog yard shed while he talked.

Geez, I thought: *what kind of stuff goes on out here in rural America?* It didn't help that just about everyone we met around there that first year said the same thing—we needed a *Big Dog*. Obviously a Big Dog figured into the area's customary home protection plan, but since we had hand guns, a rifle and a shotgun discreetly placed all over the inside of our house, I wondered how much extra help a big dog really would be? Maybe a hefty growl and bark would help deter the bad guys, but since we planned for our guys to be outside dogs at night, I wasn't exactly sure how much help a *bigger* dog (with or without a menacing bark) was going to be from inside the dog yard in the wee hours of the morning, anyway. Besides, I didn't like the thought of our dogs—big or otherwise—being put in harm's way, in charge of our protection. I figured it was the humans' part of the bargain to take care of human attackers. Still, it's hard to ignore the advice of a straight-up, no-nonsense high sheriff when it's the first thing he tells you out of his welcome wagon. And, *Big Dog* certainly had some kind of time-honored hold on country folks, so off to the Pets section of the newspaper ads I went again—this time with a very specific purpose in mind: we wanted a Big Dog.

Having already had one Labrador-mix who was a big dog (Ratches), we confidently followed an ad for lab-mix puppies to a small house on a small street in the nearby small town of Reidsville. There we were directed by the owners to a small playhouse-type shed on the front lawn. The curse of working couples is that you can't ever seem to get around to doing the one thing you really most want to do until all the other chores and necessities of "getting through the week" have been satisfied; so it was, I guess, inevitable (again) that we pulled up to the "puppy shed" in fading daylight. Fortunately for us, the owner had hooked up a trouble light under the shed ceiling, which fully brightened the interior, revealing a thick mat of fresh straw. The smell of new straw and puppies was catnip to Mary: before I could say, "Hi," to the owners, I felt her squeezing past me to get a better look. This time I had to be the one with manners, because the allure of puppies had captivated my bride.

"Is it okay if we go in?" I managed to blurt out just as Mary nosed her way through the doorway and bent down to find…Nirvana.

Her eyes lit up: she was sitting in the midst of a tumbler full of puppies! Lots of them! Some golden, some black. All pure-tee-dee-*light*-ful! Puppy snoofles and whimpers and licks and round tummies were all around her; she had those fur balls coming and going under both arms and over both legs. Occasionally one topped off a determined climb up on her shoulder by reaching the summit of her thick red hair, and tumbling down onto other pups fumbling around on her lap.

I watched as everything happened in slow motion for a minute…I have never seen my Mary happier than at that moment. There are times when a guy would like to feel responsible for his girl being the happiest she has ever been, and I think I have been treated to some of those, but the complete and uncomplicated, unreserved outpouring of genuine joy in that scene is something no camera need capture for me to recall. Holding that instant as long as I could, I finally blinked, and everything was back to real speed—grand chaos.

Picking out a pup after all that was almost an afterthought, but select one we finally did. She was all black, and since she seemed the absolute sweetest of the lot, Mary immediately named her "Chelsea" (for Chelsea Gardens in London, where she had visited one summer in the early 1970s while on a student work visa during our single days). From oncoming headlights during the ten mile drive home, I caught glimpses of Chelsea snuggled close to the front of Mary's neck. They were quiet and contented: no barfing from either of them. The cycle of bringing up another puppy was to begin again.

Chapter 3
Chelsea

Our back door steps leading down to an open carport below the second level screened porch and deck were few, but huge to a puppy just weaned from her mother. Chelsea was a trooper, though, determined to climb up to the landing outside the laundry room door, which she quickly learned was a room you had to go through to get to the *really* important room in the house: the kitchen. Mary and I are sure of two things from our experience living with a pack of dogs: the older ones teach the younger ones, and the thing the youngsters learn first and quickest is where the food comes from. Our guys may have been outside dogs for the most part, but they all learned everything there was to know about the kitchen. Things drop from counters (particularly at the end of a work day), so being well-positioned (ie., under the cook's feet) near a kitchen counter is prime lesson material in a young dog's life. Of course, when you're little and the other guys are big, maneuvering into a good spot is like rebounding with Shaquille in the paint: you can dream, but pickings are going to be sparse, and you could get stomped on.

Pictures of Chelsea's early weeks at Meadowbrook are of a solitary black ink spot on the back door steps, alone in front of the wood stove in the kitchen, by herself on the stone patio, or huddled against the double-glass doors on the patio landing. Hers was a lonelier puppyhood than others that followed into the pack: Tag was too busy developing pack leader skills to be bothered playing nurse maid to a puppy, and Windi wanted none of it. Dogs let other dogs know what they want, and what they don't want, and they don't mess around when conveying the messages. Poor Chels would sidle up to Windi for some care and comfort in a big world, and Windi's response was to get up and move somewhere—anywhere—else. Chelsea would try follow along where Windi was going: Windi picked up the pace until short puppy legs couldn't keep up. Pretty soon, young Chelsea began to lose interest in the whole, "Somebody please raise me," thing, and just raised herself. We spent more time with her than with the Borders early on, trying to make up for this lack of attention by her counterparts, but her subsequent independence from everybody else in the clan was an inevitable extension of the separateness she was consigned to early on.

Perhaps it was having been born on a small street in a small town that kept Chelsea, well, *smaller* than we had hoped. Or maybe her diminished role in the pack contributed to her short stature. As absurd as it sounded, we actually began to think that there was some law of bio-physics at work in the world of dog packs that prohibits a puppy (regardless of breed) from growing larger than the size of the pack leader. Here was a bona fide Labrador, whose parents (her mother's owners assured us) were both large dogs, stunting her growth to match that of the Borders. It was just too weird. Whatever the reason, she quit growing at Tag's shoulder height. This was to have been our Big Dog! Nope. In every other way, Chelsea had true Lab genes: she loved water and lived to play. Chelsea's genes were happy genes. She loved life, loved Frisbee, loved ball-toss games. She spent her time outside the dog yard snouffling around in the brush and field, snorting hot doggy breath into the burrows of mice and voles. Mary's theory was that she stunned them with blasts of mole breath ("Pudh, pudh!"), then dug into their burrows with quick, hard paw strikes, finally snagging her immobilized prey. Afterwards, she carried the victim (probably having given up the ghost from shock) around the yard for a while, finally dropping it onto the stone patio or patio landing to "age." When the carcass ripened after a few days, she (along with her comrades) rolled on it.

It was always easy to identify long-dead mice or voles (or, and dog-owners—you know this is coming—piles of poop): just spot the dog rolling with a purpose. Sure, dogs roll on their backs to scratch them, but that is an obvious exercise where the legs shoot up and in all directions in a carefree *wheeee!* kind of action. Applying doggy perfume, on the other hand, is a study in languourous motion, done with care and precision. First you approach the rotting, slimy item with head lowered, and sniff carefully, making sure it has achieved a degree of decomposition suitable for application. If satisfied, turn to one side, extend the neck and expose the shoulder, so that it bears the maximum squish! when you land. Then slowly wriggle forward to spread this marvelous fragrance down as much of your back as possible. After a couple more wriggles directly on your back (for style points), and a sprint back up onto all four feet, finish with a brief shake (not too much—you don't want to undo all the fine work you've just accomplished) and a final sniff to see if you've left some really prime stink still on the ground (if so, this would be a shameful waste, which requires a repeat performance). All our dogs were proficient in this activity, but Chelsea did it with relish.

She had no interest in—or predilection for—being a guard dog. Her clear purpose in life was to chase balls and Frisbees, keep in check the local mouse and vole population, get wet in creeks and bogs, and plop down all stinky, wet and muddy in front of our wood stove (thank goodness for tile floors) to cook until her fur singed. There was no room in that tight schedule for home security. One year after tossing Chelsea into our doggy fray, we were obviously still going to be "short" the country-living-required Big Dog. What else could we do but hit the road again: this time an hour and forty minutes to Haw River following up on yet another newspaper ad in the Pets section. I did my homework on the phone first: six-week-old German shepherd puppies AKC certified (our first dog ever with actual *papers*!), mother 75 pounds, father 115 pounds. We *were* going to get Big. (With a price to match. *Bring the checkbook.*)

Chapter 4
Ruffy

We were getting to be old hands at puppy selection. We knew the routine: one of us had to play nice with the owners (and be subjected to the tears and implorings of the inevitable young daughter, unhappy to see any of her puppies being handed over to complete strangers), while the other, with a keen and critical eye—surveyed the lot and determined whether anything there was worth taking. That plan was not going to work this time. The problem? All of them looked *and acted* alike; I mean, *exactly*. How do you decide between equal pups? We watched them for what seemed like an eternity—literally, several hours: there was no way to distinguish one from another. And we really wanted to guess right, here: the cost was $300. Ouch. This was no time for careless thought; we needed to be sure. We were professionals in our work: we knew when it was important to scrutinize carefully, and make a measured decision.

"What do you think, Mary?" I asked for the 100th time.

"I don't know," came the professional reply. "What do *you* think?"

I'm surprised we're still not there, deliberating, some seventeen years later. After agonizing all afternoon among the handsome, brindle-colored litter, we finally just *picked* one, exchanged cash for pup, and drove in stunned silence back to Meadowbrook. This was a big undertaking now: we had two mature Border collies (siblings, for that matter—a sure way to inspire continual rivalry in the pack) and a one-year-old (still all "puppy" at that age) waiting for now a fourth member of the group (who we were sure was going to be BIG—a lot of animal to feed and care for). One thing we absolutely agreed on: this was *it*. No more dogs. We look back on that moment and laugh.

Finding a dignified name for what promised to be a dog of great, dignified stature called for serious deliberation. Our choice turned out to be a roadside sign announcing a fading town from another era, "Ruffin"—just up the road between Meadowbrook and 20th century civilization. There was that "rrrr" thing going in my brain again, I guess, so starting with an "R," "Ruffin" seemed like a good name.

"What do you think, Mary?" I asked her with a wince.

"I *guess* so," was her answer, more resigned than enthusiastic.

After a few moments of riding in silence, I said to her, "Since he has papers and all, he's worthy of a special name. And he's going to be dignified, like Ratches. How about we put "Ruffin Ratches" on the AKC papers?

"Yeah, that'd be good," said Mary (still thinking, *All* my *dogs are worthy)*. Then she looked out the passenger window quietly for a while. Sighing inside, we both hoped we knew what we were doing. How wrong could we be, anyway? I thought. We just needed a Big Dog—what difference did it make what we named him? *Geez, you'd think we'd learn.*

We shortened "Ruffin" to "Ruffy" early in the deal, primarily because he was too cute for a formal name assigned to unincorporated ground with a railroad track running through it. His right ear was cocked at the middle, falling over to the side; from any angle, he resembled a field hare more than an aspiring German shepherd. He was as quiet as he was handsome, and we anxiously watched by the day to see whether he was going to, you know, grow. Four months later, he was hardly any bigger, and his ear was still adorably (but now a little alarmingly) cocked to the side. He didn't seem to be growing into an adult: still reluctant to venture out into the field, he waited at the point where our back yard was separated by a low, curvy stone wall from the enormous field beyond. To a puppy, that field must have looked like the ends of the earth, with huge weeds, brush and straw, stretching out to what must have looked to him to be forever, with who-knows-what beasts and scary monsters waiting out there to gobble him up? I shuddered for him. *Good boy,* I thought, *smart fella...stay near us and the house until you're big enough to join your cohorts out there in the wild.*

Not yet growing (bolder or bigger), he was at least doing one thing new: biting the begeebers out of everything: our shoes, table and chair legs, rugs, and parts of my body (any parts—whatever happened to be near his teeth). His bitey mood was getting out of hand; my arms and legs were the stuff social services investigations are made of, and he was still small. What were we going to do when he became big and strong? Ruffy was treating me as just another member of the pack, somebody to rough-and-tumble with, and eventually to overtake in the climb to be as high in the pack pecking order as possible. I had no hope of ever training or disciplining him if I could not get this "bitey" business under control. To do that, I would have to establish myself as an authoritative figure. Trouble was, he already had an authoritative figure he looked up to: Tag.

Tag, probably sensing that this newest arrival to the pack would be a handful if ever allowed to be out of line, wasted no time bringing Ruffy along in learning the "do's" and "don'ts" of the Meadowbrook pack. More than disciplining him mercilessly, Tag took him under his wing in a way distinctly different from how he interacted with the others, maybe because he had found another "guy" to pal around with. Ruffy clearly enjoyed the special attention of the pack leader, and the two soon went everywhere together. "Mutt and Jeff" they were: fairly short Tag, with his growing buddy shadowing him around the field, around the house, in their dog yard, everywhere.

It was up to Mary and me to let the big guy know that he had to accept some instruction and correction from *us*, as well. Thing was, he was Tag's all day while the humans were away at work, so when the chips were down, he invariably glanced over at Tag for direction whenever I was trying to exert some control over him. So long as Tag went along with whatever I was trying to impart, Ruffin did too. *That's reasonable*, I thought: Tag took on the pup-raising chores—he should have the final say. Admittedly, it was a little unnerving to lecture a hundred-pound dog, only to have him look over at Tag, questioning (*what* about *this, boss? Okay with you?*) It's hard verbally disciplining when you're trying not to laugh. All I wanted was to have some say at times in what Ruffin could and could not get away with doing. But right now, to him I was little more than a chew toy, and the communication gap was widening by the day.

Time for action: Mary had an idea. While I busied myself at home with the logistics of paying bills and attending to chores around the house and acreage, the love of my life had been closely studying our dogs' behavior. For her, dogs were endlessly fascinating buggers, from whom we humans could learn a lot. One of the things she had paid special attention to (enviously) was how successfully Tag had achieved domination over the others in the pack. How had he done that? By biting them on their muzzles. Happily, Mary exercised control over me with reasoned thought and a sweet nature, instead. So sweetly, and in a carefully constructed line of thought, she laid out a plan.

"Skip, you know how Tag bites Ruffy on the muzzle sometimes? He does that to get his attention, and to discipline him. It's his pack-leader way of training the pack members. You've seen it work. Why don't you try that?"

This was how we were going to cure "bitey mouth"? What? It took me a few seconds to register that.

"You're kidding!"

"Well," she explained, "at this point, it's important that you get his attention to regain control; otherwise, he'll *never* listen to you."

I looked at her. I tried to say something helpful, to clarify the plan. "Are you *serious*?"

"Yeah." She looked at me matter of factly.

Those little prickles of fear began to dance on the back of my neck. I couldn't believe what I was hearing from someone I...trusted.

"Where—uh, how would I—I mean, how do I...uh, *do* that?" I stammered.

She was enjoying this way too much. With a little grin, she said, "Hold his nose and gently bite him on his muzzle; that will get his attention, and show him you are in command. If you bite him back, he'll start respecting you, just like he does Tag."

Oh, well—yeah, that makes sense. Just bite him on the muzzle. The muzzle? This was a German shepherd! Sure, just 16 weeks old, but still, he could, you know, *hurt* me! Geez, his teeth were razor-sharp (as anyone who has ever been nibbled or outright bitten by a puppy knows, young dog teeth are serious attention-getters). Bite him on his *MUZZLE? I don't* think *so.*

"He's going to let me *do* that?" I pressed. You hate to be a wuss in your wife's eyes, but I was being invited to chomp down the muzzle of a dog—a *German shepherd*, for cryin' out loud. Let her think what she wanted about my manliness. I was being directed to go eyeball-to-eyeball with a set of teeth. *Insane.*

"Well," she replied with a tone that closed the conversation, "desperate times sometimes call for desperate measures. It might not work, but you have nothing to lose."

Except my face, I thought.

I have always remembered that whole sequence vividly: it was one of those times in your life when things are so goofy that time freezes in stop-action so the event imprints for later assessment, because right then you are incapable of making any sense of it whatsoever.

Long pause. "Okay," I said, "I guess I'll try it." (*No way I'm trying that*, I thought. *No way!*)

My science-type spouse (chemistry major at UNC-Chapel Hill, with biology aptitude) was obviously eager for this experiment to occur, so she could observe—from a distance. *Charming.* That is exactly what happened, before I could come to my senses. Mary sat on the sofa, while I sprawled out on the rug next to Ruffin. After he predictably ignored my attempts to get his attention, I somehow wrestled him into a three-quarter Nelson. I grabbed the end of his nose with one hand, the back of his head with the other, shut my eyes tight, and silently uttered a mighty prayer as I gently (but firmly, as Mary instructed) gripped the boy's muzzle with my teeth.

I was expecting a full-out backlash attack. That's what *I* would have done if somebody bit down on *my* muzzle!

He took me totally by surprise: he went limp. I waited for an attack that never came. He stayed limp.

I realized I had been holding my breath. I opened my eyes slooowly…caaarefully…*nothing*. Just one limp puppy, but a limp puppy watching me with round eyes wide open! I verrry slowly exhaled…then released my teeth, then my hold on his nose and head. Giddy with relief, but quick to take advantage of a situation, I narrowed my gaze at him, looked deeply into his eyes, and said with mounting authority, "*I* am boss here," like I meant it. I hoped it, anyway.

Over the course of the next several weeks, whenever His Biteyness returned to form, we repeated this procedure. It took only a few more times, and he finally quit his biting on my body parts. I never did that with another dog, and I seriously hope never again to have to entertain the notion of doing so. When I invited Mary to do that to Ruffin as well, she sweetly declined, explaining that Ruffy was not giving *her* any trouble. At that moment it dawned on me that whenever dog discipline was called for, she somehow found a way to discreetly step out of the way and let me roar forth to tackle the assignment. I had never noticed that before.

As a post script, the next time we took one of our dogs in to see Doc Ally for a checkup, I started telling her what I had done with Ruffin. Her back to us, attending to shots and whatnot at the work counter behind her, she paused, and chuckling, turned around to face me, now amused, shaking her head side-to-side, and said, "There are more traditional techniques for establishing dominance over your dog, you know."

Deflated, I murmured something about, "thinking it might help," and trailed off, while Mary was still trying to shush me from admitting the whole episode.

The doc resumed her shot preparations, administered them to the dog on the table, and then started to laugh again. As she put the materials away, she once again turned around to face me, squinted her eyes, and asked, "Did it work?"

****

Biting Ruffy on his muzzle was a turning point in our relationship with our dogs. For the first time, we fully understood a fundamental element of pack behavior: passed down from eons of wolf generations in the wild, dogs in a pack have a leader, and that leader metes out discipline by biting muzzles—how hard depends on the severity of the offense, and however long it takes to sufficiently get the offender's full attention and recognition that whatever earned the muzzle-bite was *wrong*. We had seen Tag do this countless times on his other three pack members, but it had not dawned on me to try it myself—it just wasn't in the collective human gene pool. Hitting, slapping, verbal redress, sure—but nose biting? As it turns out, muzzle-nibbling carries great significance in the animal kingdom: if you're an otter, for example, getting your nose sharply bitten confirms that you better start getting ready for a family, as you have just been claimed as a love object and mate.

Ruffin never looked at me the same after that. I was, finally, an authoritative figure for him. Okay, so I never replaced Tag as his true leader; truthfully, I never really tried. It worked well, the way Tag fashioned it: don't mess with success. Ruffy liked Mary and me just fine…but he *belonged* to the Boss.

In his second year, Ruffy fulfilled our expectations: he got *big*. At 105 pounds, the veterinarian folks cautioned me to back off the food throttle, especially in the summer months, when his heavy coat kept him hot and less willing to exercise. Ruffin didn't think too much of that, and his kitchen begging techniques grew more imaginative and insistent. We stuck to our guns, though, and he dropped to a range of 90 to 95 pounds; after that, he began to explore the woods more meaningfully, dragging home a distended tummy on several occasions, and looking very green around the gills. Animals in rural area woods are either killed by hunters, killed by natural predators, or just die of natural causes. Hunting was commonplace throughout the year all around us, and if a carcass was left incompletely disposed of on the ground anywhere within scent range, Ruffy was on it…then into it. He usually had company from one or more of our other dogs on these unhealthful forays, but he was the big eater. Those were the nights that we were glad our pack was an outdoor group: with bedroom windows open, we were occasionally treated to disgusting regurgitative sounds from the dog yard. Good thing his stomach seemed to be as tough as he looked: it had its job cut out for it.

Ruffy turned out to be Meadowbrook's "big dog," but not necessarily its protector. The distinction is easy to explain by examples. His was a *magnificent* bark: it was hefty, from the chest, and it suggested that the chest and the beast who owned it was huge and meant business. The cool thing was that if you couldn't first see him and could only hear his bark, you would think that this animal would take on a full-size truck—and win. Then, when you saw him, you'd think this guy could take on a full-size truck full of raw-boned country boys—and win. His look was *that* leveling. Unless you knew him. Ruffy, it turned out, was your typical gentle giant—big, but friendly. When he was in the open back of our pickup truck, parked while we were at lunch or at a store, his size and aloof manner discouraged most people from getting close to him, but those few (usually children) who were unafraid to approach him found him to be exceptionally tolerant of petting. For a wandering set of fingers that found special spots behind his massive ears (both of which had finally straightened up after the first year), the scratcher was treated to faint whimpers of appreciation. Strangers coming up our driveway would draw his deep, chesty bark, followed by a hasty retreat to the rear (behind Tag, or us, whoever was farthest away from the threat). Some guard dog.

Still, there was that one episode when a colleague of mine visited us overnight. Scheduled to ride with me to a business conference the next day, Baron arrived at our house at night after all the dogs had been put to bed in their yard. Arriving that late, he had not seen any of them, and they had not seen him. So when Baron sleepily opened his bedroom door (directly off the kitchen) early the next morning, he startled Ruffy (who was dining nearby) such that the big guy in one leap pushed his nose about 4 inches below Baron's belly button—and held it there! No growls. No snarls. Ruffin was a study in quiet intensity. Baron had already raised both his hands in instinctive surrender pose, and was now staring befuddled down at this large German shepherd head. Neither being moved a whisker. I happened to be at the kitchen sink with my back to all this, but the sudden movement from Ruffin caused me to turn quickly, and seeing his muzzle holding Baron in a decidedly compromising position, all I could do was...laugh. My buddy glanced up at me without moving any other part of himself *(he* was *not* laughing), and asked me, softly, what he should do now? Since Ruffy had never treated anyone quite like this before, I wasn't at all sure what he had in mind, so I hesitated before answering. Finally I gently called to him to come to me, that it was "all right," and (as Baron told me many times recalling this story thereafter) "after what seemed like an eternity, this horse of a dog lowered his head and went back to his breakfast bowl." Baron replayed the scene without embellishment (clearly, none was needed) when my wife joined us downstairs for breakfast a few minutes later, and then again several times during our drive later that morning. At each business event after that where our paths crossed, Baron laughingly remembered his intimate introduction to Ruffin, "the biggest dog I've ever seen!" So he *was* a guard dog. (Or maybe he just didn't like having his breakfast interrupted.)

The Borders at Christmas; Tag (top) and Windi (bottom)

Ruffin and Chelsea at play

Tag and Ruffy's Circle Game:
Penalty (bottom)

Chapter 5
Freckles

Country living is different from city fare. As a human, you are living shoulder-to-*whatever* with the rest of the animal kingdom. You are in *their* home—a guest in *their* house. Splash around in a calm pool part of a creek, and *they* have to wait until the sediment settles back down before they can get a clean drink of water. Make a bunch of noise around the yard mid-evening, and startled birds will have to find their way back to their nests when they think things have quieted down, making it safe to resume their sleep; they get up early every day, you know. Lizards spend their lives driven to explore everything, so taking in stride their incursions into your bedroom or foyer once in a while is recommended: just throw a trash can over them, slide a baking sheet under it, and trot the ensemble out the front door (a reptile version of "catch and release"). Get over your "*What's that?*" reaction to nighttime screeches and cries in the woods: those are mealtimes. And scold them all you want, but getting dogs to quit pouncing on and littering their mice/vole/mole catches around the yard is a waste of your time and their patience: they were once wolves who did this to survive.

Human routines must adjust to rural life. Trotting out in your underwear after dark to roll the city trash container to the curb because you were already in bed before remembering that trash day was tomorrow(!) was not really an option when you lived a half-mile through dark and spooky woods from your county trash container. We tried to remember to put our trash cans into the back of our truck while it was still daylight, so we could see what we were doing at the other end of our driveway when pouring their contents into the county container each week. (Forget about doing it first thing on the scheduled pickup day: beating those fellas to your can was hopeless; apparently, they got up before the birds, and no matter where you lived, you were the first stop on their morning route.) With daylight around us, we could spot anything happening around that container, which (because we kept the lid on it tightly shut) usually was…nothing. Except one late afternoon in late autumn, when there was something…something moving skittishly around the container, trying to keep out of sight.

Turns out it was a small, gaunt, all-white female retriever or setter. It looked unsure of itself, and more than hungry, it seemed very uneasy, skittish—maybe sick. But not rabid (like I knew what that would look like: a dog frothing at the mouth in *Old Yeller* was the extent of my worldly wisdom when it came to rabies). Mary, Maiden of the Order of St. Francis, took food and water bowls back to the end of the driveway, and (after many efforts) coaxed it to gingerly sample some. This went on for a few days, Mary and I taking turns ferrying food and water the half-mile to where we figured our lost, white dog might continue to hang out. We added a cardboard box and a blanket for shelter. During those first few days, the skittish creature was not always visible, but we left a food bowl, and when we checked back on it a short time later, it was empty. We had a hard time convincing her to trust us enough to get close to her. She kept her distance. She also kept her mouth open constantly in an unnatural way, although there didn't seem to be anything stuck in the back of her mouth or throat that would account for this strange look.

At some point, days into this dance, she became bolder, and I managed to snag her and whisk her off to the vet's office for a complete exam. Due to faint spots on her skin along her back and shoulders, and a couple of tiny dark spots on her muzzle, we named her "Freckles," although from more than a foot away, she appeared to be all-white. Her hair fine and long, legs thin, tail wispy, face long and lean, she fortunately turned out not to be as fragile as her delicate features suggested.

After doing some blood work, Doc Ally's partner re-entered our small examination room with a somber look on his face. Freckles had some intestinal problems (from poor diet), but worse, she had heartworm. That accounted for her mouth being open at such an odd angle all the time: she was literally starving for oxygen. Left untreated, her condition would deteriorate until breathing became so painful that death would be a welcome relief. I remembered at that moment what veterinarians and animals health advocates regularly remind us: people who abandon their pets (alongside roadways, in woods) are condemning them to a long and painful death—some of the worst kinds of torture. Guessing her age to be eighteen months to two years, the doc said her youth might work in her favor, but heartworm treatments are tough on any dog of any age, and there was no guarantee of success. At the somewhat advanced stage of her condition, he estimated her odds of recovery at no better than fifty-fifty.

He told us what the treatment regimen would cost. *Ouch.* "Do you want to go forward with it?" he asked.

Mary and I looked at each other. This was a young, delicate animal of sweet disposition—scared, and in serious trouble through no fault of her own. "Yeah," we said.

"Cross your fingers," the man of science told us. Over the next several weeks of carefully prescribing medicines and monitoring results, in the words of the good doctor, a miracle happened. She survived.

Even then, however, not everything was fine. Doc had a couple more things to tell us: Freckles' backbone was fused (by what appeared to have been some sort of injury) in places, which explained why, when she ran, the back half of her body seemed to slope down toward the ground; she lacked the fluid movement ordinarily associated with free-wheeling running, where the back arches and flows in a smooth and rhythmic manner. Moreover, he said, her right leg had been damaged, so that it didn't maneuver properly; she was basically walking and running on three legs. The combination of these characteristics made most everything Freckles did look...odd. Her awkward gait smoothed out after she warmed up: it was a transformation that she obviously worked through with gritty determination until she was once again running with abandon. Knowing that she would quickly stiffen after exercise, she ran for as long as she could: she ran to be free—from pain, from memories, for the joy of life. Overall, to our astonishment, she got around very well. She took getting knocked around inadvertently by the other pack members in stride, learning how to bob and weave in and around the stampede up and down the back stairs before and after suppertime. Freckles had found a "safe house" at Meadowbrook, where she could be herself, infirmities and all. One of the magical things about that place was the field: whenever she ran through it, banged-up, deformed Freckles was a renewed pup—strong, alert, happy!

And, as we soon discovered once her heartworm was history, she was *fast*. Long ears and legs flapping at all angles, she was a white blur running across our field, turning lightning quick at a whim, joyously cavorting after butterflies and birds (she was a genuine bird dog). She was the picture of life on the run—

the very essence of freedom. Watching her was to realize that the boxes we humans put ourselves in (by our lifestyle choices, or inadvertently by habit) are a high price to pay for commitment to society's expectations of responsible living. Envying her flights of fancy from the moment she left the laundry room door for the day, I found myself visualizing her approach to life while I was at my desk in the city day after day, and wondering how I might find my way toward that.

During our weekend walks through our woods, Freckles would suddenly appear as a white apparition on a ridge, looking down us. She had come into view from nowhere: she always just appeared, stationary, like she had been there all along. Whichever of us spotted her first would turn to call to the other, "Freckles is here—look!" In the time it took to turn back around, she was gone. She played this appearing-and-vanishing game with us all the time, even through her later years. We had a "ghost dog," like the "Gray Ghost" of Civil War fame—occasionally spotted, always elusive. What a strange little being: wouldn't come when you called her, yet tantalized you with her "almost" presence. She was a creature on her own in this world, but wanting to maintain some sort of connection to us—among, but not *with*, us.

We learned right off that Freckles was not a dog-yard dog. She was a digger, and (amazingly, given her hind quarters' problems), an adept leaper. These skills matched up nicely with her will not to be enclosed during the day: we'd put her in the dog yard with the others, and before we got into the car to run errands, she was sprinting down the field. Living with dogs, we learned over time that dogs should be allowed to do whatever it is that makes them feel in control of their lives whenever possible; the rest of the time we humans force them into schedules and behavior that suit us. Dogs are generally expected to wait endlessly in captive places while we do people things for hours and days on end. Showing affection to dogs is often limited to a few seconds of patting them on the head, then hoping they find "something to do" the rest of the time. The best of us manage to squeeze out a couple minutes once in a while to toss a ball. Even walking the dog is frequently an exercise deemed by the dog owner to be good for him or her as much as for the dog, so Fido must either speed up or slow down to match whatever pace is preferred by his master. A true dog walking would have humans walk on surfaces preferred by the dog (cool grass instead of hard, hot asphalt), and perpetually stop—sometimes for long periods—while the canine adequately explores some fascinating blade of grass or clump of brush. If we humans had the full range of olfactory receptors dogs have, we would be right there alongside our faithful companions, noses into everything, discovering the true richness of the world (a cat was here, a new type of dog was there, somebody just had a burger, and *whoa!* chipmunks had a party *all over this place*!) So, when Freckles made it clear she was a field dog (and since we couldn't really do anything about it, anyway), that was that.

We wondered what the deal was going to be at night for our Happy Wanderer, though. Living in the middle of large areas of woods is fine, but staying out in them overnight, unprotected by a fence and shelter, is something suited only for wildlife—not pets. There are too many nocturnal creatures that can harm a dog during a time when dogs should be getting sleep. Freckles answered that question for us. We had put a dog house outside our laundry room back door steps, figuring she would want that shelter if she wasn't going to be spending nights schmoozing with the rest of the pack inside the dog yard. But no, from the outset she walked up the wooden steps to the landing outside the laundry room door, intent on heading into the house for the night.

"Okay," I said, "come on in, then."

That part went well, but the rest of the trip into the house didn't. Somebody in her past had apparently done a number on her in a way that involved doorways. She cowered, lowered her head, and though she clearly wanted to enter, wouldn't budge through the doorway. After considerable coaxing and my holding both the storm and back doors wide open, she finally screwed up her courage and in a flash bolted through the opening, slipped wildly on the tile floor, crashed into the washer and dryer, slipped and tumbled her way to a three-quarter wriggle finish, finally "sticking the landing" with a *floomph* under the utility sink! Of the many times I wish I'd had a video camcorder, this was the time I missed not having one the most. I was a little irked, though, when I noticed that every time she did this routine, the oh-so-delicate plumbing connection under that sink began to leak afterwards. I could fix it, sure—but it required the whole bag of the usual handy-home-owner tricks (nudging the pipe "just so," holding your nose just right). This was annoying, and it needed to stop.

Drastic measures were needed. I piled rubber boots and plastic buckets under that sink in an effort to physically block her out of there! Success? No. Freckles was willful. *All* our dogs were willful. A family trait. Watching her frantically climb over and into all that stuff, and lying down in a tangle that couldn't have been at all comfortable, I became aware of how badly damaged her psyche was from her previous existence. She obviously needed a tight enclosure she could feel safe in—like a burrow. Ultimately she acclimated to our home enough to trust her sleep to a cushioned bed in the open a whole foot away from the utility sink. Even then, she pressed herself up against the rear door that led into the garage; we didn't use that door much, anyway, so it worked out...just one of the zillion things you do to accommodate your furry partners.

Freckles' behavior continued to give us glimpses into her past life. One day I happened to be sweeping the laundry room at the time Freckles wanted in; she was fine until, halfway into the doorway from the outside landing, she spotted the broom I was holding. Panicked, she literally slammed herself sideways away from me into the door frame, yelped from hurting her ribs, then raced back outside and careened down the steps, out of control with fear. After that, we kept brooms and mops out of our hands whenever we were near her. I am glad I never met the people who had Freckles before we did.

Already full-grown, Freckles didn't need mothering like the others. And it wasn't in her nature to need to be pals with the other dogs, so she remained almost completely aloof from them. Almost. There was that once-in-a-while thing with Ruffy. Even Her Aloofness could not resist that thick brindle coat, strong countenance, firm masterful ears, and that *je ne sais quoi* that melts even the most distant and self-reliant females. Ruffy, it seems, was quite the stud. The picture of this tentative, delicate, living-life-around-the-edges-of-the-pack figure suddenly plopping herself down in front of Ruffy in full doggy play mode (front legs down with a thump, head lowered but eyes sparkling, tail up and entire hind end wagging expectantly) was hysterical! But not as funny as Ruffy's reaction. His head jerked back a bit, and he looked up at us, whimpering, *What's this? What am I supposed to do here?* A pretty young thing was making a bona fide play for her guy, and all he could muster was his usual, barely audible, plaintive little whine, "Mmpph." When he turned away, she galloped around the other side of him to greet him over there; when he shuffled a little ways away, she sped along after him, resuming her playful stance and wiggles, undeterred. *Ain't love grand?*

Other than her occasional moves on Ruffin, Freckles was our associate pack member, content to live each and every day in the field, sometimes making forays into the woods, chasing butterflies, pointing out birds (which she did best and most often in front of the bird houses…*so* that's *where they are!*). Rain or shine, cold or hot, stormy or clear, Freckles and her field were inseparable, and life was good. Well, good for *her*, anyway: when she found the inevitable muck pockets near the creek, she wallowed, and filled the laundry room those nights with Eau De Yuk. Fine and silky, her hair usually shed that black sludge within a day or two; and anyway, it did no good to consider bathing her: any attempt by us to (1) catch her (like all dogs, she was an excellent mind-reader), and (2) administer soap and water, would have been torturous to her already fragile psyche…we couldn't risk trashing the tenuous relationship we had forged with her, especially over a matter so insignificant to a dog as personal hygiene.

Life was cooking right along with our somewhat unusual gang of five. Routines were being established, and their doggy personalities were developing into recognizably—and distinctly—individual beings. Five was a lot of dogs to feed, provide medical attention for, and make time to love. The breadth of what we had taken on was beginning to sink in, which made our next move…unthinkable.

Freckles: first seen (top); field running (middle); at birdfeeder (bottom)

Chapter 6
Scamp

For the first time in our married lives, I was taking time off from work to join my wife on one of her business trips. Her offer was irresistible: time with my sweet-bear away from daily responsibilities of home and work, in Charleston, South Carolina, two weeks before Christmas. I imagined myself wandering the streets of this charming, historical town, maybe picking out a few Christmas cards, poking around in gift shops decorated for the season, dining with my special someone by candlelight, strolling back to the hotel under holiday lights, as carols drifted through cobblestone streets. A real Normal Rockwell affair; a Hallmark movie.

Packed and ready, the only thing left to do before heading our car south was truck the dogs to our usual boarding kennels (about a half-hour farther out in the country). Those kennels made for a pretty good doggy camp: each run was part indoor, part outdoor. In the outdoor part, the dogs could watch horses on surrounding hills, and sniff fascinating smells on breezes that blew continuously there. Owner/operator Karen absolutely loved dogs, so special meal treats and other forms of extra attention were guaranteed. She had a good heart for animals, which was about to turn our lives upside down the morning we dropped our guys off into her care.

This time there was a box on the floor in the middle of her office, and in the box two small, tan-colored puppies sat, huddled against each other, facing the world that had crashed around them. This brother and sister duo had been tossed into the roadside ditch outside her kennels a few days earlier, she told us; the male had already been spoken for, but so far nobody wanted the female. (That's the thing with many country folks, we had learned: females got pregnant, so females were a problem.) While the good innkeeper attended to our tribe, I bent over the box, and a pair of Cleopatra eyes gazed back…eyes that mesmerized Roman generals and conquered nations. Chest out, this orphaned creature did her best to project self-confidence, despite her tiny frame. What an amazing combination: tough and vulnerable. But it was those eyes. *Game over*.

Back in the office, Karen pressed us hard to take her. I gently reminded her that we were in there that morning in the first place because we were leaving for an out-of-state trip, so we couldn't take anybody!

Smiling, she said, "I'll keep her here for you, no charge; you can pick her up when you get back."

A bunch of thoughts went through my head in a millisecond; I think only one flashed through Mary's—*No. No, no. No, no, no.*

"Karen," I said, "please try to find her a home while we're gone; we have five dogs already. We don't need another dog; we really don't."

I was distracted the entire drive to Charleston. My eyes must have seen the road, but my mind was back at the kennels, gazing down into the deep pools of that puppy's eyes. Having grown up with small dogs, I missed not having a small couch companion. *But another dog? Argh.* Still, I parried and thrust with Mary over the idea of bringing yet another dog into our lives.

"They all get along so well now, Skip," Mary reminded me. "Why push it?"

"It would make a perfect six-pack," I offered. *That was lame. Try again.* "And," I hurriedly added, "I have always wanted a couch dog; you know, one to sit and sleep and watch TV beside us on the couch—a *couch* dog." I thought if I repeated the phrase enough, it would start to make some sort of sense to us. Mary, who has always been incredibly patient and forgiving of my idiotic notions, outdid herself during the next several days by innocently ignoring my musings about a new puppy. To my credit, I tried hard not to bring the subject up every time I opened my mouth. It helped that she was at meetings most of each day.

While Mary was off attending to business, I set up shop in our hotel room with my portable typewriter, composing Christmas cards as music streamed through my earphones. But it wasn't the music that had my attention: it was an orphaned pair of eyes that bore into me from the first moment I saw them. Mary returned to the room early from one of the business sessions, and began to read my Christmas card letters. Every one of them contained long descriptions of our recent experience at the kennels (meeting this irresistible new, abandoned puppy with the most amazing brown eyes). As she read, I continued typing, holding my breath, pretending not to pay her any attention. Somewhere behind me, I heard a sigh.

We played a hang-man game on the return trip, thinking of words that (*big surprise*) pertained to thoughts on getting another puppy. I started, thinking of the word, "Sixpack."

The game afoot, Mary countered with, "Vet bills."

"Couch dog," was my next offering, wondering if that would melt her some.

"House-breaking" came back.

This was going to be harder than I thought. Suddenly we were home.

Thing is, I already had a name in mind, from a dog I had been given for a short time when I was four years old: I remember loving that fellow, but he was going to be really big, and in retrospect, my parents honestly didn't need that kind of responsibility at that time, so we gave him away. Probably a good thing, actually. I am told by my mother that one afternoon she told me, "Throw the dog into the basement." The term, "throw," was a colloquialism of hers for "take and put somewhere," but I was only four...so...I...tossed Scamper the Bouncing Puppy down the basement steps. Horrified, Mom reportedly was more careful with her words after that when giving me instructions. Maybe subconsciously I've been trying to make it up to dogs ever since.

When we picked our gang up at the kennels, Karen told us nobody had wanted her (yeah, like she *tried* to find her a home while we were away). "So, she's ready to go home with you," Karen finished, a big smile on her face. Mary and I were both a little numb, but go through with it we did: five in the back, one in Mary's lap, we took *six* dogs home. Then, per the all-too-familiar drill, we headed off to the Reidsville Veterinary Hospital for another round of first exam, first shots. The name the receptionist wrote down on the new patient's chart was "Scamp." Years later, that same receptionist, having established her own relationship with Scamp, aware of Scamp's genetic mixture of many breeds and background of having been dumped on the side of a road as a six-week-old throw-away, tagged her "Scraps." That nickname, more than a few others I coined for her over time (Scamper-doodle, Scampracity), stuck.

For us grown people, a five-acre field is a big place. To a puppy, it's HUGE, and the rest of the 41 acres, plus neighboring woods, must have looked terrifying to young Scamper. Nah. Not to this one. She couldn't wait to get at it. There were brothers and sisters out there to play with; she could hear them outside—she could see them oh-so-close at meal times in the kitchen. She could see them, that is, through bars.

It was winter—too cold for a youngster with short hair to be outside all day—so we incarcerated her inside. The cage we provided for her was advertised as suitable for a Saint Bernard, which made her in it appear even more lost than the orphan she already was. A huge affair, it blocked the opening between the dining room and the kitchen, but the compromise was worth it to avoid tripping over it every time we padded from refrigerator to stove to sink and back. We needed to go about *our* business without worrying every second where she might be doing *hers*. Not a bit happy about the arrangement, she decided one day enough was enough: she took the bars between her baby teeth, and rattled that cage back and forth so loudly we could hear it from upstairs. How she did what she did next, I really can't explain under the laws of physics, but she actually managed to move that entire ensemble clear across the kitchen! That was one willful puppy; I wondered what the full-grown version of this one was going to be like? Taping the cage to the tile floor accomplished a couple of things: the stickum stuff in that tape ate through the surface of what I guess turned out to be *cheap* tile; and it toughened the youngster's muscles as she learned to first lift the cage *up* before trying to move it across the floor—all that from *inside* it! An Arnold Schwarzenegger puppy. *Wowser.*

With more than the usual incentive to house-train as quickly as possible (she was wrecking the kitchen floor), it wasn't long before we turned her over to the guys outside during the day, but still allowed her to stay inside at night, along with Freckles. Sleeping accommodations for willful Scamp were necessarily extensive. We blocked off the dining room/kitchen opening with several 25-pound dog food containers, and closed the dining room/foyer opening by keeping the adjacent stairwell closet door open. These are inventive things you do when you have dogs: trash the otherwise lovely flow-through openings to the dining room to protect the dining room carpet from dogginess. We rationalized that we didn't really need those doorways, anyway: we used the dining room (arguably the prettiest room in the house) only two times a year for those traditional family Thanksgiving and Christmas dinners. If we built again, our next house would not have a separate dining room, that's for sure. Scamp's bed was fixed up against the opened closet door, where she felt protected in a small space, and knew that our bedroom was directly above her. "Goodnight, Scamp—sleep well," was the last thing I said each and every night as Mary and I climbed the stairs to bed. Do that for a half-dozen years nightly, and something in your heart seals permanently around it.

Sprung from kitchen-prison, Scamp immediately latched onto her adopted mother. Whereas Chelsea missed out on the receiving end of that experience, she was given full opportunity to dish out motherhood—like it or not. Perseverance, thy name was Scamp: wherever Chelsea went, whatever Chelsea did, in whatever position Chelsea slept, there was tag-along-Scamp in lock step. *We* found it adorable: Chelsea, not so much. Chelsea's only escape from this incessant call for a role model was to check out the tall grass areas in the field, where little Scamp found the going more daunting than even her iron will could overcome.

The toughness of our newest pack member was never more evident than during her first big walk with all of us, when we hiked down to a major creek fed by our two boundary streams. The banks of this creek were deep and steep, gouged by repeated flash flooding. Twelve-week-old Scamp found the winter air exhilarating: she fairly flew along ahead of us, showing everybody she was a full player in our merry band. Her lack of woodsy experience caught up with her suddenly when her front legs tripped over the edge of the creek bank, and she tumbled headlong into a mighty *splash*! Images of a quickly drowning pup flashing through my head, I raced over to where I thought I saw her drop off the bank, figuring I would have to scramble down in there myself to fetch her back up. But no, as I got to the spot where she had disappeared, up popped the top of her little head, front paws scratching and digging for all she was worth to try and wrestle herself up and over the tree roots and soft riverbank dirt to freedom. She looked like a drowned rat.

The air temperature that afternoon was a not-so-balmy 20-something, the skies were gray, Scamp was drenched through that short hair to the bone, and we were at least an hour from home. My instinct was to scoop her up against my jacket and hold her close until she warmed up.

"No, it's better if she runs on her own," piped Mary. "That way, she'll burn more calories and keep herself warmer, and she'll also dry faster." She had read that somewhere.

Some friend you got there, Scamp, I thought. But it made sense, so with a murmured apology, I let her down to make the best of things. The neat thing was she didn't give me any kind of a what-are-you-doing-to-me? look of shock: instead, she immediately began trotting—very, *very* purposefully. *Tough love*. And this was one tough cookie. She looked c-o-l-d at the beginning, and ran along with stiff movements; but after a while, she loosened up as her hair looked a little drier, and her face relaxed a bit. We had aborted the marathon nature hike and headed for home immediately after Scamp's "swim." By the end of the walk, she seemed to be reasonably comfortable. Still, when we reached our house, she made first dibs on front row, center at the wood stove, and didn't budge for hours.

Scamp continued to grow up with an iron will, and a constitution to match. Remarkable for such a small dog, she was game for anything, and carried herself with dignity and strength right up there with all the rest of the pack. I think all of us tend to grow in a direction and to a degree that we see ourselves, and that self-perception becomes either a limiting or an enabling factor. For Scamp, no hurdle was too high, no task too challenging, no adventure out of reach. On a farm, this requires strength as much as desire, and Scamp began to develop some unbelievable muscles. She looked like a bowling-alley girl, a biker chick. You just didn't want to mess with her—she could hold her own with anything and anybody. Her tail was boss (hair as thick as our German shepherd's coat, which was saying something—I never actually *saw* Ruffy's skin...I knew it was under there someplace, but I never made it through all that wonderfully woolly stuff to get to it.) And she had a squint to her eyes that could stop a rhino charge. She was queen of the pack, all pint-size of her notwithstanding. This may have been helped along by her status as an indoor dog at night. The others seemed to understand Freckles' pass as a product of her neuroses, but Scamp's special status was clearly offered by us as recognition of something she had that they did not. It may have confused them, but they never challenged it. She didn't mind letting them know about it, either: the smug little smile she laid on them when they were shuttled into their yard each night, as she whirled to scamper ahead of us up the back stairs into the house, was not wasted on anybody.

So...we had a pack.

We had no idea what that meant. They would teach us. And sometimes easily, sometimes stumbling, we would learn.

Scamper's first week (top two)
Scamp grown (bottom)

Part Two

Meadowbrook Life and Times

Chapter 7
Boss Tag

Breeders and other dog owners have always known that in a household of two or more dogs, one of them *will* be leader. If two siblings are selected, it is best to pick one of each sex, in which case the male will almost always fill the leadership role naturally, quarrels between them will be fewer to arise, and those that do will tend to be settled quickly. We followed that advice, and were glad we did. Tag took charge from the outset: pretty soon he had added *us* to his list of charges: fine with us—we needed it. "Tag in charge"—one of his many honorary titles.

We found out just how serious young Tag was going to be about his role on this planet when we took him and his sister to Ocracoke Island, part of the Outer Banks of North Carolina, for our annual mid-winter visit there. This was an annual pilgrimage that Mary and I had made for over a decade, as a way to clear the head and restore the spirit after twelve months of metropolitan congestion and bustle. It felt natural to continue that tradition with our new dogs—successors to Ratches. *He* had loved it—why wouldn't *they*, as well? It turns out they did, but in a decidedly different way. Whereas Ratches padded along beside us (*behind* us in a headwind) walking the empty beach, content to scatter sea gulls when the spirit moved him, and sleep beside us for hours at a time in the dunes, Tag found the whole experience exhilarating for the multitude of responsibilities facing him. There were way too many things that needed arranging and coordinating for one Border collie to tackle—but he would give it his all, trying!

We hadn't even gotten as far as the island before he had a chance to show his stuff. We were having car trouble, and while we were stopped at a roadside garage, waiting on service, the Borders meandered through the sandy brush of "down east, North Carolina." Off their leashes (*What could that hurt? Our dogs are well-behaved...*) before I could finish that thought, Tag and Windi spotted the garage owner's old hound, and mayhem broke out. Tag barked and charged the poor, small-town, calm-mannered pooch, while Windi circled around to cut off any escape. Startled and more than a little anxious at being chased and herded on his own ground, the poor fella did the only thing he could think of on the spur of the moment: he hopped up onto an old trailer, and held his shaky balance on that incline while our sweet puppies ran around and around it, barking their heads off. (Border-speak: "*We gotcha, we gotcha! Whee! You're—not—goin'—anywhere; you're—not—goin'—anywhere! Wheee!*") I wanted to crawl into a hole and cover it up behind me. Mary and I made pitiful efforts to distract them, but Border collies once in the midst of a job are loathe to leave it. Even professionally trained members of this breed (who have discipline drummed into them early in their lives by their owners) will test their handlers' patience by trying to "finish the job" as *they* see it. Sheep-herding trials in show events have embarrassed more than a few handlers whose contestants have given it that extra zeal and consequently unraveled an otherwise marvelous herding run. For us novices at Border collie handling, reigning them in was a totally impossible challenge.

Like a fool trying to wrestle a greased pig, I turned things into more of a circus chasing after Tag, but finally tackled him. With the leader corralled, Windi soon gave it up, and we had both dogs on leash. We ignored the disapproving stares of locals, and did our best to make it appear as innocent unawareness. *Please fix our car, anyway; I promise we'll* never *drive through here again—honest—even if it* is *the only route to Ocracoke. Please forgive us our Border collies. Argh.*

Once on the beach, we pulled out our trusty yellow kite that had been waiting all year for its annual return to the happy skies of the Outer Banks. Our dream vision? Sail it high into the sky-blue winds over sandy dunes and waving sea oats. Tag's mission: seek and capture. The usually breezy conditions on Ocracoke sputtered this time, so when the unsuspecting kite dipped low to the ground for lack of wind, Tag was (ta-da!) right there on the spot to pounce on the tail and haul that rascal down. We have a photo of him proudly sitting squarely on the downed kite, the world's biggest grin on his face. *Did I do good, boss, or what?*

We never tried that gig again; instead, on a summer day later that year, we picked a place closer to home—a day trip to a remote section of Wilson Creek, North Carolina. On flattened white ledges at water's edge, it was a perfect spot for a picnic and an afternoon commune with nature. Skip, Mary, Tag, and Windi—our family. How idyllic, how cozy, how… "BARK, BARK, BARK-BARK-BARK!" (Border-speak: *Incoming!*)

Boaters in individual, inflatable kayaks appeared just upstream and were bearing down on our little band at a pretty good clip. The creek narrowed where we were, so the merry group of kayakers were about to meet the Border patrol close up and personal. As usual, Windi was first to sound the alarm: "BARK, BARK-BARK, BARK!"

Tag was only too happy to join in, and as each kayaker passed unavoidably within a couple of feet of our watch hounds, he not-so-subtly leaned away from the noisy greeters. Regrettable enough that the kayakers had their time with nature interrupted by dogs behaving badly, it was even more worrisome to me that one strong poke by sharp claws into rubber tubing, and somebody was going to swim the rest of that trip. As we tried shushing our troops, Tag shot us a look. *What are you* doing? *These are* invaders—*gotta run 'em off! Don't you know anything about anything?* Border collies are the smartest of dogs: they just don't always share human goals. Mary and I are, admittedly, two of the most stubborn individuals in the world, but against a willful Border collie (which really *is* a redundancy), we were no match. So the Borders barked, the kayakers paddled faster, and I chased both dogs around and around on the slippery rocks. Eventually we ran out of boaters and resumed our lunch. We never tried our luck picnicking with our black-and-whites there again. O for two, we were fast running out of places to "enjoy" nature with our dynamic duo.

Over time we learned that there were two places—and only two places—where we could count on *The Tag & Windi Show* and the world to be on mutually comfortable terms: at Meadowbrook, and in the bed of our truck with the other dogs. And, to be honest, the safe-and-comfortable world of the truck bed took a little training first. Tag followed orders beautifully: we told him to stay in the truck, so that's what he did. What he could not control was Ruffy's enthusiastic lunges from one side of the bed to the other while we were all speeding around on country curves on weekend errands. During one of those outings, the big guy spotted something that motivated him to whirl and lurch sideways. The whole truck bounced, and Tag was unfortunate enough to be between where Ruffy *was*, and where Ruffy was intent on *going*. Out went Tag, head over keister. He must have hit the pavement hard: when we screeched to a halt, made a U-turn, and returned to where he was, we found him sitting—dazed and quivering. Not a whimper, though he had skinned the hide off the underside of his muzzle and scraped hunks of fur and flesh from one leg and part of his chest. *Ouch.* We gently held him until he stopped shaking and allowed us to carry him into the truck cab, where he would ride with us straight home so we could tend to his wounds. Actually, that was Tag's second time out of the truck: the first one was in his puppyhood, when during one of our back roads training sessions, he followed his sister up and over the tail gate. She apparently found the allure of other dogs too much to ignore, so out she went, Tag (the good, protective brother) right behind her. We quickly stopped, and began the frantic work of trying to round up two Border collie puppies bent on corralling a growing number of tough country dogs that suddenly began appearing from everywhere. Lecturing them sternly as we tossed them back into the truck bed, we moved that show out of there in a din of barks from the riled up gang around us. An awareness that they had narrowly escaped something pretty horrible may have dawned on them as we barreled out of there in a cloud of dust: we had no more trouble with that pair venturing out of the truck thereafter. Experience—the best teacher, *if you live through her class.*

At Meadowbrook, Tag charged himself with protecting our place as his first order of business. Every day, all day, when outside of the dog yard, he ran continuous circles around our house, wearing a track wider and deeper as the months passed. When inside the dog yard, whether to keep in practice or driven by instincts passed down to him from hundreds of years of breeding, he ran the same circle along the inside of the 400-foot perimeter fence. Even during our family walks through the woods and along creeks, whenever we stopped for a few minutes to sit and enjoy the ambience of nature, Tag began a large circle around us, making sure the area we were in was secure. As he trotted steadily along, he punctuated those circles with periodic glances upward, checking the skies for predators. This was a routine he carried through life: his energy for this was inexhaustible. He protected. We were charmed, and grateful. It might seem silly to humans who have never been exposed to this kind of attention from a dog, but to those of us who have, the assuredness that you are being well cared for builds its way into your psyche, then into your heart. That it comes from your dog is all the more endearing—magical to some, I suppose, but we just accepted it as a natural part of our Meadowbrook life. I, at least, never gave it a thought that it might end some day, and when it inevitably had to, we felt an additional sadness...we felt more vulnerable to the world. Tag took care of us while he was here.

"Wheeee!" That one word, tossed out and held as long and at as high a pitch as I could muster, shifted Tag into his highest gear. Pedal-to the-metal, he *tore* around the house, while Mary and I cheered. The boy's pads barely touched the ground when he was in "wheee" mode. Land-speed records fell as Taggie ran flat out, hurling off the stone patio, cutting the turn hard around the trembling red maple at the corner of the house, disappearing around the far end and along the brick walkway across the front. For those seconds he was out of sight, it was like the moon shuttle orbiting around the back side of the moon—no contact, just silence, and an eager anticipation of his rounding the other end of the house to complete the circle. Heaven help anything in his path as he roared into sight through the open carport back across the patio. These bursts of speed became his trademark: his ears laid back, his whole body lowered and flattened, as the after-burners kicked in. His grin after doing one or more three-sixties off the patio, readying himself for another round in either direction, confirmed how much he loved it.

With the later coming of Ruffy on the scene, Tag's race-around-the-house turned into a game. Ruffin watched Tag do his whirling-dervish act with fascination. Pretty soon the big guy couldn't stand it any longer: he had to get in on this. So, he began standing closer, then closer still, to Tag's path, jutting his muzzle out just a bit as the Taggert raced by to try to "tag" him. As the '60s song says, "You don't pull the tail of a junkyard dog." When Tag noticed this encroachment, the combination of "Don't touch the pack leader while he's doing his thing," and his love of "serious" play flipped a switch in there somewhere. As he flashed by Ruffy, Tag suddenly whirled, dashed over to Ruffin, cornered him between a lawn chair and table, and chomped down on the big guy's muzzle. *Ow-ooch!* Amazingly, Ruffy let him do it: then again, Tag *was* boss. In typical Border collie fashion, this new wrinkle instantly became a new routine: race around the house a few times, let Ruffy get close to an ambush, then whirl and chomp on the Ruffer's nose. *What fun!* Even better *if you can get a little whimper out of that giant. Who's your papa?*

The rest of the new game, which the two of them worked out in short order, was for Ruffy to be able to block or disrupt Tag's blitzkrieg stride somewhere in the vicinity of the patio, and cause Tag to reverse his direction around the house. Sounds simple enough, but there were subtle, yet definite, distinctions at work. If Tag felt that Ruffy tried to *set a pick* off the patio furniture, carport support beams, or patio stairs, that brought out the referee in Tag. (The hapless Ruffin was immediately herded over to the standard penalty box—the niche between a patio chair and table, and made to lower his nose, so that Tag could chomp him on his muzzle. This was no slap on the wrist, either: Ruffin's whimpers of pain were sometimes spiked with one loud cry. It always made us grimace watching and listening to this, and even though it lasted only a few seconds, we often started calling out to Tag to break it up. *Our* sensibilities were offended, and it wasn't even *our* noses being shredded! Amazing animal, Ruffy. He loved his Taggie.

While Ruffin agreeably went along with this muzzle-chew, Tag, for his part, conceded that some of Ruffy's moves deserved recognition. Ruffy worked on his twist-and-turn skills, and occasionally was able to cleanly block Tag's spirited dash across the patio. If the cutoff move was smooth enough, Tag gave him credit, did a three-sixty (sometimes two in a row, which brought ooh's and aah's from the gallery) just to make sure Ruffy didn't leave a loophole in his stance, then whirled and raced off in the *opposite* direction around the house to resume the game. Points were scored at that moment, and Ruffy knew it: his posture straightened, and he swaggered a little as he flopped those huge paws at a victor's pace to take up a new position to ambush Tag on his next pass. Not every circle brought Ruffin out into ambush mode: he gauged Tag's speed and mood, and gambled carefully when he thought he might successfully turn Tag around: to guess wrong, he well knew, had *consequences*. Ruffy's favorite spot to lie-in-wait (if Tag was coming counter-clockwise through the open carport) was right on the carport-patio border, slightly behind the parked truck. This was risky, though: if Ruffy (from any position) suddenly darted forward from the side to jab Tag in the ribs (instead of acceptably heading Tag off), he had committed a foul, and he instantly knew it. Sometimes he just couldn't help himself, but he learned to control that urge. Too many painful sessions in the penalty box will do that. On and on the game went until Tag was tired. When you're pack leader, you get to say when the game's over. *It's good to be the king.*

Running circles and exacting discipline made for great fun and healthy exercise for the Boss and his crew, but in the wild, animals have a deadly serious purpose underlying most everything they do. When he could be persuaded, Tag mixed in fun with his routines: but as pack leader, the job was everything, and you never knew when you were going to be called upon to do it.

    A routine walk down the field for all of us one weekend afternoon—gray skies, a fall nip in the air, sharp smells of decaying leaves and rotting limbs of fallen trees, Scamp and Chelsea behind us in the field snouffling for mice, Freckles bounding through the woods someplace in her own Middle Earth adventure. Far ahead of us roamed Tag, and close behind him, Windi. Ruffin at our side. Everything as it should be for a timeless interlude of peace, feeling alive with autumn's signals that winter was on its way. Tag startled us, breaking the calm with several sharp alarm barks. Then a flurry of urgent barks from both Tag and Windi brought Ruffin out of his saunter and into a run toward them, ears fully forward and alert. Not being able to see through the brush at the end of the field, which formed the property line between us and our nearest neighbors, only heightened our anxiety: something was wrong, or dangerous, and it had the Borders' full attention…

    Our neighbors had a pair of Rottweilers—a mother and daughter affair—who were decidedly caricatures of the breed: strong, menacing in appearance (unless you were family), and equipped with jaws of death. Mom was okay, in that she pretty well minded her own business and didn't move away much from her house. Daughter, on the other hand, felt compelled to guard her 52 acres with the goal of removing all intruders; her countenance suggested that she enjoyed her work—looked forward to it, in fact. I ran across her one overcast day when I was tidying up the boundary bushes. Mid-pruning, I felt an overwhelming presence, like when I was scuba-diving on our honeymoon off the coast of Tobago in the midst of schools of fish and bunch of coral: suddenly, the water was still, and equally suddenly devoid of fish. I felt instantly alone, and looking around quickly, I found out why: a barracuda had slipped quietly into the area, and everybody who knew better cleared out, leaving the two of us to stare at each other. Offering little prayers as I eased back and out of the picture as gently as I could, I look back on that moment with a flush of relief.

    The younger Rottweiler stood stone-still facing me, head lowered, not fifty feet away. You read about hikers suddenly face to face with a bear, and not knowing whether to run, stand still, look submissively down and away, make a bunch of loud noises, what? I was just over her side of the property line, and she knew it. That made me—vulnerable. My first thought: turn and run like hell. Yeah, right. I'd be overtaken in two to three seconds, and ripped to shreds even faster. That gory visual settled me down some. Okay, no running. What else? What else? Look casually around...don't look straight at her...don't want to challenge her. No threat from me...no harm from me...I'm...just...checking out the woods and...no problem here...just..... *And then it came to me:* look down and to the side, and, like I'm looking for something I've dropped, ease back and sideways, like I'm lost in my own world of finding a dropped pair of pliers or something...just...keep looking for it...that's right...eeezy does it. *I was back a ways on my own property before I had the courage to glance up and see if...* my Lord, she was still there! *But farther away from me. She hadn't moved a muscle. I continued my studied escape until I was well away from the far end of the field. Only then did I feel I could at last turn my back on her and walk quickly toward the house. That was the first time I remember taking a breath. Heart literally pounding in the center of my chest, feeling the sweat of fear, I took a few short breaths, then exhaled with relief—a moment I will never forget.*

...Now Tag was extremely upset at something from that same area at the end of our field. Ferocious barks from him quickened our pace for a few steps until we saw the cause of his concern: daughter Rottweiler again, this time standing *on* the property line, lowered stance, staring hard at Tag and Windi. Ruffin by now was halfway to Tag, coming at a full run. Tag whirled around, and sharply barked him to return to guard us. Ruffy abruptly halted his advance, and appeared confused, even hurt. Tag took one step toward him, and barked sharply again. This time, Ruffy got the message, returned to us at a full gallop, turned around when he banged into our legs, and held us there, per Tag's instructions. We were worried for our Borders, so we started to run toward the action about a hundred feet away. Nope—we weren't going anywhere. Ruffy deftly and forcibly planted himself sideways to block both of us, looked up at us purposefully, and held his ground. Satisfied, Tag resumed his guard barks, and together he and Windi finally persuaded the Hun to retreat into her own territory. Tag, the Boss, was teaching Ruffy the Protector, how it's done. Protect the house and territory, but above all, protect the humans. Communicating quick and decisive commands to each other, man's best friends knew their jobs, and were up to the task. More than a lesson in canine instincts, Mary and I had been treated to a lesson in pack behavior: the dogs of Meadowbrook working together to accomplish a lot in a hurry in the face of real danger. We were beginning to realize the capabilities of our Meadowbrook partners.

It is commonly said that in Britain, Border collies can run a hundred miles a day easily when herding. Old-timers with thick Scottish brogues to this day will tell you that a Border collie will run to ground to try to finish a job; a good handler has to be careful not to ask too much from his herding dog, lest he lose him to his heart. During our two travels to Scotland in the early 1990s, Mary and I saw Border collies in action doing the real thing on rolling hillsides. Leaping over and wriggling through holes in six-foot high rock walls, these dogs fairly flew over the terrain, continually moving the entire flock, rounding up stray sheep, knowing by training and instinct what needed to be done. Witnessing their intense concentration and absolute commitment to completing their appointed tasks, it is easy for us to understand the appreciative words of author Donald McCaig *(An American Homeplace,* Crown Publishers, Inc., New York, copyright 1992, reprinted with permission), which we happened upon sometime later, and which have hung, framed, on our living room wall ever since:

> One December evening you'll go out
> to bring in the bred ewes, and it'll
> be driving snow, and those hummocks
> way at the far end of the pasture
> might be sheep and might not, too,
> and the light will be failing. Quietly,
> you'll send your dog into the dusk,
> where his knowledge and heart will
> bring your sheep safely home.
> That's why stock dogs have
> one-syllable names: Ben, Nell, Pep,
> Lass, Cap, Hope. You can cry
> their names into the teeth of the wind.

Born to run, Tag's endless circle runs continued *inside* the house, too. When not "on guard" under the desk (A Washington Irving replica Partner's Desk—open kneehole front to back), he ran his circles around the sofa in the living room while we did our kitchen chores, watched TV, did picture puzzles in the corner, worked at the desk, read, played music. He most often had a far-off look in his eyes as he made round after round, no doubt hearing the mystical call of his ancestors from the Scottish moors or craggy Welsh hillsides. (I learned over time that whenever he suddenly leaped up from his watchful position under the writer's desk and began running his circles more frantically than usual, he needed to go outside for a minute; torn between being too conscientious to quit his post, and understanding that you didn't whiz inside the people house, he did the only thing he could think of: distract himself by running—endlessly running—like a Border collie would do in the vastness of sheep pastures in the Old World.) Despite our best efforts to make the house ready for sale years later, the living room's hardwood floor still bore unmistakable evidence that a Border collie pack leader once lived there.

Chapter 8
Windi-Woo

While vacationing in the North of Scotland, we slowly wound our rental car along the typically narrow roads through moors, alongside lochs, and over endless hilly terrain of marsh, heather and peat. Every turn brought a chance at something new to us—some new way of looking at life, mostly due to the slower pace there by people unburdened by corporate insistence on purchase power as a measure of success. Late one afternoon we came around a bend to find...a road full of sheep! We slowed, then stopped, turned off the engine, and watched a young couple following along, hand in hand in the setting sun. They walked comfortably, unhurried, a Border collie trailing companionably between them. With endlessly practiced moves, two more Border collies, fanned out on either side, easily herded the flock home at the gentle close of a day. It was one of those moments you remember for the rest of your life. Our goal in living ever since has been that Scotland scene: to walk lightly of spirit, hand-in-hand, with someone you love, and have a good dog at your side.

Border collie lore has it that in a household of multiple BCs, one will assume charge of the people, while the others perform the outside herding tasks. Being the house dog bears no shame: indeed, even among the hardest-working dogs in the world, a Border collie that is responsible for the people of the household holds as high a place of honor in the pack as the sweaty herders...it's just a different job, and one that is taken as seriously as fending off a wolf in defense of the flock. While Tag took on the rest of the world, Windi quietly guarded *us*.

Windi's job looked pretty cushy to the casual observer: she could lie around on the air-conditioning vents all day in the hot weather, which for the queen o' the undercoat was a royal blessing. When it was sofa time in the evening, she took up her post at Mary's feet. She was more playful than schmoozy with me, nosing a tennis ball into my lap at the supper table whether I was through eating or not (our house operated on Eastern Border collie time), and backing up into the foyer for the usual hundred tosses or so.

Midway through our Meadowbrook years she and I brought Tag into a modified version of "Wheee!" that we could play inside. It was the Tag and Ruffy game played the same way, except Tag raced around the sofa instead of the house. I sat on the edge of my kitchen chair, Windi at my feet, both of us poised to bark at Tag when he banked the far turn toward the back of the sofa, exposing him to us through the open double French doors. Windi anticipated Tag's arrival with quivering whiskers and quick, sideways glances up at me beside her. *Ready, Skip? Ready? Oh, boy, this is fun! Ready?* As Tag flew into view, Windi barked once and lunged, hoping that would turn him back in the opposite direction. Sometimes it did, but not always. He was slightly bigger than she was, and he was all muscle, so when he was intent on blowing by her, he could do it, and you didn't want to be in the way of that freight train at full throttle. Also, if things felt a little testy, Tag could throw his own bark into the mix, which, if Windi didn't back down from, could end up being one of those, "I'm in charge, and I'm going to chew on your side fur until you cry, 'Uncle,'" kind of events. (And, per the rules of dog-dom, the pack leader always wins.) This game was fun for Windi, and Tag good-naturedly went along with it. He let *me* get into the game once in a while, too: I'd get down on all fours in front of the sofa, and try to head him off there like Windi was trying to do behind it. He barked more playfully at me than at Windi, and at the end of the contest, there were cookies all around. *No wonder we never got much housework done around there. No time.*

Windi seemed to us to be the most mystical of our gang. Her ESP—with her brother and with us—was phenomenal. Thinking of something to which your dog attaches an emotion, you stir something psychically in the dog's brain, and voila!—you have silently communicated with your pet, whether you intended to or not. Dog owners will tell you this. If you entertain the notion of giving your dog a bath, that rascal will disappear instantly, and will be very reluctant to come to your call. Same thing when it's time to take bowser to the vet for a checkup. Conversely, when we contemplated taking a drive somewhere (other than to the vet or kennels) in our truck, the whole pack showed up underfoot out of nowhere, prancin' and dancin' with those eager, *"Oh, boy! Where we goin'? Can we go, too? Let's go!"* expressions on their fuzzy faces. We never packed for a vacation without having to look over at glum, heads-to-the-floor dogs, morosely following us from room to room: they knew full well that it was soon going to be kennel time again. Dogs know things by our habits, sure; but they are keen listeners to the spirit, and are tuned in deeply to the world of thought.

Windi worked at communicating with us telepathically—something she did effortlessly with her brother. Tag regularly looked at her—intensely, searching for confirmation, sometimes for courage—before deciding to run off into the field or woods on a momentary adventure. She unquestionably had the largest working human vocabulary of all our dogs, but after her second year or so, we had dispensed with chatter most of the time: she could read our minds. Early on, we trained the furries to come to the clang of an old navy bell we attached to the underside of our deck; but as the Borders matured, we found that Windi listened to our thoughts (we sent a focused message over the think-net through the woods, and within a few minutes Windi led the happy wanderers back onto the field and to the house), and the need for the bell faded.

Windi's presence in the house was not intrusive, but it was abiding—and thorough. She had a steadying influence on Tag, and a calming one on us. She had this…charisma. Try to define that in the human world: can't do it in the dog world, either. Here's another thing I can't really explain: I took to calling her "Windi-woo." It felt comforting, endearing. It just sort of rolled off the tongue one day, and it seemed to suit her. When I felt silly, or she looked frisky, it turned into "Windi-woozle." Both names felt soft and friendly to me, and, I hope, to Windi. *I wonder what she thought of them.* She, like her brother, like all the members of the pack, were eternally forgiving of our human silliness, shortcomings, thoughtlessness, and poor judgment. She just seemed to get a kick out of being with us—especially Mary. She played with me; she adored Mary.

Chapter 9
Ball Games

People make up games to entertain themselves, hone skills, expand knowledge. Dogs do that, too, and like us, they need the time and means to do them. Consigning a dog to a cage or pen most of the time does not give the animal much chance to do anything but contemplate chewing his foot off and go insane…which given enough time, he will do. If people put themselves into their pet's place for five minutes, the treatment we dish out to these guys would radically change for the better. But out of careless disregard, inattention, or (more likely) a habitual reluctance to face awful guilt, humans tend to be as unaware as possible of the plight they condemn their dogs to. Chaining them to a stake in the ground or to a doghouse, or forcing them to spend hours upon hours alone in a small enclosure, is nothing short of abject cruelty, and should be outlawed. The misery visited upon "man's best friend" is too horrible and common to contemplate, so as a race, humans prefer to ignore it.

For the furries at "Sunnybrook Farm," though, life was pretty cool, even while we were out doing people things. They had 460 feet of woven wire fencing—partly shaded, partly open—featuring six separate dog houses with flow-through ventilation (courtesy of borer bees and aged siding), army surplus blankets in the cool months, fresh water bowls, fallen limbs and hoofies (cow hooves) to snack on, birds, insects, reptiles, and small mammals to check out all day long, and fresh country breezes carrying a zillion messages—all decipherable and fascinating to the best noses in the animal kingdom. Most importantly, they had each other for games and companionship. It wasn't as good as the freedom to wander for miles, exploring at will: but neither was it as bad as the freedom to wander for miles and get (a) run over by trucks on nearby highways, (b) shot by irritated landowners or farmers, or (c) lost. So, the compromise was set: stay in your yard during the work days when Mary and I go out in the world, and when we get home (and on weekends), everybody gets let out to romp in the field and woods. So, what was the first thing they wanted to do when sprung from their dog yard? Sure. Go in the house.

I figured they needed a little exercise before chowing down after a day in captivity, so I introduced some field games. Whenever it wasn't (a) dark, (b) raining, or (c) snow or ice all over the place, it was game time as soon as I got home and changed my clothes.

I let Windi and Tag out of their yard first. Tag's self-appointed mission was to run circles around the house as fast as he could, over and over and over. He never quit except to change direction and run the other way for a while. Occasionally he'd charge right into me to get my attention, tongue down to the ground. I'd stop my play session with Windi to give him some head rubs and make him stay still long enough to get his breathing and heart back into some sort of minimally healthy range, then release him to do it all over again.

Windi's game with me was frisbee football. I'd call out a pass play (um, *hello*—it was *always* a pass play), and hurl that disk as straight and far as I could down the mowed area on the right side of the field in one of six patterns (right, middle or left—short or long). To be truthful, here, the play was often "called" only after I saw where the dang thing was headed anyway. Unconcerned with that, Windi was the picture of focus: as soon as I reared back with the disk, she sped off, ready for anything (she was quite aware early on that it could end up sailing just about anywhere—my consistency was in my, uh, *in*consistency). Again, though, that didn't matter: she was that good, and loved the game. I was getting to the point where I think she actually understood when the game was on the line, having followed the heightened sense of drama as we marched our offense down the field with precious game-ending seconds ticking off the scoreboard clock, our guys down by only a few points. All we needed was that final touchdown, sometimes a two-point conversion, to send the home crowd into a frenzy! I swear nothing in the human world of sports gave me more thrill than those agonizingly tense last-drive plays, when the future of civilization hung in the balance. "Go long, Windi!" I cried out, hoping my arm would deliver a perfect strike down the center of the playing field. We had out-of-bounds, which were fairly obvious: rough woods on the right, clumpy field ground and weeds to the left. Usually that worked to our disadvantage, but sometimes the defense was called for pushing our star receiver out-of-bounds, so the catch was good, and the drive continued. Sound a little goofy? It got nuttier.

Sometimes my throw was just bad, and we'd have to accept a lost down, or two, or...more. But, when the chips were down, and Windi didn't make the reception (usually attributable to the quarterback), the referee had thrown a flag—pass interference! *Awright! Still alive, baby!* Here's what we do, Windi: short pass to the right, then we'll hit them with a surprise bullet into the end zone, left. And that's just what we did. The best ones, though, were those marvelous long bombs that sailed into the sunset, when Windi sped flat out down the long stretch of that miraculous, legendary field and at the last second looked up, left the ground effortlessly, snagged and brought down the prize for a game-winning, no-time-on-the-clock catch! Those moments were golden. She was stunning. I was spent (literally sweating, even on those chilly late autumn afternoons). She saved her out-of-breath, heavy panting until the game was over and we were (once again) victorious. Returning the Frisbee to me, she knew when the contest was ours; we sat side by side at the edge of the asphalt pad and looked out over the grassy field of play, recovering, savoring the glory. The heroics of our efforts and teamwork still ring in my memories of Meadowbrook, and undoubtedly on the breezes of that magical field.

Meanwhile, we had others waiting their turn. I picked up a tennis ball, and let the others out—one at a time. This was tricky. Frothing at the mouth, they *all* wanted to be *next*. Using a foot, knee, elbow, whatever, the challenge was to keep two in while letting just one out—Chelsea. (Freckles, of course, was still out in the field or woods, where she'd been all day. She never had any interest in our games: she had games of sorts going on in her wacky head all the time, away from us, which suited her just fine, and frankly made things that much easier for me and the Frisbee/ball-playing troops.) Chelsea did all kinds of spin-arounds, half-jumps, and snorts until I made the first toss out onto the playing field. Gone was the football stadium and out-of-bounds boundaries; in its place, a ball-toss plane, where the sky was the limit. The Chels could get under any ball toss, no matter how far or how rugged the terrain: this was her event, and she was *fantastique*! When engaged in doggy games, we humans need to figure out our part in it: and that part is not what we think *we* might prefer to do—no, it's what the *dogs* want us to do. Makes sense, doesn't it? Chelsea's requirement was that I send the ball out at such an arc that it would bounce once—and only once—so she could snag it at a full run. Think about that. My toss had to be the right speed, distance, and arc so that she could run flat out and meet the ball at the exact point when it fell to her, head high, after only one bounce. That took some coordination, and I never worked so hard at anything in my life to get the timing right. In her early years, my mistakes didn't matter as much: Chelsea was young, and could run all day...my screw-ups didn't cost her any real lost time. But as she aged, she had a limited number of gallops down that field, and each one needed to count. So, I had to get better, and for the most part (mercifully for her), I did.

It is a thing of beauty to see an all black, shiny blur of fur race down a grassy stretch and chomp that ball out of thin air in a startlingly timed instant. I have watched a lot of professional football, and as stirring as seeing a racehorse receiver and missile of a ball connect a split-second ahead of the defender is, Chelsea's athleticism did that one better. Her combined muscle tone and speed, with fur dancing through the air, lent a slow-motion, ethereal quality to it all, and I was privileged to live it with her. With every splendid catch—the ones that accomplished the timing exactly as she wanted it to be, she showed me and the world just how proud and gloriously happy she felt. She dropped her speed to a slow-canter in a big, wide victory circle before bringing the ball back to me. (This became a dog-inspired catch phrase of ours through the years, whenever we noticed somebody really proud and pleased at what had just been accomplished, doing a human version of a big, wide circle, deservedly feeling pretty good about things at that moment.) The hero was welcomed back to my ecstatic chants of "Chel-sea-champ! Chel-sea-champ! Chel-sea-champ!" until I was too short of breath or hoarse to continue.

The telltale indications that we had had ball-game time were that I was sweating and hoarse, and the dogs' tongues were down to the ground. It was about impossible to get Chelsea to quit: that dog literally would have run until she dropped. Mary caught us playing too many tosses once, took an alarmed look at Chelsea, and tackled me for the ball.

"That's *enough*," she directed. "Her tongue is *purple!*"

Good Lord, she was right: it was *purple. That can't be good.*

"Her heart could give out, Skip," she added. "Geez!" (Okay—she didn't say that word; born in the South (Gastonia, NC), she had more cultured expressions, like, "Don't overdo the game with Chelsea, honey—she might fall over in a big ol' heap, bless her heart.")

The problem was—like in Windi's football game—we never, *ever* quit on a failed toss. On occasion, we had to shorten the throw to give weary legs a chance at ultimate success, but we always, *always* quit on a high note. Better to sleep on later that night. Even when it was purple-tongue time, getting Chelsea to quit was a ridiculous affair; I had to go through all sorts of contortions to get her back into the dog yard so I could let Ruffy out for his chance at stardom. (Leaving Chelsea out while I tried to play with others did not work at all; we had roller derby on paws.)

Ruffy performed his ball-toss event with his usual decorum. Ears properly pricked, he calmly watched me toss the ball high, then loped on over easily and snagged it on whichever bounce seemed comfortable for him to manage, usually making one of those nonchalant moves with his head to the side or behind him to make the grab look ridiculously easy. Effortless—that was Ruffy. I don't think he ever broke a sweat, unlike Chels, who was frothy-mouthed by the time she was through. Course, Ruffy was a big guy with a big stride, so covering a hundred feet for him was a cake walk. I think the only reason he did the ball-toss game was because everybody else seemed to think it was big stuff: as with most things he did, he accomplished this game with complete confidence but not a great deal of overt enthusiasm. Mister Cool.

It wasn't hard to know when it was time to change players. Focusing on the game at hand, I became oblivious to the background cries, yips, and barks, but the sudden, "Rrrr, rrrr, rrrr," to the percussive beat of a woven wire fence being pulled mightily back and forth between Scamp's teeth (little Scamper!) startled me every time. The image of that fairly compact pooch intent on taking down the dog yard fence was not so much funny as sobering. She remembered how persistence had moved that taped-down cage all the way across the kitchen: what's another bit of wire in the face of a serious demonstration of will? Call me silly, but I didn't discount the real possibility that given enough time, she would have that fence uprooted and moved to our neighbor's orchard, so when that racket started, I pretty quickly figured Ruffin's playtime was over. Ruffy had other ideas.

When I let Scamp out to try her hand at the game, there was no way I could stuff Ruffy back into the dog yard, given his size and ab-so-lute determination not to go back in there once sprung for the day. Also, Ruffy was a formidable challenger, so I had to adjust the game a bit to give Scamp at least a little opportunity to participate. I faked a throw down the straight-ahead field (which Ruffy went for a time or two), and then tossed the ball to the left out into our back yard for Scamp to chase. When Ruffin soon caught on to that, Scamp had her work cut out for her.

I tried to make the toss a long one, giving Scamp a chance to use her speed (she moved on deer legs) before Ruffy rumbled onto the scene. Ruffy moving in full gear was a locomotive; Scamp carefully weighed her chances at getting hold of the ball and zipping out of the way of this giant bearing down on her without getting clobbered. She was as bright as she was quick, so discretion clearly displaced valor when the prospect of a tie to the ball was much more than remote. Watching her dip her head down to close on the ball while casting a wary eye on stampeding Ruffy closing in fast was hysterical. There was ball-bobbling in a last-ditch, frantic effort to pull it out, and there were veer offs to avoid an unthinkable collision (100+ pounds versus, oh, say, 25). Not a pretty prospect. Scamp got in maybe three or four tosses before Ruffy pretty much took control of things. And then that, as they say, was the ball game. I tried reasoning with Ruffin; it didn't work. Eventually, Scamp began running off with the ball at the end of the first toss, which certainly took care of the Ruffy problem, but also prematurely ended the session for everybody. It got to where she wouldn't bring the ball back anywhere I could find it, so eventually Scamp was given other special time instead of being allowed to participate in ball-toss. Interestingly, she seemed to accept this change, and explored other pursuits for a few minutes before we all headed into the house for supper. As with all groups, it seems, not everybody is necessarily suited to play or do the same things all the time; individual accommodations are sometimes called for.

Having a shorter commute, I was the one usually home first after work, so the games were in full swing by the time Mary pulled into the carport. In the longer-daylight months, I tried to wait until she came home so she could see some of these antics, but most of the time she had to settle for the winding-up period. Still, she noted thoroughly satisfied grins on all faces, tongues hanging out, my hoarse voice, and knew there had been some fun going on there to start things off for the evening. Those vibes filled the air at Meadowbrook many, many nights. I know that if I should ever return to that place, and could stand in a quiet moment at the edge of our playing field, I would hear again the roar of the home crowd, and the happy sounds of the Meadowbrook players.

Chapter 10
Border Patrol

You learn quickly that Border collies must *and will* have missions in life. As has been written and said about that, if you don't give them a job, they'll find one. This is one of the reasons that people who find themselves charmingly beautiful creatures to adorn their homes or apartments as house dogs are assuring themselves of disaster: the risk is great that the dwelling will be trashed, and the dog will grow fat and become neurotic beyond human tolerance. That is the unyielding truth about high-energy herding dogs: they need jobs and space to do them in. They are what is meant by high-maintenance dogs. The good news is that they will adapt to almost any sort of assignment you give them that involves physical exercise. The bad news is that they will come up with one if you don't think of one for them, to any extent possible given the surroundings they have been offered or restricted to.

Given our expansive field and large woods surrounding it, Tag and Windi had ample opportunity to find a mission: it turned out to be keeping a close eye on the neighbor's mother-and-daughter pair of Rottweilers. I have to hand it to them: our dynamic duo were right to monitor their counterparts just over the rise at the far end of our field: like our Borders, these Rottweilers had been bred for specific purposes—and home protection was at the top of their list. Given their definite size advantage, they were fully up to the task. One of them (the daughter) projected a seriously menacing disposition. To their credit, Tag and Windi approached this self-appointed assignment cautiously, but determined they were to carry it out—daily. Here's the scene: everybody's supper is finished, the sun is low in the western sky at the far end of the field, the air is soft, and the Border Patrol begin their routine mission: check on the bullies across the border at the other end of the field. To do this, they began a slow, ambling walk in a crooked line across to the left side of the field. When they reached an opening into the woods just shy of the fence I had installed across the end of the field, they dipped into the tree line and were gone. That fence (which extended several hundred feet into the woods on both sides) was designed to persuade our dogs not to penetrate our neighbor's land in that area, but it did little good: Border collies need to make *sure* that potential marauders are *in their place*, so they conscientiously walked the perimeter of the fence line. It wasn't long after the fence was up that Tag and Windi found the left end of it and calmly continued their border-patrol forays *around* it, and deep into enemy territory until they could assure themselves that the Rottweilers were either secured in their pen or in their "people house." Border collies have no innate interest in being Border collie boss over other dogs or other animals: they just need to know that those other beings are *not* where they should not be, and *are* where they should be. Once that was confirmed, border patrol was over. They could return to the house, and life was good for another night.

This nightly outing took on a more social flavor after a while, as first Ruffy—then the rest of the gang—followed the Borders along the crooked path and disappeared into the woods each evening after suppertime. I had, in the past, tried repeatedly to keep Tag and Windi from crossing the land boundary into the neighbor's property. I scolded them, hid in the tall grasses in that area as they approached, then rose up suddenly and sternly admonished them, "Go back! Go *Back*! *No*! *This* (shouting, pointing a horizontal line right to left along the property boundary) is where you *stop*!" I repeated this nonsense ad nauseum until I finally gave it up and installed the fence. Now, a short time later, here was not just the two mission commanders doing their nightly thing, but they were leading their partners in crime into the act. As they carefully stepped along in single-file nearing the entrance into the woods, they typically picked one place to stop; first Tag (as leader), then Windi, and on down the line of whoever was a part of this renegade group on this particular evening, would each in turn nose their heads around and give a glance back to our house, now easily seven hundred feet behind them—one last look to see if we were going to reprimand them and call them back. Most of the time in the early going, we did just that, requiring lots of effort on our part (whistling, clapping hands, calling loudly). It was tiring—and annoying. Finally, as years passed, we realized the futility of our efforts. Obviously they were determined to do this routine nightly, so whenever we were busy at the precise moment they reached that glance-back part of their tour, and thereby missed our tiny window of opportunity to retrieve them from their intended course, they resumed their appointed mission, and we were none the wiser. They wore us down; eventually, all we could do was laugh darkly at their persistence and decreasingly guilty "check" on us before continuing to heed the call of *their* wild.

As with children, you can discipline and teach dogs only so much: after a while, they are going to go off with other kids, and do what they like. You can only hope they use the good judgment you tried hard to instill in them to avoid really bad things happening. That's fine with kids, but these are dogs, and if you live as partners with them (instead of disciplining them into Nazi robots, obedient to your every whim and will), they will exercise their judgment at times—not yours. Windi did that once, and paid dearly for it.

Chapter 11
It's a Jungle out There

You learn the habits of your pets pretty quickly if you pay attention to them at all, and this is especially important to do when your furry partners are Border collies—they have got to be the most predictable and consistent creatures on the planet. Live with a Border collie any length of time at all, and *you* are going to be one of the most predictable and consistent *humans* on Earth. Anyway, it was routine that Tag and Windi returned together from their adventuring into enemy territory at the end of the field. On one and only one occasion, Tag followed the crooked path back to the house alone, and at a faster-than-normal clip, tripped up the back stairs to the sliding glass doors landing (the "patio landing"), turned around, sat down, and stared intently at the end of the field. *Uh, oh. This was probably not good.* First, it was different. Secondly, when you see a Border collie staring (not just watching—there's a difference), there is always a reason: they are not just hoping for something to happen…something already has—and it is something you are going to want to know about, as soon as possible…

****

Animals are preoccupied with something for a reason: it's something worth being preoccupied about. Muffin, our one-year-old cat, had begun sitting in our bedroom closet. Proportionate to our little Northern Virginia house, this closet was tiny—just room enough on the floor for a cat to sit in, staring at a wall intently, which she had begun doing for hours at a time. Naturally, in our hustle-bustle human existence of newly-marrieds trying to race through life with two jobs and house-keeping, Mary and I gave Muffin's new habit a glance, then dismissed it as quirky cat behavior. We didn't have time to fool with a ditzy cat. After a while, though, you had to wonder what the heck she was doing, sitting in a clothes closet, staring at a wall—an outside wall. It got me thinking: the house was old, and there had been rain leaks in other outside walls, making the old-fashioned wood plank siding soft, and...oh, no! Bees! Gotta be. The world's largest nest in the side of our house! When you are young and a little stressed from owning your first house, trying to get a career started, living in a new place—that's a lot of big things coming at you fast in your tender years—you tend to imagine the worst that could happen. I waited until Saturday morning to investigate—no way I could face whatever it was on a "school" night.

Outside, behind a tall bush growing up against our bedroom end of the house, I found what I feared I would find: a hole in the siding. I shined a flashlight down into it, and got a surprise: a nest of baby birds! Well, at least it wasn't killer bees come to make a Hitchcock film in our happy home. Still, I had read somewhere that bird nests were chock-full of unpleasant things, like lice and biologically unsafe yuk-stuff; you can't just leave bird nests inside the walls of your house. But what low-life would toss baby birds out of their cozy home? Good grief.

Mary: "Can't we just leave them there until they fledge? It doesn't take long before they'll be gone, anyway." What I love about her.

"Yeah, I guess."

Muffin continued to monitor things from inside our master bedroom clothes closet (all nine square feet of it) for another week or so. Then, as abruptly as she began her round-the-clock ritual, she abandoned it. That was my cue to check the hole again with my flashlight—to find birdies gone, clean out and spray the nest with disinfectant, and repair the siding. All done, good as new, move on. But with a memory: when your pet focuses on something, pay attention. There's always a reason.

****

...Tag, back by himself, sitting on the patio landing, stared intently at the far end of the field. Waiting a few minutes, we finally walked outside and asked him, "Where's Windi?" He glanced up at us, then kept his eyes riveted on the length of the field. Very focused.

"Tag—where's Windi?" a little more edge to our voices this time.

Nothing—he continued to stare straight ahead.

We'd lost Chelsea for a day once; she had been off on one of her field-and-stream episodes, where one mouse trail leads to another, and pretty soon you're somewhere else—somewhere you don't recognize and can't smell home from. That was a horrible, long night for us, and I imagine for Chelsea, judging from the way she burst out of the entrance near the far left end of the field the next morning, ears flying, tongue all the way out, as she raced down the field to welcome *us* back! Since Chelsea had found her way back, we had real hope of Windi doing the same thing: our Border collies didn't tend to wander. They always knew exactly where they wanted to be, and it was always near our place—such is their nature, to guard, protect, secure. We decided the only thing we should do for the moment was wait, and trust (hope) Windi would be along shortly.

That's exactly what happened. About twenty minutes later, she wound her way with deliberate steps along the familiar crooked path down and across the field to our house, like a tired, old prize fighter shuffling away from the gym after a particularly tough workout. Without stopping, she stepped purposefully onto each stair step, and joined Tag up on the landing. He sniffed her in a funny way—a careful, not-quite-understanding-what-he-was-smelling way. That should have been our first clue.

"Come inside, sweetie!" Mary called to Windi from the laundry room door.

As Windi slowly padded one paw at a time across the kitchen tile, she left a trail of blood spots behind her.

"Skip—she's *bleeding*!"

That got my attention. She *was* bleeding, and from a lot of places: her sides, her back, her chest, her head. We rushed to the vet, and several days later, she was returned to us, sporting short rubber tubes in a dozen open wounds, looking like a biology experiment gone bad. It turns out that Miss Windi had been bitten repeatedly. Although we never asked our end-of-field neighbors about it, we felt confident that one or both of their Rottweilers had managed to corner her, and probably after being rolled over and over as she tried to escape, she somehow managed to get free and back onto our land to safety. The bites were deep, and the risk of infection had the veterinarian concerned. Changing the tubing and administering antibiotics were two tasks we preferred to leave to the pros, so Windi was a guest at the local animal hospital for several nights until she could be home without constant medical attention.

Through all this Windi was a warrior: we were told she suffered the necessary, but sometimes painful, veterinary care stoically, without so much as a whimper. You could tell things hurt—even days later—when she was returned to us: she had trouble deciding how—exactly—to sit and lie down without incurring pain. Over the ensuing weeks, the wounds quit draining and healed. She had the distinction of being the only member of the clan who had taken on the dreaded Huns—and survived! I think she gained elevated status among the pack for valor: we certainly never looked at her the same thereafter. She was tough. Tag was indisputably the pack leader—no easy job. But Windi was the muscle, the hunter, the fighter, when needed. Tag would organize things, but Windi had his back.

****

For a working couple, things happen at night and on weekends. So, when things happened to our dogs, we needed professional help when the local veterinary office was closed. In the city, an after-hours emergency clinic took your business…and your paycheck. And that was fine, except your pet was a stranger to the doctors there, and they didn't have immediate access to your loved one's medical history. In the country, we didn't have access to an after-hours facility: we had something better. The doggy docs there had an instruction on their answering machine whenever their office was closed: state your emergency, leave your name and number, and a doctor would call you back momentarily, midnight Saturday, Sunday morning, anytime the office was closed. Whatever doubts I initially had about this system were erased the first time we put it to the test, and every time thereafter. And when you live in the country and have a pack of dogs for your family, you put that system to the test a lot. Bees and snakes see to that.

Yellow jackets that nest in the ground (Mary and I took to calling them "ground bees") are especially nasty buggers that are easily riled, and once irritated, came after you *en masse* and with the single purpose of putting you down. Humans with allergies to bee stings lose their lives annually to such attacks. During a weed-eating chore one afternoon alongside our driveway, hundreds of feet away from the house, I inadvertently disturbed a nest of them, and did a personal-best back to the house (the gas-powered machine was still running when I returned to the scene with two cans of hornet spray). Low to the ground and endlessly curious about the world around them, dogs are especially vulnerable to a vicious swarm of ground bees.

Windi and Chelsea got to know just how awful ground bees could be. One weekend morning, Windi came tearing up the upper deck stairs, frantic for help from something tormenting the devil out of her. We were sitting on chairs, relaxed and reading in the sun, when this Windi-whirl blasted into the moment. Mary started to pet her and tried to calm her, when she noticed a ground bee burrowing into Windi's long, thick hair, heading deep toward the skin. *Yikes!* We quickly discovered that there were at least a dozen of them. I ran to get leather gloves, while Mary sacrificed her hands trying to mash as many as she could. Between us, we finally managed to squash or toss all of them, but it took what seemed like an eternity. I know poor Windi had to have been stung repeatedly before it was over. Recalling that incident still makes our skin crawl.

As bad as Windi's encounter with the bandits from Hell was, Chelsea's was worse. Late one Sunday morning she plodded toward us across the back yard. After long runs through the woods, she always moved more slowly than usual, but her approach this time was different: her steps were unusually labored—and awkward. As Mary and I continued to work in the flowers, I looked up several times, wondering why Chels was taking forever to come over to us. On about the fourth look, I was horrified to see that her muzzle was about three times its normal size, and she was wheezing badly.

I wasn't even sure it *was* Chelsea. "Mary, is that Chelsea? What's wrong with her face?" Her muzzle was continuing to swell, and she was now having a tough time breathing. It looked like Chelsea, except for her head. Honestly, her muzzle was now distorted so badly, I thought her head might explode. She looked like some sort of alien planet dog-creature-thing.

Mary guessed she had probably been bitten by a snake or something. We left an emergency message with our local veterinary clinic, and a doctor called us back within minutes. After Mary described the symptoms, the doc concluded that Chelsea had been an unwelcome visitor to a nest of yellow jackets, and prescribed Benadryl and careful monitoring for the next few hours. If things didn't get worse, we were to continue monitoring her through the night, making sure that she was able to drink water. If she began to have more difficulty breathing or showed other signs of a worsening condition, we were to bring her to the animal hospital, where the doc would meet us—even if it was after midnight. Surely veterinarians have a place in heaven. Chelsea's breathing gradually improved, and by the next morning, she began to look more like a dog than a hippopotamus.

Chelsea also managed to run up against the wrong side of a snake's disposition. Once again, the happy weekend gardeners were playing in the dirt, enjoying a relaxing time in the middle of our forty acres; once again Chelsea unsteadily walked toward us from the woods; once again, the veterinarian office was closed. This time, Chelsea's gait was terribly erratic. Up close to us finally, the gravity of her condition became very apparent: although her muzzle was only slightly swollen, she appeared stunned, her eyes not focusing on anything, and thick streams of mucous drained from her nose and mouth. This time the emergency phone call returned from the doc suggested that we had a snake bite on our hands, and that he would meet us at the clinic as quickly as we could get there. If there was one thing we learned early how to do in our new country home, it was do NASCAR from our house to the animal hospital.

The first thing the doc did was press a moist towel around her muzzle until he found two widely spaced, bloody points—where fangs had found their mark. Taking into account where we lived, the terrain of our property, the nearby creeks, and the time of year, the doctor guessed that a copperhead was the likely culprit, which ordinarily would have made Chelsea very ill if it didn't kill her. There was good news in this particular instance, though: because a fair amount of time had passed since the attack without additional, complicating symptoms, he suggested that Chelsea had suffered a "dry bite" (the snake had not released its venom). After pumping antibiotics into her to treat the puncture wound, he advised us simply to watch her carefully for the next 24 hours. He said she was lucky, and that she would probably be fine in no time. She was…and she was. Breathing sighs of relief had become something of a routine for us city-turned-country folks. Because of our dogs, we were learning to be tough in our awareness of things that can and do happen in rural life—things that are always lingering around the corner to test your readiness to act without panic, but with dispatch.

Things like Tag showing up after a run-in with a snake on our target-shooting range, sporting two bloody marks on his snout. We had seen small snakes around that area before, but apparently Tag either hadn't stopped his investigation upon spotting them, or he had been unlucky enough to run into or over one, startling it into a strike. Ever thoughtful, Tag managed to accomplish his emergency on a Saturday *morning*, when the veterinary office was *open*.

We called them, and were invited to come in right away. Rural vets are a fairly laid back group, accustomed to just about anything that country animals might adventure into. They take most everything in stride, having seen it all in their practice. So when one of them instructs you to come in *immediately*, you know to do it.

Minutes later in the examination room, the doc couldn't conclude that a snake had bitten Tag, but if it had, it appeared to be another dry bite. Good news: antibiotics to guard against infection from the puncture wounds, and back home we went to monitor him for a day. Given the size of the bite marks, the doc suggested that Tag had rousted a young snake—a good lesson for our pack leader: something not fatal, but memorable.

Through the snake episodes, we learned something about treating snake bites: unless you can identify exactly what type of snake has bitten your pet, the veterinarian won't (can't) administer an antidote. Serums for poisonous snake venom, we learned, are manufactured to counteract a *specific* venom: using an inexact match would be at best useless, and could do more serious harm. Without knowing exactly what sort of snake our dog had discovered, all the doc could do was administer antibiotics, and advise us to try to keep her calm to let the natural healing mechanisms do their work. We always added a little prayer to those remedies. St. Francis had his hands full with our little group.

****

The occasion we administered a home remedy was the most family-interactive of the wildlife happenings at Meadowbrook. It started like any other ten o'clock-time-to-put-the-dogs-out-for-the-night kind of thing. It was Saturday night, still very warm from a really hot summer day. An otherwise simple, fairly quick, uneventful chore, the bedtime routine on this particular night had quite a surprise waiting for us. *In country life, things are always lingering around the corner to test your readiness to act without panic, but with dispatch...*

Usually taking the dogs out was my job, but Mary took a turn this particular time. In her usual bare feet, she opened the floodgate (laundry room door), tried not to get stomped on by the pounding of paws as the stampede thundered past, and started down the stairs to the carport. She hadn't made the last of the five steps when she saw a commotion on the asphalt ahead of her—directly between the carport and the gate to the dog yard. Tag, Windi, Chelsea and Ruffy were doing a bob-and-weave, circling around something low to the ground. Mary stepped closer, and to her horror saw that a copperhead had been surprised (apparently having stayed on the driveway long after dark to continue soaking up the day's warmth), and was doing its best to figure out, in survival mode, what to do next. For their part, the dogs knew *exactly* what to do: terrorize the snake! This, Mary knew, was *not* a good idea.

"Skip!" came the yell from outside.

I'd heard that tone before—it never meant good news. I tore out the laundry room door, and witnessed...pandemonium: in her bare feet, Mary was dancing with a copperhead! This was love for her dogs, not brightness on parade.

"Get a hoe or something!" she yelled, as she tried to do too many things at once. Frantic to keep the dogs from nosing around the now highly disturbed poisonous snake, she tried to direct them into the dog yard while keeping the snake corralled without inviting a snake strike herself.

For my part, I wanted something more than a gardener's helper to take on an irritated copperhead, so I ran back into the house to the guest bedroom off the kitchen. There, in the top drawer of a clothes chest, we kept a Rueger .45 that could fire mini-shot for just this kind of occasion. Problem was, there were .45 shells in the cylinder (designed for home protection). It took me a few minutes to open the stupid (plastic, apparently child-proof) container of mini-shot shells, and load all six chambers. I could hear my beloved screaming at the dogs the whole time. When I finally re-emerged on the back porch, Mary had miraculously managed to get the dogs into their yard, and was making voodoo dance gestures with her hands and feet to prevent Mr. Copperhead's escape from the pavement. As I barged down the steps onto the carport, I watched the snake's broken coiling movements: he was not a bit happy with Mary's tactics, frustrated one second at Mary backing up from a strike, and thwarted when he tried to slither forward toward the dog yard or grass to safety.

Mary was equally unhappy with the delay in my returning to the scene. "What've you been *doing*? I'm trying to keep this snake on the driveway so he doesn't get *away*!" (Reading her mind was easy: *If the snake gets away, he's going to lie in wait and pick us off one by one in the ensuing days; best finish him off now, while we have him in our sights.*)

Stand back, woman—this is dangerous, man's work. "Stand to the side, Mary," I said, brandishing my weapon with an Old West flourish and as much authority as I could muster, never having fired a gun in my adult life for any purpose other than target practice. "I don't want a ricochet off the driveway to hit you."

"Then watch out for the *dogs*!" she replied, now with one more thing to be worried about.

Good point, I thought; in the excitement of gun and snake, I had clean forgot about the dogs. "I know, I know," I murmured...but (and no way this escaped Mary's notice) I had to move sideways about six feet to angle the shot *away* from where Ruffy & Company, their noses pushed up against the dog yard gate, were eagerly anticipating whatever was going to happen next.

Mini-shot sprays out wide fairly quickly, so I got up as close as I dared without inviting a strike, aimed the cannon at his head, and *bang*! No movement, but one can never be too sure with bad snakes. So I aimed once more and again pulled the trigger. My ears were ringing from the blasts (and we were *outside*). I began to have the faintest appreciation for how badly my eardrums might be injured by the blast of gunfire *inside* a house. Sobering thought. I hope I never find out.

Mr. Snake was not moving, so after a few seconds, I approached him with the hoe, and carefully nudged him. Nothing. He was in the next life. When I got up really close to him, I could see that he was, well, aerated. The first shot had probably taken care of all the business that was needed; the second one made him all but impossible to pick up and dispose of in one piece. Our work here was done. The showdown at the OK Corral had ended with no bites. And no sleep for any of us for a long while afterwards that night, either. It really *was* a jungle out there.

Chapter 12
Seasonal Stuff

For us people types, the seasons mean something: we get to do different things depending on what season we're in. There are different holidays in the various seasons, which demand different things from us as we celebrate them (or run away from them, as our individual circumstances invite). The changed weather inspires adding things to our routines while removing others from the menu.

Watching and living with our dogs as we all moved through the seasons during the Meadowbrook years, it was clear they regarded and reacted to seasons in much the same way we did. The crisp, fall air exhilarated them, and got them exploring the field and woods more energetically, with tails at full wag and faces expectant. Winter brought shorter excursions, especially if there was wet snow all over the place, which clogged the paw pads, and quickly formed ice balls that clung to long fur and weighed heavier with every step (ouch). Spring brought birds and insects not seen in a while for the always popular game of chase-and-bark. Summer slowed things down: it was time to find and claim the most coveted shady places, and enjoy looong snoozes.

****

Spring and summer in the North Carolina Piedmont are pretty much indistinguishable. Except for those few glorious weeks when spring ushers in the new blooms of forsythia and redbud, contrasted with summer's sustained heat and humidity, the two seasons in this region have plenty of similarities—especially if you're a dog. From a doggy perspective, the main and happy point is that ground made slushy from ice, snow and overnight freezes has finally given way to a warmer dampness under paw, and bluebirds are scoping out their next homes.

We had two bluebird houses—about fifty feet apart—in our backyard, both facing east (recommended in all bluebird house-building guides), and set out among a combination of dogwood, sugar maple, cherry, and crab apple trees we had planted to begin the long transformation of this end of the field from a corn patch to a backyard. Apparently these satisfied the highly particular set of bluebird demands, as one or the other of them was perpetually occupied during nesting season. Also apparent, however, was that we had spaced them too close together, as the prospective tenants always checked out both of them, then continually "guarded" one while building a nest in the other. Although we never actually got to know any of these birds personally enough to recognize one from another, we were pretty sure the same pair returned after fledging time to begin another round of egg-laying. Subsequent nestings always alternated between the two houses, sometimes three times in a season. This was Freckles' happiest time of year—paws down. Frecks ran the field and woods for a while each day, then flopped down in front of an occupied bluebird house and stared at it until she fell asleep in the afternoon sun. Life just doesn't get any better than that.

When the baby bluebirds were getting ready to either fall (or be kicked) out of the nest, another patient watcher quietly came on the scene. He was the reason I installed a metal baffle two-thirds of the way up each bluebird house post. It looked exactly like a squirrel baffle that you'd put under birdfeeders, but was much larger in diameter, because of distances that this particular intruder could reach when motivated by the prospect of tender, young birdies for supper.

Black racers were some of the most aggressive snakes in the area, and although non-poisonous, could pack a punch nobody liked very much. I didn't realize at first that a snake baffle was a good idea until I saw one of these fellows slither effortlessly up the birdhouse post, and help himself to whatever was inside the little round hole intended exclusively for bird access. (I think that first episode gave Mr. Black Snake eggs—not actual baby birds—for dinner.) Baffles went up the next day, and all was well, I thought. Not for long. It turns out that snakes are infinitely patient.

After a different nesting had produced baby bluebirds, the black racer was back, lying comfortably under the baffle, waiting for a baby to come sliding down the metal umbrella, to bounce (Ooof!) on the grassy carpet below. *Talk about food falling from the sky. Talk about fast-food drive-through.* This was ridiculously easy, and impossible for Mary and me to prevent. Nature, however, occasionally gives the innocent a break; how that was accomplished in the bluebird-snake scenario, I don't know. But there were plenty of happy times when we heard and saw a baby and mother bluebird chirping to each other at dusk, and no snake to be found: he was probably full from recent raids on other nests elsewhere in the woods, or perhaps gorged on a toad or mouse from around our tractor shed. (I was messing with something around that shed one day when I turned the corner to walk behind it, and there in the shade was a fairly large toad stuffed backwards in the mouth of Mr. Black Snake. As much a fan of letting nature "be" as I like to think I am, that was too gross for me to ignore. Freshly annoyed at snakes culling the bluebird population in our yard, I was in no mood to put up with this disgusting display of "Gotcha!" so with a long stick, I tickled the snake around the side of its head and mouth until it let the poor toad go. Apparently weighed down by the old maxim, "Don't bite off more than you can chew," Mr. Snake wasn't able to do much to defend against my probes and keep hold of "lunch" at the same time. Undoubtedly frustrated at having to choose between escaping my obnoxious presence and losing his prize catch, he opted for his own freedom, and loosened his grip on the relieved toad, which hopped quickly away, no doubt with a fresh perspective on life. Translating his glare at me: *$%@#$!* If I hadn't been so big, I'm pretty sure he'd have tried his luck with me as a toad-substitute on his dinner menu that afternoon.)

Worrying bluebirds through fledge times was tough on Mary and me: the same cannot be said of our dogs—they enjoyed having baby birds to try to find and play with around the yard. Chelsea turned out to be the more focused and talented birdmeister, ferreting out baby bluebirds after carefully listening to their chirps and nosing them out of what they had thought were good hiding places among the ever-present weeds. We would never know of these successful hunts without the sudden, noisy disturbance of parental bird squawks. We came to recognize that alarm bell, and were quick to tear out of the house and go to the source of the racket, where we inevitably found Chelsea repeatedly tossing a baby bluebird up in the air and letting it bounce on the grass. *What fun!* I guess it's true what I've heard about Labradors and other good bird dogs: they have soft mouths. Good thing for a terrorized baby bird…it sometimes gave the cavalry that little extra time needed to arrive and abort disaster. Sometimes, though, the poor thing was in shock from being slimed, or just tossed around a little too much, and was beyond our help. Typical of Chelsea's eternally happy nature, she was okay with our interference, figuring I suppose that there were more baby birds where that one came from, and tomorrow was another day. A dog's life is simple, and happiness is always just around the corner.

When Freckles wasn't running the field and woods or keeping tabs on our bluebird houses, she enjoyed one of the most delightful gifts spring and summer offered her: butterflies! To Freckles, they were perfect—something delicate, flitting and daring in no planned direction. Frecks the Ditso-Dog, with wings. Two of a kind, those marvelous beings—both exquisitely beautiful to watch in motion. A stone, ground-level patio spread out at the bottom of a wide but short set of steps leading from the patio landing outside the double-glass sliding doors we looked through from our kitchen table, and adjoined the concrete carport under the second-level screened porch and deck. Raised beds flanked the patio: filled mostly with canna, they served a dual purpose of decorating the back length of our home, and providing butterflies with plenty of landing pads. On a patio warmed by the mid-day and afternoon sun, Freckles could lie in five-star comfort, endlessly fascinated by these magical creatures.

Once in a while, a butterfly landed on the patio and tantalized Freckles by staying there a while, slowly opening and closing its wings in a dazzling come-hither display. This was too much for mesmerized Frecks: she ever-so-slowly raised her back haunches, held the pose for a moment, then moved one front leg forward (slooowly), *held it*, then another leg, *held it*, and did this at a barely perceptible pace for as long as several minutes. Inside our house, I was afraid to risk making any sound that might interrupt this, so I whispered to Mary to join me to watch. When Freckles managed to get within a foot or two of the butterfly, it suddenly took flight, but only for a few yards. Freckles snapped her head up and around to follow the path to its next landing, to begin another round of stalking. With unbelievable patience and isometric strength, Freckles continued her stealthy approaches until the weary butterfly finally moved on far enough, or high enough, to end the game.

Twice I witnessed the unimaginable: Freckles was rewarded beyond her hopes: the butterfly hopped over and landed *squarely on her muzzle*! Time and dog froze. Freckles' eyes crossed as they tried to focus on this tiny wonder sitting on her nose; the rest of her remained perfectly still. She must have been stunned. *I* was. I will never, as long as I live, understand how that happened. And to have seen it on two different occasions...Freckles was a magical dog.

"Snapping bees" provided Tag and Windi with hours upon hours of some of the most completely joyous times in the history of dogdom. Through spring and summer, bees of all sorts busily went about their business around our house, and the Borders were ready for them. Standing on the patio landing, Tag and Windi crouched at full alert to lunge and snap their jaws at passing bees, whose incessant buzzing was irresistibly alluring. *Almost got that one, Tag!* cried Windi.

"Woof," *That was close!* answered Tag. (*Double snap*) (*Snap*) Sprays of dog spit, punctuated by the clack (snap) and double-clack (double snap) of teeth, steadily escalated to a state of frenzy as our Border collies became lost in a world all their own. As a general rule, we tried not to interrupt our dogs at play, but when the pupils of Tag's and Windi's eyes became fully dilated, and their mouths were foamy, we figured it was time to call a timeout. By then, they were losing their footing, stumbling on the stair steps with every lurch toward an escaping bee. When they were that zoned out, taking them away from "snapping bees" was darn near impossible.

"Barking hummingbirds" was a modified version of snapping bees: hummers didn't come nearly as close as bees to the patio landing, so the Borders learned early on that lunging at them was mostly for effect, and snapping jaws was a waste of time. The plan to ward off these intruders? Healthy barks! (After a while, a dog will grow hoarse from repeated barking. Sadly, I have heard that pitiful progression from suburban neighborhood dogs left outside or tied all day to a clothesline; they resort to mindless and endless barking until they grow hoarse trying to get someone to change their plight, or at least come over and give them some attention.) I wanted my dogs to enjoy themselves, but enough was *enough* already! My nerves frayed, I inevitably called the game, not so much to prevent hoarse hounds, but mostly on account of ICSIA (I Couldn't Stand It Anymore). For their part, hummingbirds never seemed the least bit bothered by the whole barking business: they were focused on keeping each other away from the feeder—quite the spectacle, ferocious dive-bombings by such tiny beings with such snarly dispositions. *If nature teaches us anything, it's that there's not always a lot of "playing nice with the other kids" in the animal kingdom.*

DOGS OF MEADOWBROOK

****

Two things signaled a definite turnover from spring to summer: Scamp and Chelsea found shade early in the day (and rarely ventured from it), and Ruffin's coat turned into a molting mess. Thick year-round, Ruffy's fur became clogged with undercoat, which then sprouted disgraceful patches. He couldn't help it, of course, but he looked diseased. I pulled out his clumps of old, smelly undercoat until he wouldn't put up with that any longer. I tried to brush the stuff out, but whichever type of tool I tried, it quickly became clogged and useless. Besides, it was much more satisfying to pull clumps out of his hide; I told Mary this once, and the look I got back suggested in the strongest possible terms that I find some other way. *Okaaay.* BATH time!

In a dog's world, BATH is always a fully capitalized word. Dog owners learn early that you don't ever say that word out loud. You don't even whisper it. You can't even *think* it. Any dog owner who has paid even minimal attention to his or her pet knows that dogs have a corner on the market on ESP. We watched our Border collie siblings look down the field while standing shoulder to shoulder on the patio landing, turn quietly to each other, then simultaneously tear off down the steps, fan out and race to meet at an appointed spot at the edge of the woods. Communication among dogs is often accomplished without sound: they can just gaze at each other for a second or two, and the message is conveyed. They have learned to bark at humans to get their attention, but among themselves in a familiar environment, they communicate quietly. Undoubtedly, this is born of hunting and guarding instincts passed through the generations of dogs and their wolf forebears; but it also carries the useful attribute of being just plain easier.

At a hundred pounds (give or take), Ruffy added a bit more than the usual challenge to bath time. I changed into bath attire (a bathing suit—because, as dog owners know all too well, when doggy takes a bath, *everybody* takes a bath). While my trusty assistant (Mary) positioned herself ready with the hose, I sort of *sat* on Ruffy's haunches, and the three of us made a movie worth taping. Lots of suds, lathering, rinsing, and near-escapes later, Ruffy was clean*er,* if not clean. The main objective had been accomplished: his undercoat had been dislodged, so that it could now finish its emergence to the outer layer of his fur, and fall off—*everywhere.* For the next several days, huge balls of freshly washed undercoat floated in the breeze along on the patio and out into the grassy back yard. Our place looked like the "after" shot from a sheep-shearing contest. Later on, when scraping old birds' nests out of the bird houses, we would find some of Ruffy tucked in there among twigs and grass. Brushing our German shepherd was essential during these periods, if we were to spare the inside of our house from being buried under fluffs of very fine, silver-black-brown-white hair.

"Tick check" held a fascination for the whole family. Spring through August presented all of us with a serious bit of business: find all the ticks that came into the house on any of us—Mary and me, included. As much fun as Mary and I had checking for ticks on each other, the furries seemed to enjoy it even more. The routine started innocently enough: the room in the house with the best light for spotting these tiny, disgusting creatures was the downstairs bathroom, just off the kitchen, near the guest bedroom. When I drew scaled house plans for the builder, I didn't take into account the thickness of walls—exterior or interior. After the builder and lender approved the plans, the first thing constructed was the outside frame. After that, the contractor's carpenters began erecting walls for the various interior rooms. As work continued, each wall progressively shrank the net available space in the remaining rooms.

Since we were living in a rented house on the other side of Greensboro (a good 25 miles away from the new house site), we didn't want or feel the need to be *troubled* by *little things* that might come up during construction. The understanding we had with the builder (who had a well-deserved good reputation in the area) was that he should, "take care of things," and call us only when something major came up; otherwise, we would see him every couple of weeks, and in the meantime go about our working lives to earn the gazillion bucks he and the bank were going to be charging us for this modest new home. One evening the builder called us, and casually mentioned that the thicknesses of the walls were being taken out of the small, downstairs bathroom—was that okay? Well—sure, I guess. He didn't sound too worried about it. So—yeah, okay. The next weekend we drove to the site to make our usual weekly inspection: there we found that the downstairs bathroom, already small on my scaled drawings, was now *tee-ninetsy*. Big sighs from both of us. A little late to do anything about it now. We just sucked that one up and let it go. "Nothin' to be done anyway," as my grandpa would have said—what was done, was done. Well, this one was *extra crispy*. The resulting downstairs bathroom was…well, "small" doesn't cover it. You could perform every single imaginable, normal bathroom function in that room without moving more than a foot in any direction. It was…*compact*.

Bringing the first dog into that tiny cubicle for the first tick-check in the history of tick-checks in our house was an orderly affair because of pack leader Tag. Of *course* it was Tag first; we had to set an example, and Tag knew it, accepted it as his lot in life. So I sat down on the open toilet lid, asked Tag to come forward into the well-lit close quarters (which he—as always—obediently did), and with tweezers in hand, I proceeded to examine him for ticks. When I found one, I plucked it off him and tossed it between my legs into the toilet bowl water. When done, I flushed the disgusting creatures down into whatever next adventure awaited them, hoping that they would not show up again some day as of urban-legend monsters.

I dismissed Tag, invited Windi in, and repeated the procedure. These were Border collies: they *love* routines—especially new ones. A really great day for a Border collie is having all the sheep in the world to herd, *plus* a *new* routine. So getting them to join in tick check was a piece of cake. Chelsea, Ruffin, Scamp (and of course, the reclusive Freckles), however, were leery of this whole business of bright lights, tight space, and tweezers. In addition, I undoubtedly had that tone in my "Come here" that suggested whatever it was that I wanted was probably a human version of something *good* for them, which (in dog-think) most often meant anything *but* fun for them! With much coaxing (involving the usual dog-treat bribes), and having shown the others what our good Border collies had done and survived, everybody but Freckles was enticed into the summer nightly routine. (I had to do a hands-and-knees version with Freckles in the laundry room on her bed; every night she pretended we had never done this before. *Gotta love your dog.*)

Be careful what you ask for in life: you just might get it—in spades. Tick check became quite the social event at our house. It wasn't long before I no longer needed to announce, "Tick check;" all I had to do was grab the tweezers, turn on the bathroom light, sit down on the john, and *whoomph!*—I had the whole cavalcade of dogs trying to squeeze past each other through the narrow doorway to be first in line. That's nearly 400 pounds of *Get outta my way!* testing the construction integrity of that little room's doorframe. Mary figured they felt the difference (and benefit) of having ticks removed from their heads, backs, chins, ears, chests. In probable confirmation of her theory, Tag would return to the bathroom for a second round, which I first attributed to him merely wanting more head and body rubs. But nearly every time, I found at least one more tick that had escaped my first inspection; when I removed that one, Tag left and did *not* return for a third session. *Hmmm.*

****

Emerging from the season of ticks and hot humidity, doggy noses came fully alive in the fresher, crisper air of autumn. Energy levels picked up, and everybody ate more enthusiastically. There were more things to do in the woods, mostly because there was more urgency to the goings-on of the woodsy critters. Squirrels were moving with more purpose, deer were showing up in greater numbers, and skunks and woodchucks left their scent on everything. Now in their middle years, Tag and Windi settled into a routine that ordinarily kept them fairly close to home. Tag ran a tight circle around the house that formed a race track—an inch deep, securing our perimeter. Windi kept a closer eye on Mary and me, usually from an air conditioning floor vent. But at the first hint of that fall chill in the air, all bets were off. Something in those winds pulled the Borders' olfactory triggers, and off they went in any direction to check out—everything.

Cruising the woods was easier in the fall: leaves were falling, clearing the view ahead. And the varied scents of nature in decay were a dog's version of (pardon the expression) catnip. Dragging tongues and self-satisfied grins greeted us upon their return from one successful foray after another. Scamp joined Chelsea's foraging along the edges of the field for mice and voles: in the cooler air, these outings that had been cut short by oppressive heat a month earlier now lasted for hours.

Ruffy moved between the two groups, or (in typical German shepherd fashion) lay down on the patio landing and watched *whatever*. Dr. Ally told us during Ruffy's first exam as a seven-week-old puppy that German shepherds were watchers. "They watch," she said simply. "They like to watch stuff. It's what they do." Turns out she was dead-on with this guy.

My mother could spend a whole day sitting on a beach or in a mall, being entertained by the constantly moving show around her. "Sit here with me," she'd say; a young boy, I wondered how in the world sitting and watching could be considered any brand of fun.

"People are fascinating—just watch for a few minutes," she insisted. It didn't take five minutes before somebody proved her point.

Mom and Ruffin. Two souls talented in the art of intelligent observation.

Fall for Mary and me meant it was time to cut and stack firewood, doing our best impressions of the fabled ant, lest we be caught short by an early winter. We learned that lesson the hard way one January, when an unusually heavy snow-and-ice storm blitzed the area, trashing power lines, and cutting off our electricity for five days. Our wood stove did its job, but only as long as we had firewood to feed it. The two huge wood racks to the side of the dog yard had not been fully replenished in the fall (I guess I had thought the gnomes and fairies were going to do it), so we were constantly behind scratch that winter. Midway through that five-day deep freeze and power outage, I found myself chain-sawing dead trees some distance from the house, then dragging the cut up logs through icy snow for hours at a time. I felt a renewed appreciation for our country's pioneers. Operating without well water (no generator) was no picnic, either, for all kinds of imaginable reasons. During this stretch, we envied our dogs' outdoor lavatory lifestyle: making daily drives to local stores to beg fill-ups for our five-gallon water containers to refill the backs of our toilets got old fast. The one thing besides the wood stove that worked fine was our garage: maintaining a constant temperature range of 15-35 degrees during the course of those five days, it was a terrific refrigerator. Of course, keeping the dogs out of there was critical: their exceptional noses were working exceptionally well. We found them, tails wagging excitedly, sniffing day and night under the second laundry room door, which, totally ignored before, suddenly lead to a huge refrigerator!

Splitting and stacking cords of wood on racks that we fashioned from long, treated boards, landscape timbers, and carriage bolts, always brought the pack together—under foot. They *loved* this fall ritual. While we worked, they moused. Discovering and uncovering mice in the field and woods was fascinating to them, undoubtedly spurred by an instinctual hunting and foraging call from their ancestors, when survival—not fun and games—was at stake. The Borders, particularly, were scarily focused doing this, practicing skills they were genetically driven to sharpen. But for them sniffing and rooting out mice from of a stack of wood was clearly an exercise in pure joy! Tails constantly wagging, grins aplenty, whimpers and sharp yips of excitement, this was energy at its happiest: they whirled and darted from one side of the cord to the other, then poked and nosed into every crevice and cranny of the woodpile, on the scent of mouse nests and stockpiles of sunflower seed heisted from under the birdfeeders. They did this for hours, totally lost in some of the most fun a dog can hope to have.

We found time to play, too, and for us there was no better season for it than fall. "Throwing the ol' ball around" in our back yard, while the boys of summer were doing the real thing in their post-season chase for a World Series title, against a backdrop of orange, yellow, red and rust-colored leaves that lined the field, was totally satisfying in country sunshine. Words cannot adequately describe the contentment we felt stealing a weekend afternoon for ourselves in the open bed of our truck, parked in privacy halfway down our driveway between our house and the road—colored leaves drifting down on us as we and all of our dogs (except wandering Freckles, of course) snuggled, grinned, and napped. As we all lay piled on top of each other, hands and jaws snagged leaves close enough to catch on their twisty dance down from golden beeches and fiery red oaks towering above us. Those moments were precious—and we knew it. Lost in our own secluded, beautiful world, we spiritually embraced nature, and wished it could last forever.

****

Winter brought the whole family together like no other time of year. With the house closed up against the outside cold, we savored the aromas of chicken dinners and freshly baked chocolate-chip cookies. Dark by the time we made the commute home from work, everybody gathered inside for the evening events: for the dogs, it was chew on a cow-hoof, squeak a squeak-toy, do a bit of preening (*slurp! slurp! sluuurp!* that was some sound—endless, loud slurps (after a while, we were in stitches listening to that), maybe catch a nap. Mary's and my deal was to watch TV, do desk work, listen to music, and talk over a jigsaw puzzle on a card table in the corner of the living room, or sometimes just look out into the blackness of the field. Somewhere out there a fox or two was beginning to stir, deer were nibbling the barest bits of leftover corn from a one-acre patch we tried annually to wrest from the field weeds, wild turkeys huddled for warmth under a thicket or in a hollow place left by an uprooted trunk of a fallen tree. The dogs couldn't have cared less: they were contentedly spread out throughout the living room, and underfoot at the supper table.

Winter's cold, ice, and snow didn't keep us inside all the time: Mary and I actually looked forward to long, cheek-numbing adventure forays through our woods and into neighbors' deeper woods on many winter weekends (made the wood stove and soup feel all the better when we pushed our way, frozen-faced, back into the house an hour or two later). We were treated to the indescribable beauty of icy ledges along the creeks, guessing who made animal tracks in the snow, stumbling across icy mounds and spikes of dirt pushed up by the overnight freeze, imagining the lives of so many animals managing to survive the bitter cold day after day, night after night. Union and Confederate troops had camped in this area during the Civil War over a hundred years earlier, in some of this same kind of weather. Most of all, we relished the feeling of being together with each other and with our dogs, who in their proud and spirited gait, and happy glances back at us as they led the way, were clearly pleased to be showing us *their* world.

It wasn't hard to get a little lost during these outings, which was probably an appropriate penalty for trespassing: walking just ten minutes in unfamiliar thicket frequently had us wondering which direction then led back home. For miles around, the terrain and trees looked the same. *No wonder Chelsea got lost out here before*, I thought. I laughed to myself when I actually considered leaving trails of breadcrumbs; birds, squirrels, chipmunks and mice (not to mention our traveling party of constant snackers) would have removed those markers in record time! Instead, I became more vigilant about noting where we were every few minutes: it took some of the excitement out of exploring new territory, but the tradeoff of getting back to our wood stove before dark had a certain appeal.

As much as we enjoyed our wanderings through woods that weren't ours, we didn't have to go farther than our own field for winter fun. In an early Meadowbrook year, when Tag was still a youngster, a moderate snowfall blanketed everything over a weekend, and Mary was moved to exercise her artistic talents. Directly out from the house about a hundred feet into the field, she sculpted a snow dog. While she worked, Tag paid her no attention, instead making his usual several hundred runs encircling the house—on patrol. When she finished, she invited him to come out into the field with her; of course, he obliged, although probably wondering why she would interrupt the serious business of securing the house perimeter. Halfway to the snow dog, he noticed it, pricked up his ears, and ran over to it, tail wagging. It was about his size. He sniffed it carefully in all the right places, and then…lay down beside it, for a long time—even after Mary returned to the house…to keep it company, or keep an eye on it, I guess. *I know it's not moving… but you gotta watch out for the quiet ones.*

The single most-memorable time brought by winter each year for us and for our furry group, however, was Christmastime. There was magic in the air. It was Christmas magic that delivered Scamp to us. It was Christmas magic that persuaded Tag to inexplicably take a rare break from dutifully running circles around the living room, pad slowly over to me while I was lying down under the newly erected Christmas tree messing with the lights, nestle his back and rump against mine, and go to sleep(!) It was at Christmastime that Freckles blew our minds when she emerged from the laundry room (she never, *ever* came out of that room any other time), walked (deliberately, without that frantic sideways dodge of hers) all the way through the kitchen and into the living room where most of our Christmas decorations were, gently sniffed everything in turn, looked up at us (we hadn't moved a muscle, stunned by her behavior), smiled, wiggled, and wagged her tail. Then, suddenly remembering herself, she quickly trotted back to her laundry room bed. It was a long moment before Mary and I could speak. When we did, we figured that something about Christmas in her past must have imprinted a good memory. Maybe. But I tend to chalk it up to good old-fashioned Christmas magic. In the mystical world of dogs, that would hardly be a stretch.

The exact order of events most evenings during winter in the Meadowbrook household was this: after the dinner dishes were done and lunch was made for the next day, we all retired to the living room. Places everyone: Mary and I on the sofa facing the fireplace and TV, Tag to our left under the desk, Windi at Mary's feet to her right, Ruffy to my left on our beautiful wool rug ("Don't *ever* let your dogs on this rug," admonished the terribly serious salesman), Chelsea and Scamp curled spoon-fashion around each other, inches from the wood stove behind us in the kitchen, through the open double French doors. We closed those doors when we had the fireplace cooking, but the loss of heat and trouble it took to build and maintain a fire there gradually shifted our interest toward the wood stove. Chelsea and Scamp could not have been more pleased. It was a race to the front row: that wood stove was doggy Nirvana: toast and roast until you're done on one side, then turn over. I used to stare at them, perplexed at why I was not seeing smoke curling up from their fur. Surely their black noses would crack from the dry, intense heat. Once in a great while, with great, measured effort only after they gave the matter long and careful consideration, would either of them haul herself up with a sigh, trundle over to the water bowl, tank up, pad back, and fall to the ground with a mighty *clunk*, exhale and grunt, soon to be out cold for another few hours, or until bedtime.

If the fireplace was happening, the C&S pair trucked on into the living room, Chelsea parking herself directly in front of the heat, Scamp plopping her fine self between Mary and me—our couch potato, Miss Queen of the Sofa. Soon, with the embers glowing brightly, all dogs but Tag were asleep—he was quietly alert, on duty, keeping watch over all of us. The zzz's in the room were palpable: we could not—*could not*—stay awake under those circumstances, good movie or ball game on TV notwithstanding. Discipline alone got us up and doing the nightly go-to-bed chores on school nights, but on weekends, we freely gave in to the marvelous feeling of "Sleep where you drop, for as long as you like." Somewhere between late evening and midnight, somebody finally stirred (usually Tag—keeping track of at least some semblance of a reasonable bedtime), and gradually we all groggily managed to find our way to finish the day. Marvelous times, looking back: the family unit, fur pack and all. Winter, with all its inconvenience and harshness—its slushy, icy, darkness—turned out to be the best time of the year.

WILLIAM SCHWENN

Playing field gone amok (top);
Scamper's first adventure (bottom)

Truck Load; (top, left to right) Ruffy, Windi, Scamp, Chelsea, Tag (middle, left to right) Mary, Tag, Chelsea, Ruffin and Windi; (bottom) Chelsea playing Mom to Scamp

(top) Patio porch; Scamp and Chelsea—Ruffin on patio
(bottom) Carolling; (left to right) Freckles, Tag, Ruffy, Chelsea, Scamp, and Windi

DOGS OF MEADOWBROOK

(top) Patio Porch: Tag and Windi (Scamp looking on from inside);
(bottom, left to right) Chelsea, Tag, Windi, Ruffin

WILLIAM SCHWENN

(top) Ready for Town; (left to right) Ruffy, Chelsea Tag, Scamp, Windi;
(middle) Frosty autumn morning;
(bottom, left to right) Chelsea, Ruffin, Tag, Mary, Scamper

DOGS OF MEADOWBROOK

(top) Dignified Ruffin
(bottom) Tag, Freckles, Ruffy, Windi, Chelsea, and Scamp

Chapter 13
Magical Field

    Illusions: slight-of-hand, "Now you see it; now you don't," making that coin, egg, tiger disappear before your very eyes—that's the stuff of magic. Live long enough, and if fortune smiles on you, *wonder* replaces these tricks of the trade…and that, too, is magic.

    Patter of light rain falling on leaves right outside a bedroom window, adding to drowsiness a cozy layer of contentment as you awake to a gray morning. The haunting *hoo-hooo, hoo-hoo-hooo* of a determined night owl moving in on its hapless prey. Light flakes of winter's first snowfall, turning a field encircled by hardwoods and evergreens into a giant snow globe. These are marvels of nature—treasures of unbelievably complicated design, simply offered to all creatures who would know this earth as our fragile and endlessly fascinating *home*. Meadowbrook had these and countless other magnificent treats for the senses. What Meadowbrook also brought were moments and things that were nothing short of magical.

****

    Rising up from near the bedroom end of our house one special night was the same moon we had watched for years in our country place, only this time there was to be a total lunar eclipse. The skies were nearly cloudless, and as the moon was clearing the short pine trees, Earth's round shadow began edging its way across the moon's surface. Soon, a once brilliant full moon was darkened to a pale ghost of its former self. Now only inches above the trees, this huge ping-pong ball hung in perfect stillness. We held our breath, awed by something going on bigger than our world, afraid we might miss even an instant of this incredible event. The ashen, off-white sphere remained fixed, stopping time. Through our binoculars, the depth of another part of our universe was humbling. As we watched, we spoke only a little to each other, and in whispers when we did.

Our reverence may have affected our furries, as they moved slowly around us when they moved at all. Mostly, they sat at our feet, and looked around uncertainly—probably wondering how a brightly lit yard and field had so quickly been plunged into near blackness. We tried in vain to get them to look *up* and see this dramatic moment, but a dog's life is simple: take advantage of the rare event when the whole pack—humans included—is out prowling around the grounds in pleasant weather with apparently no agenda other than to enjoy each other. *There are mice, voles, toads, whatever, on the ground to be sniffed and jostled: no point in looking up.* No doubt there were untold instances of special happenings in the dogs' world, when *they* tried in vain to get *our* attention to *Come, look, join in!* and we didn't understand. Well, for however many of us looked up and saw its wonder, this was one truly memorable presentation brought to us, in part, by Meadowbrook. We took pictures, but haven't needed them. When something magical happens, you never forget it.

****

We moved to our country place the second Saturday in April, 1987—two days ahead of Mary's birthday. After all the financial stress and physical strain of preparing for the big change, I surprised myself (and exasperated my spouse) at delaying the actual move of our last furniture—including our bed— one last night. Leaving the city and all its conveniences, proximity to my tennis buddies, and familiarities, turned out to be (for lack of a better word) scary. To me, anyway. Mary was and had for some time been raring to leave the noise and closeness of neighbors behind—the sooner the better, for her. But she stuck it out in our rented box in Greensboro one last night, when all we had with us was our bed, a floor lamp, and our toothbrushes.

She woke me early the next morning with, "Hi, I love you. *NOW* CAN WE GO?" So we left without breakfast. I can count on one finger the number of times Mary has left our home without at least some semblance of breakfast. Off to the country we flew: anxious me, with my uncertainty intact, eager Mary with her nose out the window the whole way.

Some folks refer to their dogs by what their dogs do in or for their households: they have hunting dogs, herding dogs, lap dogs, and ride-along dogs. Jon Katz, in his charming tale, *The Dogs of Bedlam Farm*, (Villard Books, 2004), first introduced me to the term ride-along dogs, noting that these are "proud and lucky dogs," accompanying their owners (often in trucks) everywhere they go. The ride-along dog's prime responsibility (and joy in life) is to hop in the truck and stick its nose out the passenger window while the driver runs errands or goes visiting. That was us that bright, sunshiny Saturday morning: me, and my *ride-along* girl.

After work a few nights earlier, we had been filling the new master bedroom closet with our over-abundant supply of hanging clothes, testing the pole and support brackets: they failed miserably, so we added some. During one of the trips between the bed and closet to add still more weight to the sagging pole, I suddenly felt drawn away from our immediate business to look out our second floor bay window, where I met the steady gaze of a doe. That deer had probably been looking at us for quite a while. Standing alone there halfway up and in the middle of the field, she was our first greeting committee (unless you count the fence lizard on the batter boards just before the house foundation was poured seven months earlier, who *I* thought was cute, but didn't draw as good a review from Miss Mary). I quickly called to Mary, and we stopped our work to stand quietly for a long while, enjoying a silent commune with one of nature's most tender and beautiful beings. Our reverie was broken by a mighty *crash!* Behind us pole and brackets finally gave it up, bringing the weight of too much apparel down with them to the floor. After hurrying to check the damage, we returned to the window—but the deer was gone. I worried I would never see another one. I had a whole lot to learn about country living.

During the weeks after we moved in, we were surprised at the variety of critters who called the woods around us their home: they came in all forms, scurrying, slithering, trotting, racing, flying, flitting, darting, hopping, stalking, ambling, picking their way into and out of the woods, through and around the field, across the hilly furrows of former corn rows that would eventually flatten under my persistent efforts to convert a small part of the house end of the field into a yard. We knew there were many other residents out there we would, if we were lucky, *never* see (skunks, poisonous snakes, fuzzy spiders), but nothing prepared me for the jolt I received looking out our master bathroom window less than a month into our new country life. Floor-to-ceiling and five feet wide, the glass fairly filled the wall, creating a spectacular view of our field and trees, and sky above them. Through that massive opening, we could take a bath in the swirl of jets and look out onto the length of our five-acre field, and all the beings that might happen to be munching, standing, or walking on it.

Offering breathtaking, panoramic views by day, the master bathroom window was a different story in the blackness of the country nights. At night, with any bathroom light on, the windowed wall became a mirror, and poking your nose right into it to try to see out didn't help a bit, either. All you saw was inky black nothingness. It was unsettling to know that everyone, every creature, every *everything* could see *us*, but *we* couldn't see *them*.

Imaginations can run wild in that sort of setting, but nothing short of Dracula plopping himself upside down onto all four sides of that window could have startled me more than the night I had finished brushing my teeth and had turned back to switch off the light, to be greeted by a sudden bursting into view of a giant luna moth! With a brilliant, multi-colored "eye" on each of two giant lime-colored wings, it looked capable of barging right through the glass and devouring me in a few choice bites. Images of equatorial jungle life from issues of *National Geographic* popped crazily into my head. Never having seen this specimen of flying nightlife, I garbled something that brought my biology enthusiast wife into the room. Seeing her delightedly surprised gave me some assurance, but I realized we "weren't in Kansas, anymore." I was a while staring at this winged beast before I could finally let myself appreciate the majesty of its beauty; transforming fear into curiosity, into acceptance, into marveling, takes time…and this one took its full share.

"Wow," I finally exhaled; "that's really something."

My pitiful attempt to capture the striking beauty of the moth notwithstanding, the magical moment of being welcomed to its world stuck with both of us. Part of that magic is that we never saw it again, despite thousands of nights of our having our bathroom light on in the late night hours during seasons when luna moths are supposedly out and about. This was a one-time encounter—another basic component of true magic.

****

From Wikipedia, the free encyclopedia:

Ball lightning reportedly takes the form of a short-lived, glowing, floating object often the size and shape of a basketball, but it can also be golf ball sized or smaller. It is sometimes associated with thunderstorms, but unlike lightning flashes arcing between two points, which last a small fraction of a second, ball lightning reportedly lasts many seconds. Sometimes the discharge is described as being attracted to a certain object, and sometimes as moving randomly. After several seconds the discharge reportedly leaves, disperses, is absorbed into something, or, rarely, vanishes in an explosion.

Ball lightning showed up at our Meadowbrook home on an unimaginable scale. We were having trouble getting to sleep late one night. It was summer, it was hot, and it was humid. I must have had one eye open amid restless tossings and turnings, and whispered to Mary, next to me, that the fireflies were "really big, and really bright, and moving really *fast*!" A few minutes later, we were sitting on the carpet in the bedroom bay window, staring in disbelief at the show going on all across the field. One after another, balls of greenish-white, intensely bright light shot toward us from the far end of the field, along the line where the trees met the grass, about thirty feet above the ground. Some of these balls of light made it nearly to our end of the field: others disappeared halfway along their streaks toward our house. This unbelievable light show continued for probably twenty minutes. We couldn't even muster anything more than an occasional exclamation, it was that dazzling—and intriguing. These were no fireflies: they were too big, too white-hot intense a light, and *way* too fast in their movement. They zipped sideways over the ground at varying speeds, some of them incredibly fast, but much slower than traditional lightning. Without knowing what we were looking at, we were being treated to ball lightning—that wonderfully magical show nature occasionally cooks up when all the essential ingredients are on hand and something sparks the works into play.

We never saw it again: not there, not anywhere. I suppose if we live long enough in the right kind of circumstances, we might. But I doubt it. Meadowbrook's field was special in what it offered, in what it inspired—in us, and in the dogs. I wonder what our dogs thought of that night, if they even witnessed the event at all. Maybe humans make so much of happenings like this because we allow ourselves so little time—and so rarely put ourselves in position—to experience them in the first place. Dogs, on the other hand, if left alone enough and encouraged to live doggy lives, get to be old hands at living a life in and with nature, so they can drink in all this magical stuff as just part of what happens on the planet. Doesn't mean they appreciate it any less, though, I suspect. Their lives just might be quietly richer in what really matters.

We told our neighbor lady at the far end of the field about our experience with ball lightning, and she wasn't surprised. She attributed that and a few other things that we came to realize were unusual about our place to "power points" that she told us were geo-something-or-other phenomena, located about where our two tracts of land met.

"They're all over this place," she said, excitedly pointing around us one weekend afternoon as we stood on our common boundary at the end of our field, discussing our mutual experiences in country living.

She and her husband had bought their half of what was originally a single-tract farm a short time before we bought the other half, and like us, had come there to try country living. They did well for a while, but eventually gave it up to return to people and things they enjoyed in a more populated environment. We, on the other hand, pressed on toward an even more remote setting for our next permanent home. Two couples, passing in different directions, matched up for a short time around the magic of power points.

****

There's nothing particularly magical about bats: they fly weirdly and look like something from Middle Earth, but basically they perform a public service. One expects to see them in the wild in certain settings, and a field surrounded by woods is one of those places. So, it was hardly surprising that Meadowbrook had bats. The cool thing to us was that we had a stable community of bats: they never numbered more than eight, and rarely exceeded four to six. These quirky aviators appeared like clockwork at dusk from somewhere in our front woods, soaring above the roof of our house and out over the field, engaged in their timeless chase of flying insects. From our constant battle with mosquitoes, I know our bats were incomplete hunters, but they gave it the good try, for which we were grateful. They sometimes finished a dive a mere foot or so from our heads, but mostly they exercised good manners and kept their lurching flights a respectable distance from us: for our part, we slumped down into our patio chairs as low as we could, as we enjoyed their quirky aerial show. In the cooling humidity of summer evenings, we found bat-watching to be a comforting, happy, even hypnotic time for us—especially after a long day at the office. We began to relax and talk easily about our respective work day happenings, then soon moved on to happier topics like future vacations, or more philosophical subjects like truth, justice, and what's for dinner? Putting ourselves back together night after night in a two-career household where both parties are designated office managers is nothing short of a minor miracle. For bats to have been key players in accomplishing that was, by any definition, magical.

****

A phenomenon that we have not seen since the Meadowbrook years was perhaps the most purely magical aspect of that field: animals standing at the far end of that field appeared considerably larger than they looked when standing closer to the house. Not just larger: *considerably* larger. This makes no sense, of course. Magic never does. We first noticed this when a light-tan-colored animal stood at the far end of the field one cloudy weekend afternoon in autumn. I immediately thought, *Deer,* and called to Mary to come look at it with me through the patio glass doors. The more I looked, though, the more unconvinced I was that this was a deer, after all. Something about it didn't look quite…deer-like.

I asked Mary, "Is that a deer, or—"

"I *think* so," she answered, squinting, unsure. "I don't know," she answered finally. "It's big enough to be a deer, but…"

The thing standing out there wasn't moving much, and didn't seem to be grazing like our deer usually did. She grabbed the binoculars.

"Scamp!" Mary laughed out loud.

"You're kidding? Scamper? You've got to be kidding!"

"Nope. It's Scamp."

"Let me have those." *Hmm...binoculars don't lie.*

Amazingly, over the years, we never tired of this goofy ritual.

Our dogs turned into all kinds of large animals through the trick of "expando-vision" that our field played on us whenever one or more of them had reached the far end of our field and stood there a while without us knowing they had gone there. There were times when one or both of us would actually walk midway up the field to *prove* that the animal we were seeing was not one of our dogs. But every time we were initially unsure, it was. Perhaps the swale between the ends of the field inspired an optical illusion, or maybe distance alone somehow produces that effect. Deer appeared to be massive when they stood at the far end of the Meadowbrook field—but slight and vulnerable when they munched apples off the tree in our back yard. Yet foxes and wild turkeys who made appearances at the far end of the field always seemed small in our view. Mary is convinced that this is a magical defense mechanism afforded some of the creatures who are purest of heart, which we agree *must* include our dogs and deer.

****

Black velvet. That's the only way to describe the Meadowbrook sky at night. With no city lights around to disturb the richness of endless Space above us, we saw stars the way they must have appeared to the first humans—stars so numerous you couldn't pick out constellations. Halley's Comet bold and brilliant. The Milky Way breathtaking in its vivid sweep overhead. In their majestic twinkling, stars shared their light from eons ago, across the vastness of our Universe. Stare at them long enough, and you are transfixed by their beauty...and something else. They are at once close in on you, and eternally far away; warm and friendly...cold and distant; not of this world...but of the same Creation. Humbling, terrifying, beyond human capacity to understand.

Although nature undeniably produces the most awe-inspiring moments, humans, too, can come up with some fairly spectacular magic. With a little help from the Christmas-lights industry and a local home-improvement store, we discovered that stringing a number of variably-timed, multi-colored Christmas lights throughout our expansive dogwood tree in the center of our back yard provided an opportunity to synchronize some slow-fade colors in various successions. The effect at night was an incredibly mesmerizing sequence of red lights fading slowly into blue, then fading into green, then into yellow, then back to red, and on and on. We could watch it for hours. Simple minds, to be sure, but it was calming beyond belief. Against a backdrop of recently fallen snow, or even better—a yard sheeted by ice, this slow-motion, revolving progression of muted colors in the total silence of 41 night-time acres in the middle of country was…awesomely…magical.

Chapter 14
Characters

Ascribing human tendencies, desires, emotions, and thoughts to animals is a habit common to many pet owners—dog owners in particular. "He's just a dog," raises eyebrows among the dog-loving world: No, not just a dog—he's, well, something more than that. This is the stuff that goofy debates are made of. Dogs are not humans: four paws, some kind of tail, and a tongue that curls down and backwards to drink water pretty much take care of any argument to the contrary.

But because dogs can do, feel, and think human-type stuff, our geocentricism takes over. Anything worthwhile that other animals can do—short of flight—is often regarded by us humans as something almost human, and we are quick to praise it as such. Right along with that is our human bias that says anything animals do that is unpleasant to watch or think about is animal behavior, and we dissociate ourselves from that in short order. Pigs wallow in mud and filth (how's your bathroom looking lately?) Goats smell bad (been in a crowded subway in summer after a long day at work?) Lions and wolves tear after their prey in violent attacks (ever catch the evening news?) We're all animals. It wasn't long after ninth grade biology informed me that I was part of the animal kingdom that I began to look at animals differently. Stuff I was doing as a growing lad seemed to be the same stuff other animals were doing, and for what appeared to be the same whimsical—or compelling—reasons.

Dogs, like humans and other animals, like to eat; they also need to eat. They like to play, and they invent ways to do that. They like to snuggle with each other sometimes, and with other animals, including humans. They react with distrust and fear when physically or psychologically harmed, and if treated badly enough, they will react to protect themselves. They need sleep, and they search for attention and love. They have and express curiosity and interest in the world around them. They learn by making mistakes, and if they survive those mishaps, they often do not repeat them. They signal how they feel. They communicate tenderness, instruction, affection, discipline, and aggression with each other and with other animals. The emotions they communicate run the full gamut from silly to deadly serious: like the soldier at war, who one minute fires to kill, and the next comforts a civilian child wandering through exploded ruins—the emotion of the moment depends on the moment. That guard dog who bares her teeth with head lowered at an intruder is the same goofball who throws all four legs up into the air on a lazy afternoon in a sudden return to puppyhood. What motivated you the last time you threw a jig into your stroll through the house, out to the shed, or down the hallway to your office? (If you haven't done that in a while, you might should wonder why not.) Dogs get playfully silly for the same reasons.

Getting the drift of all this? A lot of the animal kingdom has a lot in common with a lot of the rest of the animal kingdom. Dogs are animals. People are animals. Animals are animals. Until you walk a mile in someone else's shoes, paws or hooves, you don't have a clue what's going on in that other being. True or false? Birds don't love. Snakes don't feel pain. Deer don't know fear. Fish don't get hot or cold. The point is, we humans don't know much about other forms of life. Worse, we don't seem to care much about what we do that impacts other animals. Worse still, when we suspect that we may be harming them—even unintentionally—while we pursue our human objectives, we tend to concoct some theory that makes everything okay, which is easier on our consciences than merely looking the other way. That, and our human ego, probably accounts for much of our zeal to transform our wishes into beliefs, and beliefs into "facts," and hold fast to them. Nothing solidifies belief like ignorance. The less we know, the more we seem to need to enhance our ignorance with certainty: so the easy answer is to make something up, and defend it to the death. This might be okay if we were discussing how many stars there are in the Universe; but the game gets unconscionably cruel when ignorant belief supports, justifies, and encourages human treatment of animals and their habitat in ways we would regard as unthinkable if done to our fellow humans. Laws aside, put a human being at the other end of the fishing hook, hunter's rifle, or arrow, and see what you think. Put yourself in a crate or cage for hours, days, weeks, months, years on end, and how might you feel? Starve, kick, mutilate, yell at constantly, ignore continually, leave outside in the rain, sleet, snow, burning sun, or forget to provide fresh water for your dog or other animal in your care, and think for a second, how you would feel in that creature's place?

By habit or some speck on the DNA of human genealogy, some humans are persuaded that killing other animals is okay, and those of us who like our hamburgers, chicken fillets, fish platters, venison stew, and steaks add ourselves to the unsavory practice of growing and "harvesting" our cousins in the animal kingdom to satisfy our own appetites. Taking reasoned thought along these lines to its logical conclusion, humans should all be vegetarians, at least until studies further confirm already existing evidence that plants, too, feel stress, need companionship, and suffer the pain of damage and loss, in which case we will all starve.

What does all this have to do with an otherwise pleasant little book on the lives of dogs? Maybe about as much as the Karma-theory of life: everything any of us does has an effect somehow, somewhere, on someone or something on the planet, and those effects pile up, converge, reinforce, and collide with other things done by ourselves and others, and pretty soon we realize we are all awash in a jumble of waves that we helped set in motion in the first place. Think this is too esoteric, or just plain nonsense? Could be. Or maybe there is something to that irritating little reminder we've all heard more than once: "What goes around, comes around." Entire religions are based on that simple principle expressed in different ways: "Do unto others," "Respect all forms of life," "Love thy neighbor as thyself." For such a simple concept, it is, amazingly, too often forgotten.

We humans like to think of ourselves as the most advanced form of life on Earth. Evidence to the contrary, it is a tempting mind set. Even if you buy into that one, wouldn't it be fair to say, then, that humans should at the very least be careful stewards of our planet? Because if we—the highest form of intelligence and life on it—don't safeguard its welfare and ability to sustain life, what chance does the Third Rock have? "Walk softly upon the land," is a phrase used by outdoors enthusiasts who truly revere nature and all its gifts: treat nature with the same respect as you would want afforded to yourself, and thereby leave for successor generations the opportunity to enjoy the blessings of our world.

Some of those blessings are dogs. I am not here to tell you that dogs are people, smarter than people, better than people. If you pay attention to dogs, you know they—like all animals, humans included—are capable of nasty behavior, unsavory emotions, and the full array of regrettable tendencies. They are what all animals are: individuals. They lead complete, individual lives: they see the world from their individual perspectives, shaped by their individual backgrounds, pursued by their individual, internal interests, driven by their unique genetic codes and personal spirits. Their lives can be as full as opportunity and external forces permit. They are as worthwhile, fun, and all-around wonderful as any other animals—us humans included. Some dogs are pretty cool— some not so much. Some dogs are friends and teachers: don't let your guard down around others. Some are affectionate to a fault, and will sacrifice themselves for you: others have their own agendas and will show up at mealtime—maybe not even then. Sound like some family or friends you know?

Pay attention to your dogs, and right away you begin to see the characters they individually are. Sure, many are full of gifts for you, while admittedly others are, we might say, lacking in redeeming value. But all of them are characters. The greatest joy in having dogs is to discover as many facets of those characters as possible. A word of caution at the outset: like people or any other animals, dogs will reveal their inner selves only when they are comfortably secure in their relationship with you. If kept at bay, ignored most of the time, shown irritation when they try to interact with you at an "inconvenient" time, they will gradually become disappointed, grow quiet around you, and eventually shift their focus in other directions. Dogs not kept in a fenced situation will roam to find a fulfilling life if they aren't provided one by their owners. Sure, that's not the only reason they wander, but it is a guaranteed consequence of inattention from the beings they would otherwise prefer to share their lives and time with. As in all marriages, friendships, and other partnerships, your *interest in* their *lives and welfare keeps* their *interest...in...you.*

****

Tag's was a character study in the traditional work ethic: *Work, work, work!* "Gotta run, gotta run!" we laughingly called after our Taggie boy as he suddenly, incessantly trotted out of sight around and around the sofa, around and around the house, around and around in his dog yard, around and around us in the woods.

"Taggie legs" was no joke: his haunches were "twisted steel," and that came to be one of a zillion phrases in our household lingo born of the dogs' characters. Our goal: diet and work out, so we, too, could have Taggie legs. No chance of that happening, but it was something to aspire to. Tag ran for practice, sometimes when he had to go outside to take care of business, sometimes just because he was *driven*; but whatever the impetus, his was a mission that was rarely on hold.

At the start of a family activity new to him, Tag planted himself in front of me, and with terribly earnest eyes, asked me, *What are we doin'?* His self-appointed job in life was to bring order to the other dogs and to Mary and me. Once he understood the plan, he could adjust his coordinator role to it, and life would once again be copacetic. Straightforward, uncomplicated, tough as nails, no-nonsense, to-the-point: that was Mr. Dependable. That was Tag. Contented when order reigned. You just didn't want to mess that up. Keep it simple, keep it predictable, don't confuse him. Tag kept us all in rhythm, on time, safe. Taggie in charge. From puppy to old guard, that boy never lost his sincere look: it could drive you nuts when you wanted to take a break or haunt you when you tried to give him or the pack the brush-off after a tough day at the office—when they had waited all day, looking forward to just a little of your time to make their day. Keeping us all on an even keel was Cap'n Tag's creed. *Okay, while you guys figure out what's next on the agenda, I'll just run some circles for a while. Gotta run, gotta run.* For sure, they broke the mold when they made this one.

Want to throw in some silliness and sly looks portending mischief? Windi was your girl. Talking the pack leader into forays was her specialty: where Tag was steady, Windi was adventurous—but only when the mood struck, which in hot weather was not all that often—certainly not when air conditioning vents were in good working order. "She's my good Scottish lass," Mary happily proclaimed through the warm spring and summer days, when the two of them talked each other into lazing around inside while the sun baked the back of the house and weeds continued to crush the vegetable garden. First things first with Windi: she and Mary paid homage to that sacred second cup of morning coffee and afternoon tea time on weekends—feet up on the ottoman, paws stretched out on the carpet, both lumps of contentment in their usual spots at Mary's end of the couch.

Windi's the one who taught us foyer ball (see Chapter 15). It was Windi's ears that most appreciated the exotic sounds of things. She perked her ears up and cocked her head almost completely sideways at the sounds of words she found interesting or funny. Then her whiskers bent forward (you could see them curl, like they were magnetized to your face); at that point, her eyes dilated, and she looked a little crazy. I tucked those words away for future fun with her, and they always worked. With Windi in the room, we were all easily entertained.

The stinkier she got (most often from wandering through creek bogs), the more affectionate Chelsea became. Miss Happy—Miss Sunshine—couldn't wait to share her odiferous self with you upon her return to the house after a disgusting session in black muck. Sporting seventy pounds of will, she was not easily dissuaded from her predictable greeting back at the house: first wiggle all over while plowing headfirst into us, then twist and turn while bringing her side and hindquarters through a full slide along our legs or tummies, then abruptly reverse direction for another full frontal press of muzzle against whatever part of us was left standing or sitting. You could *not* hold yourself upright against the exceptionally strong onslaught of this much happy muscle. These sessions always ended with you on your back, totally grossed out and laughing. That done, she looked for her bed or, if the wood stove was cookin',' the prized front-row spot there, as close as she could get to the glass doors where the heat was most intense.

Chelsea was up for a game of foyer ball anytime, but her deal was to ferret out the closest "woobie" (a fluffy squeak toy stuffed with cotton) and squeak that until we gave up trying to watch our TV show. You couldn't hear much over the incessant noise of that most favorite toy. We marveled at the variety of cadences and volumes she could produce from a "woobie:" shaking it in her mouth, trotting from room to room, lying on her side or back, she could squeak the dickens out of a "woobie" at ninety miles an hour, slowly in hypnotic strains, or in an endless combination of cadences. A maestro of woobie-dom, she was.

She had a collection, dispersing and leaving them in all sorts of places inside and outside the house. The ones left outside gathered rain and yard yuk, so by the time one of those ripened into a black/brown soggy mess, she was eager to bring it back inside for a chew on our nice clean floors and rugs. Spotting that game afoot before the woobie could land in forbidden territory was a regular challenge for us: not only did we have to be quick to notice the advancing disaster, but if we were going to prevent a very-disappointed-Chelsea face, we had to find a moderately clean substitute woobie for her. Thank goodness for Mom: she graced us with new woobies every Christmas, and sometimes just for fun during the year, so we generally had a steady supply of Chelsea's woobie fix on hand.

Always happy except when she happened to be sick, that was the Chels. Look over at her from the desk, sofa, dinner table, reading chair, or just passing through the area where she was, and unless she was unconscious, you got a big ol' wag or two in response. Bank on it. *Ain't life grand?* Chelsea's creed.

"Be careful what you name your dog," is a theme that cannot be over-emphasized. Ruffy lived up to his name, but not because he intended to be rough. He was just *big*, and judging from his obvious grin after he bowled Chelsea over every time we all started our walks around the field, down the driveway or through the woods, he rather enjoyed being big. Watching him lope with a sudden burst of speed, closing the distance between him and Chelsea at the start of those walks so he could tumble her into a somersault or two as he lumbered over and through her was so bad it was funny. We felt ashamed to be laughing at poor Chels, rolling rump over snoot (but not enough to stop). He never tried that with Boss Tags, but the rest of us were fair game. The times Mary and I came closest to visiting our friendly orthopedist courtesy of a Ruffy stampede were when others in the pack—already in his sights—cut close to our legs as they raced by to elude him; unwittingly (and very unwillingly), we had just set a pick in the path of galloping Ruffy the Water Buffalo. *Ouch!* When he banged into the back of our legs, it *hur*t: if he'd have connected from the side, they would have broken. We kept that in mind during the early minutes of every walk. Lumbering into us brought a strong rebuke from whichever of us had been clobbered. Ruffy glanced back at us with a wounded expression of having done "something" wrong, but a doggy conscience has a short half-life: he quickly forgot about whatever it was he'd done, and bounded off after his victim with renewed enthusiasm. (One of the invaluable life lessons taught to us by our dogs: pay attention to what's going on around you. *Gee—thanks, Ruffin.*)

Every once in a while Ruffy tried to catch-and-tumble Scamp, but that was doomed to fail: her hearing was excellent, and she could sprint sideways on deer feet. Chelsea usually paid for that a few moments later. The song says, "If you can't be with the one you love, love the one you're with." Ruffin's motto: "If you can't bounce the one you want, bounce the one you can." Soon after Chelsea realized she was Ruffy's favorite target, she began her walk around the field by staying in the thick, high brush outside the mowed part, where Ruffin couldn't build up any speed to bowl her over. Chelsea was accustomed to browsing through underbrush for mice and whatnot, so brambles and deadfall didn't much bother her: Ruffin, on the other hand, found such terrain distasteful and awkward. For the big guy, the rough-and-tumble business was more than just a game of pummeling your pack sister: for him, it was another notch up on the pack hierarchy for him to run the field closest to the leader. In the end, climbing the corporate ladder is what it was all about in a multiple-dog environment. So chasing Chelsea out of the (cleared field) picture was enough to satisfy Ruffin, although he did thereafter try to find ways to surprise Chelsea before she could make her way off the game field and avoid the whole business. After all, whichever world you're in—dogs' or humans'—accomplishing your primary objective is fine, but if you can have some fun along the way, well, so much the better.

Ruffin's life revolved around Tag. He emulated Tag as much as a lumbering German shepherd could copy a smaller, faster Border collie. Both had excellent vision, as dogs bred for livestock protection should, but there the physical similarities ended. Mutt and Jeff, this pair, although the adoration seemed to be mostly Ruffy's for Tag: Tag, after all, was the leader, and could show no favorites, even if he had any. Ruffy, however, was free to shadow Tag and (in true wolf pack behavior) lick his muzzle endlessly: this blatant respect was the Boss's due, so Tag put up with Ruffy-breath all day long—such is the burden pack leaders bear. Before putting himself into gear for anything, Ruffin checked to see where Cap'n Tag was and what he was doing, in case that made a difference in the Ruffer's immediate plans.

Freckles was a ditz. No offense, but she was flighty, her brain always a few yards behind her body. Wherever she flopped down—on the patio, in the yard, on her bed in the laundry room, she looked around a little dazed afterwards, taking a few minutes to gather herself, seemingly trying to answer the question her whole face was clearly asking, "What am I doing here?" A squirrel cage of an animal, Frecks lived to run, ferret out birds, stalk butterflies—that's it. That's all. Her life was ridiculously simple. She ate and slept because she felt the need to: otherwise, she wouldn't have taken time for either of those. She came into the house only because it got dark. Weather meant nothing to her: rain or shine, hot or cold, the world in daylight was meant to be run in, and because we fed birds in all seasons, she had an ample, never-ending supply of them to watch and chase year round. Darkness, though, was a problem, so when the last of the twilight vanished, inside she came, half-flopping, half-heaving herself with a *thump!* down on her bed. Regret at having to give up the day showing in her pinched face, she immediately buried her head in the blanket and closed her eyes—her signal for us to hurry up and turn out the light, so she could escape to her dreams and plans for the coming morning. A simple dog leading a simple life. A delightful creature living a delighted life. If Chelsea showed us happy, Freckles taught us *joy*. To watch her white, silky fur romp and tear across the field in whatever zig-zag pattern caught her fancy at the moment was to feel the blessing of life in its purest form. I dare say not many people have seen that kind of wonder. Mary and I can only aspire to approach what that dog continually lived. Doggy heaven must have fields like that, full of butterflies and flowers, birds on the wing, all for the eternal delight of our most fanciful dog of Meadowbrook.

The most complicated member of the pack was Scamp. They all had their moods, their moments of varying emotions, ranging from serene to anxious, flat to full throttle, contented to irritable. She had these, but in the presence of deeper thought. Working closely with colleagues and employees, or living closely with family members, if you pay attention to their eyes and body language, you can receive intricate messages from them without their ever opening their mouths. It works the same way with dogs—some more than others. Scamp always had something cooking, her attic light always on. And her thoughts weren't limited to what we humans think are the full breadth of doggy thoughts (*When's supper? Can I have another treat? Want to play ball? Let's go for a walk. I have to go out!*). Hers included the stuff of philosophers. A tell-tale moment, repeated over and over by her, was when she looked intently in first one direction, then another, and was oblivious to everything around her, prompting Mary or me to ask each other, "She is lost in thought, isn't she? What do you suppose she's thinking?" We would watch her do that for minutes at a time, after which she'd turn her head back to us, rejoining us in the here and now, trot over, and do some typically doggy things like hopping up on the sofa to nap, or snagging a toy or cow hoof to have a chew. The weirdest moments were those when she concluded her private contemplation by turning to us and looking at us with obvious thoughts or questions on her mind. Not being mind-readers, we couldn't come up with what they were. We would have been better company for her if we could. We have no doubt she shared those quiet conversations with her fellow furries—just another aspect of their world that we were not equipped to be a full part of.

Scamp explored the world like everybody else in the pack (except Tag, whose life mission was based on duty)—comfortably, at her own pace, selecting those things she felt like doing at the time, for reasons known only to her. Dogs can make you feel stupid when they see you doing something that makes you uncomfortable, yet you do it anyway. At those times, they will watch you in amusement from a safer, more comfortable place. You won't get a lot of companionship from your dog, say, when you're weed-eating in 90-degree temperatures. On such occasions, Scamp kept a skeptical eye on me from a distant shady spot (I could have done without the slightly upturned corners of her mouth). When my dad and I tore into a project of felling dead trees for firewood, chainsaws blazing, recklessly bolting out of the path of falling limbs and towering trunks, Scamp was curled up in a happy ball under a lawn chair occupied by mom, some distance away—both of whom had better sense than to play chicken with an 85-foot oak tree.

But mostly Scamp kept us company. Our nightly routine was to flop on the sofa after the work day's supper dishes were done, and the next day's lunches made and tucked into bags in the refrigerator. She politely waited at our feet while I settled into position—feet propped up on the ottoman, blanket over legs in the cooler weather. Then, with one pat of my right hand on the sofa cushion, she hopped up in one graceful leap, slid her back down alongside my right hip, careful to keep her head up for the obligatory couple dozen rubs and strokes until she was ready to snooze. We turned the TV volume up slightly about ten minutes later when she began to snore.

When Mary or I grappled with sickness, Scamp notched herself down to match the mood of the house. Her pace slowed, and she was quiet; she reduced her trips to the water bowl, so she could last the whole day without having to go outside. When either of us was home on a week day, Scamp was our dedicated indoor companion. If either of us was home alone and sick, the rest of the gang was put out in their yard, but Scamper was the designated indoor guard dog. She knew her role on those days: she held back on the laundry room door landing and watched while the others were put into their yard, patiently waiting until she was inevitably invited inside to take up her post. She was never in the way, and always company. Incongruous as it seemed for such an independent and tough little critter, Scamp, more than any of the others, needed to feel close to us in association, if not always physically. When you take time to notice things like that, you realize how little you have understood—and appreciated—how much richness of life was being offered to you all along.

The work life, and all the angst that goes with that in the after hours, cheats us of too much of what we should experience while we are lucky enough to be on this planet. While we were and remain grateful for the comforts and opportunities our careers provided, our lingering regret is that it came at a high cost. Part of that bill is a glimmer of awareness of how little time we had to experience the characters who shared their lives with us at Meadowbrook. Still, the moments we did spend with them lifted us from an otherwise okay house on a farm field in the woods to a life rich with wonder and fun, the likes of which we will never know again. Our memories, thankfully helped along by many photographs, grow more special to us with time, and give us the faith to move forward with new adventures and different characters for as long as we are able to rustle up dog chow several times a day.

Chapter 15
Home

It's a funny concept, "home." You can be home in a rented house, on a trip, in someone else's home. Home is a state of heart. Home has no boundaries on number of occupants, and is not limited to humans. Meadowbrook was home to us *and* our dogs: it was as inseparable from them as much as it was from us. Home is shaped by the characters in it; it is formed by the events that happen there. Those characters and events fashion bonds that the heart quietly gathers into itself until heart and home are one and the same. This process happens in odd little ways that you don't always notice at the time.

Part of making a home is looking out for the other guys there—doing for them, accommodating them, wanting to make their life there better—more enjoyable. Mary noticed how much the furries liked sitting on the patio landing, so they could see out over the field, feel the predominant, southwest breezes, and snooze away from the incessant biting of the ground insects. Problem was, the sun beat down on the back of the house all day long, and for at least six months out of the year, that sun was brutal. The answer? Install an awning over that landing. Now this went to the heart of a bone of contention between the lady of the house and me since its construction: I did *not* want any awnings or overhangs that would block my view of the sky! I was adamant about that. I didn't ask for much from her (*Okay, I did*), but this was one hot button with me. *No way, Jose. No awning.*

"Skip, they are so hot out there, exposed to the sun all the time, and they *love* being able to sit and lie there, looking out on everything. It's their favorite thing to do!" she implored.

Whatever else I learned about her over our years of marriage, she was always right. Not the tired, "By definition my wife is always right—that's the secret of our marriage," adage that we hear at every social gathering, but as a matter of fact, she always *is* right. She's a smart bear, and when I feel like exploring that little-used corner of my brain that harbors a bright bulb or two, I realize it—and go with it. Go with it we did, and within a few weeks, we had a brightly colored, striped awning over our patio landing. Now shaded, that landing was packed with pups, which gave us a neat show while we ate our meals on the other side of the patio doors. Giving the pack a place to continue their "watch on the world" in the pouring rain was another bonus. I had to admit, Mary's awning idea was golden. (She later pushed the envelope by asking for a long awning over the three small double-hung windows in front of the kitchen sink and counter, to the side of the patio landing, but we did that, too.)

Chelsea's spot on the patio landing was on the left side (looking out), one leg dangling over the top step. Ruffy's was on the right (no legs dangling). Tag and Windi held the center, ready to spring into action when anything dared to show itself out on the field—especially deer. Freckles wandered by, and when feeling frisky about Ruffy, would do her dance routine on the steps and awkwardly up onto the landing to pester the poor boy, but basically just loitered long enough to put in an appearance, and then was gone in her customary flash. Scamp ran up the steps, checked out (sniffed) everybody, and then gave us the paw-squeak on the glass doors to be let in. We were given one chance to escape the muddy scratch on the glass doors, but we had to be quick in noticing it: she sat in her trademark pose—chest out (which on a little dog is funny), head back, eyes boring into us—for a few seconds, expecting us to spring into action to *LET HER IN.*

We tended to notice this communal scene while watching TV at meal time. The small set was perched on the near end of the kitchen counter, away from our view of the patio landing and field. The companionable spirit of our collection of furry friends drew our attention through the sliding glass doors, and pretty soon we turned the TV sound down to focus on what they were doing: picking at burrs in their haunches, sniffing each others' ears, offering a few respectful licks to the boss' muzzle, snapping at a June bug passing recklessly close overhead, silently communicating to each other with looks that only they understood. But it was their calm gazing out over their realm that caught—and held—our attention, and as often as not, persuaded us to turn off the TV... and watch with them.

Nothing says home and family like chow time. Feeding these six guys took all of two minutes. Here's how it worked: we lined the bowls up on the kitchen counter, poured in the dry kibbles, opened a can (or two, depending on how affluent we were feeling that particular day, or how deserving we thought the furries were of a special treat with their meal, or how cold or nasty it was outside) and carefully divided the contents among the bowls for added taste and texture, then slid the bowls across the tile floor to their designated places (except for Freckles,' which required a walk into Her Highness' laundry-room quarters). The sliding of the bowls was a page right out of the bartender's handbook: I rather think the dogs enjoyed watching their breakfasts and dinners arrive at their appointed spots on the floor with a flourish.

Closely related to meal time was the family event of going outside. Any owner of a big dog knows this drill: it is variously described as, *Look out! Get out of the way!* or *Stand back!* all of which refer to the human, who stands to get trampled in the dog's zeal to leave the building. Multiply that by six strong-willed, scrambling canines all *needing* to be first out the back door, and you have a recipe for *Wild Kingdom*. Wading through the fur to get to the door in the first place to open it is tricky: they want to accommodate you (because I am fairly sure that on some level they comprehend that a human needs to do something halfway up the door to get it to open), but they also are keen on keeping their position (like any good race car driver jockeying just before the starting gun), to get a really good shot at being first down the back steps to the carport and out into the yard. That not-so-subtle shifting of poundage can squeeze a knee, or pin a leg, and over you go, on your way to your friendly orthopedist. (Our family physician told me long ago that the single most common cause of household accidents was a pet, usually a dog. "They'll hurt you if you're not careful," he cautioned, I suspect from experience—his patients' *and* his.)

Once the latch to the storm door was released, my work was done: the fuzzballs did the rest. BOOM! the door flew open, banged against the left railing of the small landing, knocking it back into the stampede, which in turn banged it again several more times against the railing as bodies exploded through the doorway and crashed down the stairs. I let out my breath after each of these episodes, grateful that I and the door were still in one piece. Occasionally one of the gang was not, getting "rolled" on the steps, or (to avoid that) jumping one step too many, and landing awkwardly on lower steps or the concrete pad, accentuated by some sort of yelp. I always cringed at that, but hobbled or not, they all usually managed to escape relatively intact out into the world once again. Tag was not so much an organizer as a *leader*, remember:

he *led* this madhouse out the door, and if you didn't want your muzzle shredded, you let him. *Things you work out as a family.*

Sometimes somebody didn't feel well. With us, the tell-tale signs were cold and wet noses; with them, noses were warm and dry. But as in the office, when I didn't have to reach out and touch an employee's nose to know that he or she was ailing, you could see by the tilt of the head, pace of the walk, or "green" look on the furry face that *somebody* had munched the wrong stuff in the woods. When Mary or I was sick, Scamp put herself into shutdown mode, hung out on the bed if we let her—otherwise, she stayed quietly on her bed all day, every day, lending a calming presence to the house until we could get well. Having that company helped the one left home while the other punched the work clock feel less lonesome and more protected. Something about having a friend standing guard over you while you slept spurred the healing process.

Dogs' senses are legendary. They can hear the slightest crack of a dog-cookie jar from anywhere in the house; one of the silliest notions an owner of multiple dogs can entertain is to be able to give a treat to one without the others knowing about it. Open that lid, and all muzzles are lined up at your feet before you can say, "Shhh," to the one you intended to reward. They also constantly watch the inside of the house from out in the yard, just in case you're planning to do something worthwhile, like say, getting into the dog-treat jar, or fixing their supper, or planning to go someplace fun (which was dang-near *anywhere*) in the TRUCK! We tried pulling the shades down once in an effort to pack for a beach trip without them getting all wired up about our soon leaving them behind (packing for a trip is tough enough without having to step and stumble over a bunch of dogs intent on getting in your way): the first time I had to go out to arrange the back seats of the car we intended to use, the troops were already assembled at the outdoor steps. *You're not fooling anybody here, bub.*

A working couple, commuting a combined three-plus hours a day, has little time during the work week to attend to other things. A pack of dogs figures in to most of what's left. Our awake home time was limited to about 4½ hours a day, five out of seven days a week, and the first hour of the work day hardly counted: brushing teeth, getting dressed, creating some sort of excuse for breakfast (my breakfast of choice was Instant Breakfast—add milk, stir, and guzzle—a sixty-second miracle of modern dining), tossing dry and canned goodies into the dog bowls, a minute or so later booting them out into their yard

(Ruffy held the chow-down speed record at twelve seconds), and kissing spouse goodbye for another day, didn't exactly constitute quality time. But that was our Meadowbrook ritual. The furries good-naturedly put up with brevity in our morning greetings, despite their natural proclivity to start each day with a more proper appreciation of the miracle that we were all still there, together, on a planet that promised at least the hope of some wonderful, new adventure that day.

When traveling on vacation through the English countryside early one morning in our rented car, we drove by a sheep farm just as the owner was opening the pen where he kept his working dogs. There must have been at least a half-dozen Border collies, but their tails wagged like they numbered a hundred! That scene—farmer greeted in brilliant morning sunshine so enthusiastically by his beloved partners—stuck with Mary and me, a reminder that life ought not be taken for granted, not even for a single day. Dogs know how to greet; we should learn at least that much from them.

Our evenings were more eventful. We generally spent the first hour with the dogs, playing field games and serving them supper. Then, while they sorted themselves out into their respective pursuits—Tag and Ruffin in their circle-the-house contest, Windi digesting comfortably on the patio landing (or inside on the air-conditioning vents if the heat index was too high), Chelsea snoofing out mice and voles on the field, Scamp giving herself a bath (a noise that proved unbelievably distracting during our dinner prayer), and Freckles running around someplace—we threw something together for supper for ourselves, made the next day's lunch, interacted with the dishwasher, and collapsed, usually on the living-room sofa. If we made it to that point by eight-thirty, we were doing well. Staring at a 5:45 a.m. alarm clock the next day, and forty-five minutes of bedtime preparations looming, any hope of logging anything near eight hours' sleep left about a half-hour to do everything else that needed doing that evening. Anything that consumed more than that tiny allowance of time infringed on much-needed sleep.

No wonder Americans falling asleep on the job had become a national epidemic: our pace of life had become debilitating, and almost everyone was caught up in it. Except for the independently wealthy, those not already caught up in this out-of-control merry-go-round ride were clamoring to hop on board to make ends meet. Something was wrong here: in our parents' day, one went to some kind of "away" work while the other stayed home, and took care of the house and family business. Life was simpler, easier mentally, and probably healthier for everyone. At minimum, dogs and at least one of their owners could have a proper English greeting each morning.

Watching a videotaped TV program helped cram a one-hour show into forty minutes, which helped. Of course, we had to do that while scratching each little furry head as it came up to the arm rest of the sofa and presented itself, in turn. Going through four or five of those took time, and some focus if you wanted to avoid giving them short shrift (and they know when you're not being sincere). The Border collies, especially, would stand there all night until you paid them proper attention and did it *right*. Frankly, after a day of people, office thrills, and a long commute, it was more enjoyable to scratch those heads than watch TV, so we ended up rubbing their shoulders, haunches and chests, as well. And, of course, doing that revealed ticks during tick season, which prompted tick check in the bathroom, and forget about TV or anything else that night. *My, how time flies.*

A ball can appear on your lap at any time. Training the furries to resist this temptation during our suppertime took some effort and real persistence on our part, but to a large degree was successful. The exception was when our mealtime took longer than our usual twenty minutes to discuss something at work, our finances, a house repair problem, or something *important* (like, should we get another dog?). The time for patience over, one of the group would hop up, grab a toy of choice (a ball from Windi or Ruffy, a "woobie" from Chelsea) and nose it onto your napkin. *Yuk. Supper was over. Gotta love your dogs.* That became our mantra. Every time I wrote a check at the vet's, cleaned up the floor from some overnight misery of an ailing pooch the next morning, bought another round of (expensive) heartworm tablets, I sighed, and with a wince reminded myself aloud why, despite two good incomes, we were always behind the eight-ball: "Gotta love your dogs."

No matter how crammed the evening became, there was always time for indoor ball-toss. The human name for our indoor ball-toss field was "foyer." In "foyer ball," the tosser sat at the kitchen table, faced the length of the foyer, and threw the ball (usually a tennis ball) on one bounce against the back of the front door. The preferred game seemed to be to catch the ball in the air off the door. When things went awry, the ball went careening off front teeth into the coat rack, bachelor table, or wainscoting, and turned things into a frenzied free-for-all. In other words, when the intended tossee missed, all bets were off: it became *anybody's* ball to get, for which the foyer paid a price. Unless subsequent owners have replaced all surfaces in the foyer-ball field, there are still nicks and slashes in the wainscoting and walls—subtle reminders in a portion of a place the dogs of Meadowbrook and their human compatriots called "home."

Chapter 16
At Day's End

There's a song by Bob Seger and the Silver Bullet Band, called "The Ring," in which a woman, many years into her marriage, is suffering an unfulfilled life; in the wee hours of the night, she sometimes looks out through the window into the distance of what might have been, then looks at her sleeping husband, but never looks at her wedding ring lying on the bedroom table. In that song, day after day, year after year, for her, another day "just ends."

At Meadowbrook, with its cast of for-sure characters, no day "just ended." The ending of each day was an *event*. Bedtime preparations for *us* were easy, and varied only slightly, depending on the season. In the cold months, I stoked the wood stove so we would have heat well into the early morning hours; that way, when I opened the pocket door at the top of the stairway overlooking the foyer the next morning, warm, toasty air greeted me, and the floor tile in the kitchen felt friendly to my toes. The rest of the year, it was just a quick matter of adjusting the thermostat or checking windows for desired ventilation. In all seasons, putting the pack to bed, however, was an adventure.

Tag's inner clock went off to the minute every night: 9:15 p.m. was bedtime for a civilized Border collie—period. No ifs, ands, or buts—if it was 9:15 p.m., you better get off your keister and get the bedtime show on the road. As pack leader, he had a busy day in store for him the next day, *every* day, so he knew he needed his rest. A dog's life is simple, and a good pack leader must insist on keeping it that way. Tag did his best with what was admittedly a tough crowd to corral into proper action at the proper time. Tag was all about proper. He meted out disciplinary chomps on the muzzle to his four-paw troops for any transgression (getting in his way, going out of order in line for something, going in the wrong direction), but when *we* were the ones messing things up, he planted himself squarely in front of us, looked sharply into our eyes, and telepathically commanded, "Pay attention!" So many times I realized afterwards that he must have been very disappointed in our unawareness of what was important to do at the time, and in our inability to do a thing properly.

Tag's first effort to round all of us up and put everybody to bed was a polite, slow walk out of the living room, his toenails clicking *tik-tik-tik-tik* across the kitchen tile, followed by a casual look back to see if we were astute enough to get the point and follow his lead. If that was unsuccessful (which it was about half the time), we were treated to his annoyed second effort (run back to where we were, stand directly in front of me, give himself a mighty shake, then run out into the kitchen, whirl around, and bark—*once*). If all that didn't work, he put *himself* to bed (at least, temporarily) in the far corner of the kitchen until we finally got with the program. It was that last, frankly exasperated sigh as he flopped down on the hard floor that usually got my attention when I had been either too absorbed in something else to notice his invitations to wind up the day, or unwilling to muster enough energy to move from my couch-potato spot.

Letting the dogs out to go to bed was (mercifully) a lighter version of the one that followed meal time (see Chapter 15); that does not mean we could get away with our part barefoot then, either. Mixing it up with over 350 pounds of muscle shifting in different directions all at once at the back door is an art that, no matter how deftly done, risks serious pain and injury to human feet that get, well, under foot. Still, the bedtime version was more orderly, gentler on everybody. Creatures of habit, like any animals, the dogs knew what was expected of them next, and they generally were happy to do it. The long-hairs trotted dutifully into their yard where individual houses and blankets were waiting for them. The two short-hairs (Freckles and Scamp) sniffed, whizzed, and quickly returned to indoor air for the night—most of the time. (Scamp varied this routine in her later years, venturing out on late-night escapades that would last up to several hours, sometimes not returning to bark me awake until 3 a.m. or so; see the Epilogue). I gave each of the outside four a small cookie treat once inside the yard, and told them all to "sleep well." The final part of my nightly dog yard ritual was to rub Tag's head, bend low to his ear, thank him for taking care of everybody that day, and remind him that "Ratches will look after you." With that, he turned and slipped into the big doghouse—the one that still bore the name of the legend painted in an arc over the door.

Sometimes I petted Freckles on my way through the laundry room after locking up, but other times she was so tightly coiled up (or was so muddy and stinky from a day in the creeks, bogs, or whatever) that I gave her a glance and kept on truckin' to join Mary upstairs. "Goodnight, Scamp," were my last downstairs words for the evening as I climbed the steps to our bedroom. (She gave me my first downstairs greeting each morning: it was a high-pitched, stretched-out, "Rrrruuhhh," that escaped her as she stretched that typical doggy stretch—front legs out first, then bend the chest down and forward to stretch the back legs, giving that last leg a little wiggle and kick to finish up. If she didn't do all that, I knew she was sick.)

Shower, brush teeth, settle down, and finally lights out for us. It surprised us that it took us a little while to realize something that had been going on after the outside portion of the pack had been put into their yard for the night: they howled melodically for at least a half-minute or so after—always *just after*—we turned out the last house light. This goodnight song was Tag's inspired way of letting the rest of the "jungle out there" know that he and his gang were on duty at Meadowbrook, and of letting us know that we were being protected while we slept. Cap'n Tag was the genuine article. Having lived with him over ten years, there is nothing in this world I am more sure of than that he was always on duty, and we felt safe in his charge. He was only 50+ pounds, but his legs were twisted steel, and he was all heart. Look up "conscientious" in the book of words, and his mug should be there. We called the group "carolers" when they performed their song from the patio landing in the early evenings of the Christmas season, and it was a decidedly different sound from their normal nightly version: their call out into the darkness past the holiday lights on the dogwood tree was more direct and forceful, as they repeated their selected tones with continually strong bursts of energy until they suddenly decided to quit. Their regular goodnight song, on the other hand, moved with more varying volume and pitch—*We are many, and we are strong*—until the last single note faded wistfully into the night.

Part Three

Beyond the Boundaries

Chapter 17
Going to Town

It's *Saturday!* The best day of the week. The day we all go to town—*all*—if you can corral Freckles. Now that was a trick. First, she had to be somewhere close enough to hear the truck start up. To a dog, every truck has its own distinctive engine sound. Our guys knew our Chevy start-up call, and its idle speak. They had all been virtually born in it: carried to Meadowbrook from their various litters in it, ferried to the vet in it, run around the countryside a few miles many nights at sundown in it just to take a ride. If the weather's good, ears and nose are out the window, slobber spraying backwards all over the paint job. (Bug splatter on the grill and hood will eat through paint after a few days; dog spit and acid do a number on the polish and paint in *minutes*.) You can always tell who has a ride-along dog in the family; just look at the outside of the passenger side door of at least one of their vehicles.

****

Early in our marriage, we paid a visit to a Fiat dealership in Northern Virginia, and met the proverbial combination of an irresistible force and an immovable object: a midnight blue Fiat Sport Spider, and a car salesman whose two principal attributes were a talent for spotting lust in the buyer's heart, and steely-gray eyes at the bargaining table. The object of our desire had one overriding feature—a back seat for our big, handsome, ride-along dog, which for a foreign sports car convertible, was not that common. We ignored the checkbook's warnings, and drove it home. For all ten of its years in our family, it sported a trademark V pattern of dots trailing down over the trunk. Another part of Mary's Scottish ancestry came to the fore: she liked cold weather. The Fiat was hers. More than a car, it was a part of her lifestyle, her distinct way of feeling the richness of her days. When it wasn't raining or snowing, that convertible top stayed down. On the coldest days, ear muffs and mittens (and the heater on full blast!) were all Mary of the McLean clan needed as she merrily shifted through the gears. Behind her, ears and tongue flapping joyously in the breeze, Ratches grinned all the way to and from wherever Mary took him. The wind whipping by carried his happy spray of saliva down and across the top of the trunk, where it dried instantaneously and etched Ratches' signature mark forever on our dog-mobile. It became his car; we sold it shortly after we lost him. On our way to trade it, we stopped at the end of our driveway, shut off the engine, got out, touched the hood, then ran our hands along the top of the trunk that carried Ratches' reminders of wonderfully happy times. Mary's tears let an incredibly special time of her life slip into the past.

****

Firing up the Chevy S-10 usually brought Freckles out of the woods and field: it was the only thing that did, other than nightfall. We learned early on not to abuse our vocal cords hollering to Freckles when it was time to take her to the vet for shots and checkups. Instead, we just got in the truck, revved up the engine a few times, and if she was anywhere around, *presto!* she appeared, out of nowhere, like always. But, if the truck bed was filled with the rest of the gang, she usually lost interest in going: seeing the others in the bed panting and ready for a big ride, she more often than not wagged, grinned, wagged some more, then wheeled around the bounced off into the field. *See ya.* The life of an independent. Our associate pack member.

Off we went to Reidsville—to town. What a troop: two off-the-leash humans in front, five excited furries in back! Through the open country, at speeds (and I hope no NC trooper is reading this) of over 60 mph in the straight stretches, we were on an adventure every time. Exhilarated to be off the work schedule, an even bigger prize was waiting for us: Short Sugar's—the premier barbeque place in the region, as far as we were concerned. It had an old-time-diner look to it, with plain-spoken, down-to-earth folks waiting tables, getting to know you, swapping light stories about themselves and ourselves, and bringing your usual when you first got to the table: buttermilk and chopped for Miss Mary, Coke and sliced (no slaw) for me, medium fries. With sports page and front page spread out on the table (you *know* who read what), happy and contented, we snarfed lunch. Two peppermint patties on the way out, and the weekend was officially underway.

While we were inside Short Sugar's chowing down, the petting zoo was in full swing at our truck. "Children" of all ages stopped by the back of the S-10, "ooh-ed" and "aah-ed" over the Borders, Scamp and Chelsea, and wondered if they could pet the big guy. They always hesitated when they approached Ruffin, and only a few brave souls gave it a try. Ruffy was splendid: he shied his head back a bit, lowering his massive muzzle, and if the courageous passerby didn't flinch or pull back, he'd gently and slowly give the extended hand a few light sniffs. A few lucky folks were able to coax his whole head forward, where it was treated to careful rubs on the muzzle and behind the ears; but these people were rare—most gave Ruffin the distance his countenance suggested was wise. Appropriately enough, he was appreciated more by being watched, just as he enjoyed the world mostly by watching it. Sitting calmly and with confidence, Ruffy was a showpiece in that truck bed. We chuckled, listening to people come in after having passed by our guys, remarking about how beautiful those dogs were, wondering whose they were, and the inevitable, "Did you see how *big* that German shepherd was?"

For people already in the restaurant when we arrived, there was a growing buzz when one person after another remarked to their table mates, "Oh, look at those dogs, honey!" or (to their child) "Look, Danny/Becky—see the doggies? Look at that *big* one!" That big one caught everybody's eye.

Truthfully, it would have been easier on our digestion if we hadn't had the dogs with us: the always looming prospect of a lawsuit from a bitten (or even just scared) child can put a crimp into an otherwise-relaxed lunch, but the risk seemed worth the joy those dogs brought to the scene. And, it didn't take long before that truck and those dogs became an institution. "Oh, *you're* the ones with *those dogs*!" we'd hear from increasing numbers of strangers, and not just when we were parked at Short Sugar's, either: this went on at many of our stops all over Reidsville. It was kind of cool; nah, it was way cool. We had an identity—from our dogs, sure, but it counted. Frankly, there are worse sources of identity than a pack of pretty special pooches. We were proud.

The owner of Short Sugar's came over to our table once with a bucket of huge pork bones. "Thought the dogs might like 'em."

We were very careful about spiky bones that could catch in a dog's throat and intestines and do serious damage or worse, but looking at these large chunks of bone, and weighing the owner's amazing thoughtfulness, we said,

"Sure, thanks," and gave our guys a Short Sugar's treat later that afternoon. On really hot summer Saturdays, the waitress showed up at our table with a bucket of water for us to take out to the dogs. *After* that, we got *our* order.

The treeless parking lot surrounding the restaurant baked intensely on sunny days, so we took precautions in the hot season to protect tender dog paws from the heat-absorbing black rubber bed liner in the back of our truck: we covered it with a light colored, plastic tablecloth. For shade on the hottest days, we attached a huge umbrella to the hand-made wooden rails that helped keep the dogs inside the truck bed. The umbrella rig easily caught the attention of the incredulous patrons. To the dogs, it was just your average family outing at the shore: *Pass the Coppertone, will ya, Tag? Hey, anybody remember to bring the beach ball?* It got a little cozy with five dogs vying for a spot in that small patch of shade, but, panting and pressed up against each other, they still managed grins when we came out to resume our Saturday outing. *Yeah, it might be a little crowded and warm, but who'd want to miss out on all this?*

The fur-pack rode merrily with us through countless errands in Reidsville—to the farm-supply store, hardware store, grocery store. They were patient riders. We could trust them for as much as an hour at a time to stay in the back of that truck. We were smug in that prideful thought until one very hot summer afternoon when we went grocery shopping. We'd been in the Food Lion maybe five minutes when Mary heard something over the PA system, "Will the owner of a large brown dog get him, please?"

I hadn't heard it, but I was startled to see Ruffy jauntily making his way down a center aisle, back to (what else?) the meat counter. The boy knew what he wanted, and where to find it. Besides, it was wonderfully air-conditioned in there. We had parked near the entrance, and I suspect he felt that cool air coming out through the constantly opening front doors, and decided it was time to check out this cool place of great smells. Completely self-assured, he floppy-paw sauntered his way past canned goods straight to the pork loin specials.

Hi, everyone. Just going for a stroll to the meat counter. Catch you later.

Mary was mortified. I tried not to act panicked, fearing that this would unsettle other shoppers even more. So with as much dispatch but as little overt distress as I could manage, I whisked alongside him, grabbed his collar, and escorted him pronto past the checkout people, murmuring apologies over and over until we were well into the parking lot. We decided that one of us should stay with the truck for the remainder of our grocery shopping. *Duh.*

Chapter 18
Field Visitors

If you build windows, they will come. Sure enough, they did. Well, yeah, they would have come anyway, but how great it was to be able to see the length of the field from virtually anywhere in the house. The country living show happened out there anytime of day and year; sometimes we were lucky enough to be home to see it. Through a heavy mist on a cool, autumn weekend morning, a pair of gray foxes carefully stepped out of the woods at the far left edge of the field and cavorted for at least ten minutes—tumbling, racing to catch each other, playing. No time to find the camera, we were glued to the windows, not daring to move a whisker for fear of scaring them off. Finally they made their way across the rest of the field, and disappeared into the woods. We never saw them again.

Deer began their daylight exploration of our field at the far end, farthest from the dogs, so they could munch unmolested the clover, corn and barley we planted. They might have also liked more of the watermelon and muskmelon, but the bunnies got to them first. We managed to salvage some corn, but bent stalks and a trail of ears into the woods and down toward the creek was pretty solid evidence pointing to raccoons as the likely culprits. As the dogs grew older, the deer grew bolder. It was amusing to watch an aging Chelsea sitting on the patio landing spot deer only halfway up the field. A twitch of the nose, a stirring of the front legs, neck and head raised up a notch, eyes fully focused, and all the while, mental calculations based on many recent chases across that open ground. Youth sprints out after anything and everything; age tempers that enthusiasm, weighing likelihood of success against wear on the body. Wiser, not-so-young-anymore Chels more frequently came down on the side of, *I think I'll just keep an eye on them for a while; but if they get* any *closer, I'm going for it. Maybe.* Give the Meadowbrook deer some credit: they didn't rub Chelsea's face in it. They could have come in a lot nearer to the house, but they respected her dignity and gave her an extra several hundred feet of deference. Of course, there was that occasional day when the air was crisp enough for Chelsea to give it a shot, if only to show herself and the world that there was still plenty of spring left in the girl. On those occasions, the deer nearest her gave her the semblance of a chance, waiting until the last second to suddenly whirl around and bound off (*slowly*) into the woods. Paws twitched as happy dreams filled Chelsea's sleep those nights.

The Borders were another story—they never met a deer they didn't chase: in the Border collie primer, that's what deer were for. And since we didn't have any sheep or goats to herd, deer would do just fine. The problem was deer didn't understand the game the same way Border collies did: the prey were supposed to circle around and be steered toward an enclosure. Our deer just made bee-lines into the woods and kept going; and unlike heavy sheep that trundled across pastures, these guys could run like the wind, even through the thickest, gnarliest woods and ravines. Still, happy grins and tongues-to-the-ground later, Tag and Windi had at least fulfilled their instinctive, alternate mission: run the intruders off! Though slowing with age, the Borders would not—*could not*—resist the urge to spring from the patio landing, and give it their all down the field for another splendid show of genes at work.

One deer show that the dogs fortunately missed (so *we* could watch it) featured a pair of males "boxing" in the barley patch on the upper right side of the field. We had seen deer rise up on hind legs to munch fruit from a tree, but this was new to us: two bucks were pawing and punching each other with their front hooves. Neither seemed to be harming the other—it looked like sparring, for fun and/or dominance. Seeing this because we happened to be home and looking out on the field at that moment, we realized a little sadly that nature's cultural events happen all around us humans, but we are not present to marvel at them.

A human *was* present, however, for one totally unexpected happening at Meadowbrook: Mary was taking a bath. Okay, let's back up…the bath was not the unexpected event. I was out of town on business, and Mary was luxuriating in our master bathroom tub. I heard about it later that night when I called home from a business trip: sitting in a lonesome room in a far off hotel, I asked her if anything interesting had happened while I was away. *Oh, yeah…*

****

She told me she had released the dogs outside after feeding them their supper. It was early summer, so daylight stretched longer into the evenings, and the air was comfortably warm. She ran the water, sprinkled in a bit of scented water softener, turned on the jets, set a book and small glass of wine within reach, and immersed herself in a world of total relaxation. A light breeze gently swished the curtains through the bedroom windows. *Aaah, nice.*

Staccato barks crashed her mood like thunder strikes. The dogs were raising a level of commotion she had never heard from them before. The pitch of barking never varied: it was deep, intense, *frantic*. "BARK-BARK! BARK! BARK-BARK-BARK!" Their tone of alarm was clear: something or someone was right there in the side yard, out of sight from the bathroom window.

Whatever or whoever it was had to have come up next to the house from the woods, and no road or path came from that direction. The sobering implications of that quickened Mary's heartbeat. A state minimum-security prison still functioned within a few miles of our house, and it was not uncommon for police to alert local communities to be on the lookout for armed-and-dangerous escapees. She leaned forward slowly and craned her neck to try again to see what or who the intruder was. First Ruffy, then Chelsea, then Windi and Tag came into view from the left, backing up in jagged, stutter-steps, heads jerking back, then low to the ground, barking furiously. Something or someone was scaring them badly, and was coming forward, not at all intimidated by their fiercest warnings or their numbers.

Oh, God, thought Mary, *this is bad. Where's our gun? It's beside the bed—my side—the other side of the room, too close to the bay window, too open to being seen from below.* Dripping, she grabbed the bath towel, clutched it to her, hunkered down and ran through the bathroom door into the bedroom. Then she stopped and hesitated: instead of going toward the gun, where she would be exposed to a wide view from below through the (back) bay window, she crept along the front side of the room, and pressed up alongside a narrow double-hung window to get a look down beside the end of the house, where the ruckus began. Sucking in her breath, she peered uneasily around the edge of the window frame. Instantly, she saw the intruder: a cow.

Must've looked like one big dog to the barkers below: they had never seen a cow up close and personal before. *Country life* is *full of surprises*, thought

Mary, and caught herself exhaling for the first time in a while, then allowed herself a little laugh. Before she could figure out who to call, the cow finally had enough of the noisy greeting, turned and walked back into the woods. Whether it found its way back home we never knew, but that was the last we saw of Mr. or Ms. Moo. Called into the house after the cow departed, Ruffin and Chelsea were content that the high drama was over. Scamp and Freckles had missed the whole thing (Scamp inside the entire time, and Freckles gone who-knows-where?). The Borders, ecstatic at having repulsed an advancing invader (a huge one, at that), pursued it a while in the woods, but soon reappeared, panting hard and sporting the world's biggest grins. *Bring on the sheep!*

****

From the first moment I saw it, the corn field had a magical feel to it. That first day with the realtor, as we walked through its knee-high, broken stalks and followed (wow!) deer prints, I *knew* this was a place of *life*—changing with the seasons or by the moment, but always *changing*. That's what life is: change. Humans are creatures of habit, whether they like to admit it or not. Many openly decry change: but give those same folks a year with no change in their lives and they'll be climbing the walls for something different to see, feel, do. I knew this would be a place of peace, adventure, mystery and fun—all rolled up into one. All of that, with a twist, had its way with my father one morning while Mary and I were at work.

My dad's perspective on life is that anything worth trying is worth doing right—that is, completely, all the way, no dabbling. After watching us for a few years play around planting a half-acre of corn at the far end of the field, yielding meager results after the bugs got through with it, he offered to spray the crop with stuff recommended by the local farm-supply store. He had researched it, and he was certain we might actually be able to come up with a decent amount of corn for once. Weather and temperature cooperated that year in rare fashion, and with Dad's periodic spraying, our corn grew to eight feet or more, and thick as bamboo. It was in this jungle of nearly impenetrable green that dad was applying the last spray of the season. The bright sun overhead reached only a little of its light down into the waist-high area of the tight, long corn rows that he was trying to maneuver through with a sprayer on his back. He had remarked after the most recent spraying how dark it was getting in those 200-foot-long rows. On this day, with the corn another couple of feet higher, he disappeared into the patch, emerging at the other end of each row to catch some air, wipe the sweat off his forehead, and steel himself to tackle another suffocating tussle through the length of the patch. This would have been arduous work normally, but constantly tangled up in rows planted too closely together, claustrophobia and intense, humid heat strained my father's nerves. So it wasn't too surprising that this otherwise unflappable man felt a twinge of fear crawl into his stomach and up his spine when he heard something else in the corn patch with him.

The first *crunch* made him stop, and listen. Nothing. Spray, then *crunch-crunch, whsss, crunch, whsss, whsss*. He stopped again, turned. *Where was that coming from?* Corn stalks and leaves pressing against his face, and dark from his chest down, this was not a nice place for nature's surprises. Ready to defend himself with the spray nozzle, he turned again. Louder now—*whsss, whsss-crunch, snap*—and coming from—where? Where? Still louder, *Almost on top of me...wha...* "Freckles! Geez, you scared me!"

Wag, wag, wag (Freckles-speak: *Cool—I didn't know you were out here! Isn't this great?*) Then *crunch, crack, snap, crunch, whsss, whsss, crunch*. The now-familiar sounds faded as she made her way back to her other pursuits o' the day. Dad had just been treated to a day in the life of Freckles, which was always new, always interesting. Chuckling, he collected himself, shook it off, and mushed on through the remaining rows. The memory of that returned at our family dinner table many times: Dad had come to our field, expecting one experience, and was given another. Life—a Meadowbrook specialty.

Chapter 19
Refuge

Animals know things as much by instinct as by learning through life experience. They know where a safe place is when they are hurt and need help. They found Meadowbrook time and again, and in doing so, gave us and our dogs images we would just as soon have done without. But the story of this place—the magic it held—is not an incomplete version of life: it is not merely the happy slice of the world. There is another side to existence on this planet, and our place played a role in that, too.

****

He limped into view from the left side of the woods near our house. His tan hair was long and disheveled; white around the muzzle confirmed his advanced age. I silently named him Whiskers for the grizzly, whiskered look about his face. In obvious pain, this badly worn, old dog brought himself along awkwardly across our backyard on a cold, winter weekend day. He looked up at me from a distance, barely managed the faintest wag of his tail, then pressed on toward me, head swaying side to side. When I went over to meet him, he collapsed at my feet, sticking one leg out at an odd angle—grateful he didn't have to go any further. He was the picture of discomfort. We took him to the vet, and left him there for tests and X-rays.

The veterinarian called me around noon the next day at my office. X-rays had revealed severe injury to Whiskers' hindquarters, but the doctor was *not* recommending surgery.

"He's an old dog, Mr. Schwenn. We see this kind of thing all the time, and it's sad, but we have a lot of other, *younger* dogs in better shape and overall health who need homes to keep from being euthanized. If you want to 'save' a dog, I encourage you to take one of those, instead." Hardly an endorsement for valuing our senior citizens.

Dismissing his recommendation for the moment, I asked him what the prognosis would be for Whiskers' recovery with surgery. I could have guessed his response. "The damage looks extensive; at best, he'll probably have trouble walking the rest of his life, and he doesn't look like he has much of that left, anyway. Also, there's a risk he'll die on the operating table; given his condition, I think that's a real possibility. Again, I wouldn't put your money into this dog." *Ouch.*

He let me think it over on the phone during the silence between us. "Okay," I finally said. "Go ahead and put him to sleep."

He tried to reassure me. "I know it's hard, but I think you're making the right decision."

"Yeah," was all I could muster, and I hung up the phone with a sadness different from any I had ever felt. Mary and I had already talked about how we might make room for this guy—a traveler in distress who found his way to our door when he needed help. Now I was consigning him to a permanent release from his pain, and it didn't feel good at all. *Some help.* These are things that stay with you.

****

Country life is fluid: something always pops up at the most seemingly bland and ordinary times. Take, for instance, bringing the dogs in for breakfast one Saturday morning: walking across the short asphalt distance from our carport to their dog yard, I didn't expect to see anything other than the usual lineup of sixteen paws eager to romp on up the back stairs and see what goodies the weekend kitchen might be offering. (Weekend kitchens featured special treats: sometimes bits of bacon, cheese, egg; the relaxed weekend cook was usually in a more generous mood than the harried weekday version; that's for sure.) As I approached the gate, one of the quartet stepped around toward the back of one of the dog houses and absently sniffed around there. Sniffing around was certainly anything but aberrant doggy behavior, but sniffing around half-distractedly looked odd, and sniffing around without much focus when breakfast was imminent was just plain strange. Something here wasn't quite right. And, as one learns when living in the country, when something seems strange, it (a) usually is, and (b) needs checking out—as quickly as possible. There's *always* a reason a dog sniffs intently somewhere on another dog (other than the, you know, *usual* place): you can let it go if you want, but you will miss an opportunity to discover a tick, sting, bite, or the dreaded smears from rolling on God-knows-what. The point is: if it's odd, check it out. It's a good rule anywhere, but an especially helpful one where humans, pets, wild animals, and woods converge.

What had seemed to be a simple morning brought me a surprise: a woodchuck was lying behind the line of doghouses, up against a huge stump—all that remained of a once magnificent tree that had been timbered long ago. The guys didn't seem terribly interested in it, so when I opened the gate to investigate, they took off for the back door and chow. Always wary of rabies or other diseases that might be problematical for Mary, me or the dogs, I took my time approaching this poor creature. His face looked pained, but I couldn't tell from what. He just lay there, breathing slowly, eyes partly open—clearly unwell. Messing with it before breakfast didn't hold much appeal, so I closed the gate, and figured better decisions would be more forthcoming on full tummies.

The Council of Two decided we needed professional advice: while I "felt" that our visitor was probably not rabid, my knowledge and experience with that deadly disease was confined to having seen the movie *Old Yeller*. Once again we called the veterinary hospital, and were told that woodchucks are not likely carriers of rabies, and that instead, this one probably was suffering from distemper or other illness that would not likely threaten the health of our dogs. So we reached the conclusion life often leaves you with: wait and see if anything happens in the next little while. We went about our morning routines, and so did the dogs. Early that afternoon, I walked over to check in on the little fellow, and he was gone. Whether he was fine or sick, he had moved on after finding in our dog yard a peaceful rest stop. He wouldn't be the last one to seek refuge at Meadowbrook.

****

One fall, during what others refer to as "hunting season," I had barely begun my drive away from the front door of our house on a weekday morning to go to work, when I spotted a doe lying on her side next to the shallow ditch running alongside our driveway. I stopped, walked over to her, and saw that she was dead—one side of its back haunches and throat spattered with buckshot and blood. Bad enough that someone felt the need to kill a beautiful animal, but using buckshot effectively tormented this innocent creature in her last minutes of life. Wherever she had come from after the hideous blasts of gunfire, this deer made her way to a safe place—twenty feet from our dog yard, in the shade near our house—before she gave up her last breath. Wrapping her in a tarp, now taking the truck that day instead of the car, and detouring by the landfill, I hoped that this animal had found at Meadowbrook the peace denied her elsewhere. Angry and disgusted at human beings who feel the need to be cruel to animals, I drove on to work without seeing the road.

****

My most uncharitable thoughts about other human beings came to the fore in an uncontrolled rage shortly after I arrived home from work late one summer afternoon, long into our years at Meadowbrook. I got out of the car, and as usual, I first went over toward the dog yard to see the guys, and promise them ball games after I changed clothes. I never made it past the partially closed-in carport, to the left of the attached garage. Mary parked her car in this carport, but even though she was not yet home from work, her car was there: apparently, she had taken the truck that day. A horrible, rotting-meat odor emanated from the darkest corner of the carport. I squinted, but being out in the sunshine, I couldn't see anything right away. I had never smelled anything like this before: so pungent was the stench that, much as I wanted to get away from it, I had to know what was causing it. As I came to the edge of the carport, and my eyes adjusted to the dark, I could make out some movement—then, finally, a dog. A big, white dog, moving his head in slow, jerky fits, from side to side. At that moment, I felt more anxious than at any time in my adult life…there was something terribly wrong going on here.

The animal sort of staggered a little toward me, but not in a threatening way—he was more distracted by his head: in another few seconds, I saw why. A curved steel arc tightly clamped over the top of his head, and a steel rod speared straight into both sides of his head. Some excuse for a human being had rigged this unthinkable contraption to do exactly what it did. Maybe this was a stray (no collar) that became too much of a nuisance at someone's garbage cans, and *this* was the only answer some sick bastard could come up with? From the strong odor of death, it was clear to me that this unfortunate animal had been suffering horribly for some time. In a heartbreaking moment, this beautiful, long-haired male lowered his head toward me and let me try to release him from the steel grip of this home-made trap. I tried, and failed, and his unimaginable pain continued.

Unable to get him toward our truck to take to the veterinary hospital, I ran into the house and called the sheriff's office for help. Whatever I said or however I said it must have gotten through to somebody over there, as a deputy's car showed up in minutes—amazing, since we lived a long ways from anywhere. The deputies tried in vain to open the trap. They told me a steel rod was through the animal's head, and that there was no chance of the dog surviving. The kindest thing—the only thing—we could do was put it out of its misery. They told me they really weren't supposed to do that under "these kinds of circumstances" with *their* guns, but if *I* had one and wanted them to do it, they would. I went inside, came back out with a handgun, gave it to one of the deputies, and turned away while the poor animal's nightmare was ended. My tears were partly for the senseless loss of life, but more in white-hot hatred at whoever had done this despicable thing.

"The world does not need the kind of son of a bitch that does this!" I was yelling to the woods around me, but I quickly realized I was making threats in the presence of law enforcement officers. Crazy with anger, I didn't care. Looking down on the corpse of a once beautiful animal, I added, "and I don't care *who* hears me say it!" At that moment, I probably could—and would—have done *anything* to whatever excuse for a human being had been responsible for this despicable thing.

While the deputies let me vent, they calmly asked if I had a shovel. I brought one out and started to dig behind the tractor shed, but a uniformed hand touched my shoulder as another gently took the shovel from me; they told me they would take care of it. I later wrote the sheriff's department a letter, thanking whoever the deputies were for their incredible understanding and help, which helped keep me from losing it altogether that awful afternoon.

It was a German shepherd mix, handsome, and of sound stature, who was visited by evil—pure and simple. For those who believe and preach that vengeance against evil is not an answer, I applaud their conviction: part of me believes they are right; the other part would have no trouble paying whoever laid that disgusting trap back in kind. No trouble at all.

Whatever philosophies can be brought to swirl around this nauseating incident, one immutable fact remains: an animal in severe and unrelenting pain found its way to a place of escape from the worst that the world has to offer. There are many forms of refuge: one of them offers one of the kindest gifts we know in this life—an easy and welcome release into the next adventure. Our Meadowbrook dogs, like I, had never witnessed something as devastating as this, and would not again. They would continue to knit an environment of tolerance, appreciation of each other, love of living simply, and having fun. These bonds apparently carried a continuous signal out beyond the physical boundaries of our Meadowbrook sanctuary: another refugee was on the way.

Chapter 20
Chance Encounter

Life-altering moments occur when you least expect them. We took maybe as many as six bicycle rides on our nearby country roads in all the years we lived at Meadowbrook. To get anywhere, we had to travel a ways on what amounted to a highway, where the speed limit did not safely match the narrow width of the asphalt, making it even that much more dangerous for bicycle riders trying to share tight space with cars and trucks whipping by. Considering the rarity of those outings, what were the odds that we would return home with our next dog?

After pedaling about five miles on a Sunday morning when heat and humidity were already chasing each other for top billing by mid-morning, we were sweating hard and ready to collapse in air-conditioning. Cornfields and pine trees lined both sides of the flat home stretch, offering us a pastoral scene only occasionally interrupted by a passing car, now that this morning's churchgoers were already tucked into their pews. The last couple of miles promised a peaceful and pleasant burning of calories. *Nope.*

In the lead, I was targeted by a bounding, brown-and-white bobble-head figure charging hard out from behind a ramshackle shed overflowing with hay bales. I slowed a little to see that whatever-it-was was giving it her all through uneven ground of weeds and briars to catch up to me. Since it looked like a puppy, I finally stopped—out of curiosity, and come on, who can resist a puppy going all out to say, *Hi,* in a place devoid of houses? As she approached, tongue streaming out one side of her mouth, slowed by dwindling energy by this time, I looked back and saw that she must have seen us coming from a good way off, and decided that with just the right angle, she might have barely enough strength to intercept us. She looked to be about 4-6 months old. Panting hard when she reached my feet, she showed more than a little desperation in her smiles and wags. Mary pulled up in a few moments, and Miss Wags intensified her greeting. She sported a *jagged*-looking coat, but I couldn't see quite why; though her hair was short, it looked spiky all over—weird. Even though she had just sprinted some distance, she seemed more fatigued than I expected from a puppy. Exhausted and worn. Something about this dog wasn't right.

Anyway, I finally said something lame like, "Okay, honey—let's go."

"Honey" didn't budge, still reaching down and playing with Friendly Fido.

Skipper the Magnificent Mindreader tried again: "Mary, we've got *enough* dogs at home; we can't have another one."

Some murmuring from Mary.

After I got going again for a distance, my tender-hearted spouse finally resumed her pedaling. But not for long. It wasn't a hundred feet when I looked back and saw her slow as our new acquaintance panicked and tore out after Mary, clearly begging her to stop again.

Now I panicked. "Just keep pedaling, Mary. You'll only encourage it by stopping!"

"Yeah, okay," she said at last, giving the frantic pooch another round of head rubs.

Then it was my turn: both of us having left the poor thing behind us a good ways, something made me glance back, and what I saw tore my heart out. The pup was standing over some of the nastiest road kill I'd ever had the misfortune to lay eyes on, a cloud of flies buzzing around it. Puppy lowered her head to within an inch of this gross pile, flinched as she quickly raised back up a little, with some of it in her mouth, then dropped it. She stood there trying to decide whether hunger was so bad as to override all her better instincts. With a heart-wrenching lunge, she opened her mouth and chomped into the guts of the oozing, black mound.

This was too much for me. I yelled as loud as I could, "Drop it! *Drop it!*"

She turned, a filthy slab between her teeth, and looked at me.

"Drop it, NOW!" I implored her. "Please, please, don't eat that!"

Amazingly, after a few seconds, she lowered her head and let the vile mess fall to the pavement. Then, just as quickly, she raised her head back up, and looked straight at me. We held each other's gaze a few moments. Time stood still.

If I do this because you said to, aren't we making a contract?

Yeah, I guess so. "If she follows us all the way home, we'll talk about it," I said to no one in particular.

Follow us home she did—all two miles, on mighty hot asphalt, managing to avoid cars and trucks along the way. The last quarter-mile of our driveway was uphill and steep, but the little gal toughed it out, then fell out on the brick path at the bottom of the stone steps leading up to our front porch—too tired to go any farther. I brought her some water, and with some effort, she managed to stand and guzzle most of it at once. I plunked down next to her, and saw the problem of the prickly fur: ticks—a boatload of them. I wondered how she could have any blood left in her. This was clearly an abandoned puppy, trying to survive, probably using that old crumbling shed as a poor substitute for home, and literally being eaten alive by ticks, which by now had grown fat on what was left of a dog that for a long time had not known the simple pleasure of a comfortable breath in this world.

"Would you get me a bucket of water and tweezers, Mary? I think I'm going to be a while." I picked ticks off this sad pup for over an hour. That's how we passed the time in the shade of our tiny front porch, sheltered by branches of hardwoods nearly touching the house. I really wasn't much hungry for lunch after that grisly task, but I needed the break, so we went inside to clear our heads and try to decide what to do next with this pitiful foundling. Refreshed water bowl nearby, I figured she wasn't going anywhere—and if she did, that would resolve the situation for us. A peek outside midway through a grilled ham-and-cheese confirmed the future: she hadn't moved an inch, except to fall over, hard asleep.

Mary apologized for stopping that second time, which only encouraged the dog to keep following us. I took plenty of due credit for interacting with the dog at the road kill scene…and for picking ticks off of it. I mean, save a life in China, and you owe that rescued victim your care ever after. Like ol' Dad always says, "No good deed goes unpunished." *Yeah, we really need another dog. The vet bills and kennel arrangements, and….*

"You know, she took a chance on us," piped up Mary, helpfully. "We could call her 'Chance.'" Only she wasn't really *asking* if we could keep her, and we both knew it. And that was okay: the series of events was tough to ignore. Waiting a long ways off from the road and a world she had long since come to distrust, she overcame her fear, picked us out, and made a mad dash in the desperate hope that she might yet find a home and life worth living. We tried to leave her behind, so she blindly turned to her alternative: an existence of poison and sickness, until it might mercifully be over. Then I interrupted that, and she somehow found the stamina to run two miles to our door. How—exactly—were we going to turn this creature away? The odds of any dog being selected from a humane shelter when it has already reached semi-maturity are not good, and this girl needed immediate medical attention, to boot. *She did take a chance on us. Surely we were meant to take a chance on her.*

Off to the vet the next day.

"You got *another* one?" the receptionist asked, incredulously.

"I...I dunno. Maybe," was about all I could manage. The doc was impressed at the sturdy constitution of this female mixed-breed pup. Her round, intelligent eyes were engaging, but the slope of her wide head suggesting that at least part of her was pit bull worried me a little. Suspicious of stereotyping ordinarily, there are nevertheless some bad things bred in dogs that environment sometimes cannot seem to completely alter or erase. Border collies can be tamed into a somewhat-calm lifestyle, but there are moments when they unequivocally heed the call of their Old World ancestors, who were bred to herd and control. In those moments, they are driven to organize you, other household pets, or themselves in ways that to them are irresistible, even if disruptive to everybody else in the place. Some breeds are quick to snap and bite even their owners of many years. Even if you don't read up on your breed of choice beforehand, minimal attention to your canine pal will quickly reveal the basic traits that lie dormant under the surface, waiting to awaken at any time, under circumstances that make perfect sense to their host, even if they don't to you.

Pit-bulls have the rap of being aggressive toward other dogs, and toward most everyone not their owner. Their reputation is to be loyal "to a fault" to a single individual in a family. Here we were about to introduce Chance to not just one other dog in the family, but a whole pack! What I hoped was that the non-pit bull part of her would moderate her enough so that she could gratefully assimilate into the group comfortably, and we would all continue to live in the magical atmosphere that our six-pack had created at Meadowbrook.

For the next year or so, that is exactly what happened. She creatively mixed her distinctive traits in with the rest of ours. She became the class clown. The flower barrel on the corner of our back patio? A perfect perch for sitting and watching the field (never mind that her hindquarters barely fit on top of it). And the wooden garden cart under the carport? Nap-time (even if she did have to drape herself over rake, shovel, and hoe already in it). Oh, and the dog yard was a nice place to visit, but you don't have to stay there; this girl had the leap of a gazelle—no running start needed, just squat, look up, assess the task, and in one easy motion clear the fence like an Olympic high hurdler. *Awesome, dude!*

    Chance ran the field with the joy of a resurging spirit, in the company of any and all of the others, and sometimes just on her own. She watched Tag carefully, learning the routines and games like snapping bees. She was careful to keep herself out of the Tag-Ruffy deal, and didn't muscle in on Chelsea's mouse-hunt. Her thing was to greet the UPS and FedEx guys. There were times when she felt like being part of the pack, so she stayed in the dog yard with them when we were away (at least we *think* she did, as on most days, I arrived home to see all six dog-yarders wagging at me from the other side of the woven wire). But when we were home on a weekend to hear the delivery truck squeal to a stop between the carport and dog yard, we looked out to see Chance beside the van, giving the driver her best Wal-Mart greeting. Not every driver thought that was the coolest thing. We peeked out the window once to see the FedEx truck stop, then idle for a while. Finally the door slowly opened, just enough to allow an arm to slip through, set the package down, and quickly slam the door shut. By her facial expression and posture, Chance seemed extra pleased with herself.

    Christmas came early for Chance. In the dwindling light of late afternoon in her first December when I drove in from work, I noticed sprinklings of something out on a small knoll just off the asphalt, in the first part of the playing field. It was a mound created by excess dirt from a nearby gardening project that I never completely smoothed out. So it gradually grew grass, and became a favorite spot for Chance to sun herself while she waited for something to happen. I forgot about it as I changed clothes, and was making my next day's lunch when Mary popped in, asking me what was on the playing field. I looked out at that mound again, and figured it was time to investigate. Good thing I did: a Christmas gift for Mom was strewn around the knoll, its brown shipping paper peppering the area, and its box chewed. Luckily, Chance preferred the wrapping and the box over the bracelet, which was lying unharmed a short distance away. We imagined Chance's leap of heartfelt joy and surprise when Santa Claus showed up in a motorized sleigh, and tossed out a present just for her! *Ain't Christmas great?*

That's how it went for over a year with Chance. Meadowbrook life was a basket of goodies at every turn. Clever, imaginative, opportunistic, she was fun to watch. We gave her love, but made sure she understood the pecking order (Tag was leader), and The Rule (nobody got mean with anybody else). The chief judge at the court where I worked, always asking me how many dogs I had *now*, also regularly wondered, "Don't they fight with each other?" He asked me this so often I began to worry about it. In his long life he "had been around," as they say, and he knew things. For him to be that amazed that so many dogs in one household didn't squabble made me question the likelihood that our good fortune would continue. I chalked it up to Mary's and my taking the right approach with our dogs—loving them all well, and making every effort to give them all opportunities to do the individually rewarding things they each needed to do to have a fulfilled life. A happy pup is an agreeable pup, we figured. Keep each one satisfied, and they'll be too comfortable to fuss with each other. My socio-political view, as well. Sometimes, though, the world has other plans. Sometimes there are, for lack of understanding or better terms, "bad seeds" out there, waiting to bully and take from others just because they *can*, or *like doing it*. Patting ourselves on the back was premature, as it turned out. The game of Chance was far from over.

Chapter 21
Missing

When good ideas go bad. A weekend fun run to Food Lion started out fine, if a bit unusual. One Sunday afternoon in early January, for whatever reason, Freckles decided she wanted to go with all of us to pick up the week's groceries. Chance had been with us for well over a year, and seemed to be a full, accepted member of the pack. That made seven dogs, and on this day, all seven were going to town. That's a lot of puppy pounds in the bed of our little S-10, but merrily we rolled off to the grocery store. Chance, we had noticed during recent truck outings, was beginning to throw her weight around a bit in the truck bed, just as she had in the living room on occasion: she had begun to do little things, that taken separately, raised our alert level a notch or two, but did not unduly alarm us. These should have: inserting herself between Tag and me when he approached me as I sat on the sofa to collect a few head scratches and commune a bit; suddenly walking over to Chelsea and Windi and standing over them in a display of dominance; causing scuffles in the back of the truck—clearing out space for herself, forcing the others to the edges of the bed. If she had exhibited this kind of aggressive behavior in the *first* few months of her time with us, I would have suspected a problem that would probably worsen with time, and I hope I would have concluded that she would have to be taken to the animal shelter to be relocated. But she was fine for over a year, acclimating to the pack in fun-loving, healthy fashion—or so it appeared to Mary and me. Now, approaching two years old, her encounters with her fellow pack members were more harsh and pointed; she was becoming a bully in short bursts. Letting her continue to ride in the truck bed with the others was a mistake.

Freckles, for her part, had ridden in the back of the truck on a few grocery runs before. Only once had there been a problem: she must have jumped out as we left the parking lot, which fortunately we noticed before driving too far away, so it wasn't long after we retraced our path that we found her, and all ended well. This particular cloudy and cold winter afternoon, though, things didn't go well at all. I remembered afterward there having been a moment on the way back from the store along a long, empty stretch of the highway when there was a sudden and dramatic commotion in the truck bed. I looked back through the extended cab window, and couldn't make out anything other than some movement among the dogs, but it settled down quickly, and I shrugged it off. When we parked the truck back home after the twenty-minute ride, I lowered the tailgate to the usual burst of dogs from the bed…but…where was Freckles? I quickly looked around, behind me. No Freckles. She had not made it all the way home with us. By now, it was getting very gray in the late afternoon, so we were going to have to find her—*fast*.

We hustled the dogs into their yard, put the groceries away in record time, and blasted back out the long driveway, beginning our painful search on both sides of the roads leading back to the grocery store. *Nothing.* For an all-white dog, Freckles could disappear in an instant—"ghost dog" to the end. We made two round trips in a futile effort, calling out the windows the whole way. Darkness ended our search, leaving me with that sick feeling in your stomach when you know something bad has just happened that you can't correct—at least not right now. That it might never be right gnawed at me all night. The next day was the beginning of a work week, so we had little chance to look, although we tried. No sign of her. We tried again and again each afternoon after work, and the next weekend. *Still nothing.* This was a nightmare. We tacked leaflets containing her description in stores that would let us. By now, we had concluded that she had probably jumped from the truck to get away from Chance…and now she was gone.

Losing a member of your family suddenly and under such a regrettable circumstance was awful. I kicked myself for not having stopped to investigate that sudden commotion I had felt in the back of the truck; I kicked myself for having kept Chance. It didn't help that the weather (naturally) turned bitter, into the worst ice-and-cold spell we had known since moving to the country. For over a week, the night temperatures plummeted into the low teens, the daytime highs barely climbed above freezing, and the skies stayed gray. In the full grip of winter, Freckles was either suffering a horribly or was already dead. We knew her skittish nature would never allow her to approach a house, even if she was starving and literally freezing to death. The rest of January crawled by. We gave up hope.

We were midway through February when one evening after work we received a phone call from a man who sounded not real friendly. He wanted to know if we had a dog that was missing. "It took me a lot of days to get close enough to her to catch her and read the phone number off the collar," he said, irritably. He pointedly asked me if I really wanted the dog, as it looked like she had not been well cared for in a long time. Stunned is probably the closest word to how I felt hearing him speak, but that wasn't adequate: I was exhilarated. I was also worried that this moment would slip away before I could get this man's address—he was clearly reluctant to give it to me.

"I'll keep the dog if *you* don't want it," he gruffly told me. His message was clear: *You are irresponsible; this is a nice dog. I don't think someone like you should have a dog.*

I didn't blame him. I could only begin to imagine the kind of shape Freckles must be in by this time, all those weeks in the woods with no shelter in the worst of winter. I put the phone down, and Mary already knew by my end of the conversation what must have happened; she already had her coat on, and we were zooming down our driveway in the truck in seconds. It was dark, so finding the guy's place wasn't that easy: we took one wrong turn, but finally found it—a modest brick house, with a small cleared area out back abutting extensive woods.

He came out first, his manner picking up where it left off on the phone. I explained to him what had happened, but he couldn't have seemed less impressed or influenced in our favor. He told me she had been afraid to come up to his house, but was obviously hungry, so he had left food way out in his back yard next to the woods, which she had taken, but then returned to the woods for the night. He told me this had gone on for days, until he and his wife had gradually gained her confidence. After he told me all this, his wife walked out the back door, her hand through Freckles' collar. After our girl spotted us, she bolted from the woman's grip, and hurled herself into the cab of the truck (which I had purposely left open), and plunked herself down on the blanket I had prepared for her behind the seats. She was *home*, and even Mr. Crabby knew it. I continued to thank him profusely, assured him I would never allow this to happen again, offered to pay him for his trouble (he refused), and edged back to the truck before he could figure out a way to recapture our dog for himself.

"If you don't want her [*if you can't handle having a dog and don't know how to take care of one*], you call me, and I'll take her," were his last words, as I put the truck in reverse and backed out without slowing.

Pulling away from there, I felt like we were escaping from a gang of bandits. Of course I was grateful for his having saved our Freckles, but I also felt we had almost lost her again. After all the torture of the past thirteen weeks, that would have been too much. That was the last time we let Freckles ride in the truck bed. Distracted by relief, and happy to have our gentle spirit back, we let this latest warning pass and returned to the routines of work and country life.

Chance being Chance

DOGS OF MEADOWBROOK

(top) Chance & Co. (left to right) Tag, Scamp, Ruffin, Chance, Chelsea, Windi; (bottom) Chance's "work"—Tag disgusted

Part Four

Partings

Chapter 22
The Breed's the Thing

Hopping in and out of the dog yard had become commonplace for Chance. What she added midway through her second year with us was scattering the other dogs (particularly Freckles, if she happened to be in the dog yard at that moment) when she leaped into the enclosure, claiming the entire area as *hers*. She didn't do this by lowering her head in attack mode, nor did she snap at the others. But by subtle movements she persuaded the others, including Tag, to move away from her. Increasingly, they chose to get up from their favorite spots and move quietly into their houses, or over against the shed, or up against the fence, to give themselves space from Chance. Tag usually began to run his perimeter circle, for something to do that (a) was always a good thing for a responsible sentry to do, anyway, and (b) gave him something to do *away from Chance* that saved face as he removed himself from her presence. Something was waking up in Chance that she could not seem to deny.

One weekend afternoon I walked up the gradual incline across the backyard from the tractor shed to find Chance and Scamp(!) having pinned Freckles to the ground, tugging on opposite ends of her. Freckles was admittedly the lowest-ranking member of the pack, if she was a full member at all. Referring to her as an associate pack member (due to her basically keeping to herself most of the time), we, too, regarded her as the least threat to any newcomer to the group. In dog culture, anyone trying to gain a high status position in a canine troop instinctively starts at the bottom and works up from there. It occurred to me that Chance could be starting a move to establish an official position in the pecking order of our pack. As it turns out, she had more than assertion of dominance in mind.

A few months after Freckles was returned to us, we arrived home late one Sunday afternoon with a full load of groceries. I noticed as we passed the dog yard that Chance was lying out on her knoll, while everybody else (including

Freckles, for a change) was inside the fence. As we put the last of the food away and were preparing to let the dogs out of their yard and into the house for supper, a terrible scream erupted from the dog yard. I stopped what I was doing, and ran down the back stairs to see Chance tearing Freckles' hind quarters apart. I yelled at Chance: "Get *away* from her! Leave her *alone*!" Chance tugged once more at the now limp Freckles, then backed off as I raced to the gate. What I saw first was Freckles' bad leg dripping wet with saliva, but otherwise unharmed. Still, despite a slight stirring to get up, she couldn't raise herself at all. I gently reached around to check her other side; when I withdrew my hand, it was covered with blood. I hollered to Mary to bring me some big towels and a blanket right away, and to call the emergency vet. We were on the road in minutes. Mary drove, as I cradled poor Freckles in my lap. She looked stunned, and scared. I had screamed at Chance until I was hoarse, and left everybody in the dog yard—hungry, and tense.

The head doc met us at the veterinary hospital, and after a quick look, determined that the attack had been severe, severing muscles to the bone in several places. He told us she might not survive the operation, but if that was what we wanted him to do, he would begin immediately. We thanked him and asked him to do it, and to let us know as soon as he knew anything.

All I could do when I got home was yell at Chance some more. We fed the dogs, and she ate with the best of them; remorse was not in her. She knew I was upset, but took it in stride. That was more than a little unnerving.

The call from the doc came the next day. Freckles survived the Sunday night surgery, but the damage was extensive. His prognosis: this dog of the field would likely never *walk*—let alone run—again. We digested this as best we could that night, in between self-recriminations that I couldn't stop laying on myself. I should have seen this coming: the signs were all there, and had been apparent for months. It's just…we'd never had experience with dogs being anywhere nearly so brutal to each other before, and I couldn't bring myself to believe this *awfulness* was possible among dogs in *our* family. I just…couldn't. That was an error in judgment that cost Freckles her life.

We went to see her a few days later when she could actually be made presentable for us. She was barely able to stand; the technician with her said they had been taking her outside some to stand in the outdoor air, and that she had been able to move slowly. But the prognosis remained the same. And, in any event, she would have to be lifted up to stand. A working couple an hour's drive away from the house, how were we to care for an immobile dog for the eleven-plus hours each day we were gone? That would be cruel enough, but the prospect of Freckles denied the only thing she enjoyed in life—running the field—seemed impossible to permit. Neither of us could conceive of a way to keep this dog with us. No one was going to adopt her in this condition, either. I took another day or so to try to come to grips with this tragedy, listening to another doctor in that facility gently trying to encourage me to think carefully before consigning Freckles to the miseries she would be facing through a process of recovery that would likely not produce decent results. At the last, I could not see a practical way for any of it to work. We finally ended it, at her side, tearfully.

I took Chance to the vet the next day (there was no animal shelter in the county, so that was the next best thing), with a request to board her and try to find her a new home. Under the circumstances, there was no way we could endanger the remaining members of our pack. The animal hospital staff understood, but after a week, they were no closer to relocating Chance. I had a choice: I could have her put to sleep on the spot, or try another way to find her a new home. I placed an ad in the paper, stressing that this dog needed to be in a single-dog household. After a few unsuccessful calls, I received one from an elderly woman who wanted a full-grown, house-trained, medium-sized dog who would keep her company.

"Does she like to ride in the car?" she asked me.

"Yes, that's one of her favorite things," I answered truthfully.

So the next evening I drove off in the truck with Chance, her bed, canned and dry dog food, and several chew toys. It was dark, and the glare of Burger King's parking lot lights in Greensboro where we stopped for a few minutes hurt my eyes. I wasn't particularly hungry, but having committed to this errand at an early evening hour after work, I hadn't had time for anything to eat yet, and I hadn't fed Chance either, figuring it would be better for her to be hungry when we first got to the woman's house so she could be fed there—get things off to a good start in her new home. I went in and came back out with two hamburgers. I settled back in behind the wheel, unwrapped both of them, gave one without the bread to Chance, who looked at it, then shrank slowly back against the passenger seat and looked sideways over at me, unhappy.

"I know," I said. "This is sad. But you can't stay with us—you know that. Not after what you did."

I realized this was doing nothing but reinforcing her mood, which wasn't going to help either of us try to bring ourselves to eat something. So I made an effort to upbeat things a little. "Come on, girl—let's see if these are any good," and I forced myself to take a small bite of mine. "Mmm," I managed, with as much enthusiasm as I could muster, trying to swallow through the swelling lump in my throat, fighting tears the whole time.

A heart can break for a lot of reasons; this was one. A combination of my play-acting, and Chance trying to make *me* feel better, she allowed herself a small nibble...then another. We ate slowly, two guys havin' a burger.

"Two guys havin' a burger, huh, Chance?" I finally said aloud.

I was not aware of time. Nobody was in a hurry. We just...chewed our burgers. And then we were done.

I would miss this being. We had formed a tight bond; despite the gruesome thing she had done, I couldn't callously throw her away. In the moments after I discovered what she had done to Freckles, I had run her into the house, where she skittered fearfully around the kitchen corner and dove onto Scamp's bed under the stairwell. As I reached her, I had raised my hand and cursed at her, daring her to snarl or lunge to bite me so I could knock her senseless for having done a terrible thing to one of life's most gentle beings. She had taken my reprimand without snapping or growling, or even threatening to do any of that, though I was barely in control of myself. However confusing the combination of instincts and emotions that must have been going through her, she had obeyed an even stronger call to yield to me as her chosen pack leader, and held her head down and body tense, waiting for physical punishment that never came.

Now I was saying goodbye. Two weeks earlier, this was unthinkable.

I arrived at the woman's address: it was a trailer home, filled with cigarette smoke. Chance obediently did her business on a leash outside upon arrival, and as dutifully padded up the stairs through the doorway into—what? *Her next life, of which I know nothing.* I called the woman a few days later to see how things were going, having assured her before I left that if it didn't work out, to call me, and I would take Chance back—no questions asked. The number gave me a recorded message, which I called and confirmed a second time, "This number has been disconnected, or is no longer in service." I drove to the trailer and found it vacant. What became of Chance is something that nags at me. I didn't do right by Freckles, and I probably didn't do right by Chance, either. For a professed lover of dogs, I was losing my confidence that I should be allowed to have them. This was a dark period, and while nothing else would feel as unsettling to me about my life with dogs thereafter, the tough times were just beginning.

Chapter 23
Tag's to the Last

Life returned to normal at Meadowbrook with Chance gone. Putting her out of my mind as best I could the next day at work, I arrived home that afternoon at the usual time to be struck by something I suddenly realized I hadn't felt from inside the dog yard in a long time: sheer relaxation. Tag, Windi, Chelsea, Ruffin and Scamp had resumed their former spots they had comfortably claimed as theirs until Chance yielded to something she could not control. A palpable sense of peace and exhaustion wafted through the fence. I looked at their faces: every one of them was soft and contented, in sharp contrast to the tight, strained looks I had somehow grown accustomed to. It amazed me at that moment how I could have watched a horrendous transformation in my dogs over such a long period of time and not understood what I was seeing. You notice others who are blind to what's clearly before them, and wonder why they cannot—or will not—see it. When it happens to you, it's scary— especially if you pride yourself in being generally aware, and in control of things around you. *How could I have missed that Chance had terrorized these creatures—they who depended on me to keep them safe from monsters? They devote so much of themselves to loving us, nurturing each other, improvising games to entertain themselves while we're attending to human business, and waiting with infinite patience until we design to give them a few moments of our time and attention. Was it so much for them to expect us to recognize real danger and keep it away from them?*

"I'm sorry, guys. I am so, so sorry I let this happen," I whispered inside the car. I wanted them to continue to have that recovery time, so I went quietly into the house and changed out of my work clothes.

Mary came in a few moments later. She hadn't even put down her things before she said, "Did you see how relaxed the dogs are? I mean, you can *feel* it rolling out of them!"

"Yeah, I did. Amazing, isn't it?" I answered, shaking my head slowly in lingering regret for not having waked up to the reality of their world sooner.

My homecoming that day helped me handle the ache I felt when I later couldn't reach the woman who took Chance. Whatever happened to that dog, there was no way she could have continued to live with us. It cost us Freckles for me to realize it.

In typically doggy style, our remaining gang quickly moved past the previous year and a half and its resulting crisis, and resumed their happy routines with each other and with us. All forgiven if not forgotten, life was good again. Dogs are good at forgiving you: they ask only that you love them. There's a book floating around by Robert Fulghum, *All I Really Need to Know I Learned in Kindergarten.* Having lived more than half my life, I have concluded that everything I need to know about life, I could learn from my dog.

Some time after we had assembled our pack, it occurred to me that because we had picked out increasingly larger dogs as we went along, the life expectancies of the first four were going to converge at some point. We could actually lose them at roughly the same time. I dismissed that fleeting, horrible thought with a shudder, but it raised its ugly head again when we returned from one of our beach trips.

Mark—a thoroughly conscientious, responsible young man who worked at the local veterinary hospital—had for several years been feeding and otherwise caring for our group in their dog yard when we were away on short vacations. We had always boarded Freckles, since she could not be counted on to show up at supper time, and we couldn't have dog bowls left sitting out unwashed to attract ants and bacteria. With her no longer with us, our entire pack was in Mark's capable hands. Each time we returned home (which was frequently late at night—the consequence of our trying to squeeze in every last hour of precious vacation time), we counted ghostly muzzles in the darkness as we slowly drove past the dog yard. This time, we counted only four. No big deal—we'll see them all when we turn the lights on, which we anxiously did, so we could solve this annoying little puzzle and get on with the tedious task of taking the sandy, wet, beach gear out of the car, and get ourselves ready to re-enter the work world early the next morning.

Flood lights on, we trekked over to the gate to exchange our customary, *Oh, boy! You're back! Yippee!* greetings. They were subdued. And there were still only four of them. "Where's Ruffy, guys?" I asked. "Ruf-fy! *Ruffy*!

Where *are* you, boy?" This went on a few minutes. I took a flashlight and checked all the houses; no Ruffin. I walked the entire dog yard—for quite a while. He wasn't there. *Surely he didn't get out. He's too big. He doesn't jump.* So w*here* is *he?*

"Tag, where's Ruffin?" I expected him to know, and to somehow be able to tell me. On TV programs, hero dogs can draw meticulous maps or discuss higher math with scientists when helping to save the day. In real life, it's just not that easy.

We figured he might have gotten out, but it was not likely. We had left our group in Mark's care often, with no problem. Maybe he had been injured or gotten sick. Mark had our phone number at the beach, and could have called us if he needed to. So maybe this was just a precautionary thing that he had taken Ruffy to the vet for safe-keeping. That was probably it. At nearly midnight, we couldn't do much about any of this anyway, so we would find out what was what the next morning.

I didn't have to call the next morning. Mark's voice was on our answering machine when I checked it for messages before we went upstairs to bed. Midway through the week, he had come to feed them supper as usual, and found Ruffin lying on his side in the shade next to Tag's house—already passed on to the next adventure. Mark said Ruffy gave no appearance of having suffered—it appeared that his heart just stopped. This was confirmed by the doctors where he worked. Ordinarily, this would have been a horrible surprise, but Ruffin had been suffering from a degenerative nerve condition not uncommon in German shepherds and other large breeds. We had given him all the treatment available, but it was going to be only a matter of time before he either could not stand, or something fatal would occur instantaneously. We had watched him over the past year intermittently lose control of his hind legs trying to walk down the back stairs, and more recently seen his hindquarters give way partially or totally as he walked toward the house across the flat asphalt from the dog yard to our back door. These were disheartening symptoms that the doctor said would periodically flare up, but would increasingly occur until we either would have to make that difficult final decision, or it would be made for us.

Although the unmitigated, searing pain that every dog owner faces when losing that very special, irreplaceable friend caught us both as we listened again to Mark's voice, I was comforted by one thought. "Mary," I began, "Ruffy was

Tag's—always. He loved Taggie more than anything. And Tag was there for him at the last. And no matter when it happened, there was wonderful shade from the dogwood tree over their houses, and he could be there beside Tag, his best pal, who he adored. His last breath was in a place of peace, with all his friends. That's not so bad. I wish I could have been there, too; but he had Taggie, and that was okay. He was Tag's to the last."

We loved our gentle giant so much; it hurt when we didn't have him with us anymore. I worried more about how Tag might react to this loss. I wondered how all of them would handle it, since Ruffy died in their presence. They were quieter for a while, but not anxious. They just missed him, too.

I hope Ruffin was taken in easily and immediately by Ratches—his namesake. I like to think they are bounding through flowered meadows together in some magical way that he surely deserves. Years earlier, Ruffy walked slowly through the half-acre of shoulder-high red clover on our Meadowbrook field. He sniffed it as he ambled, and lent a stunning black, brown, and white contrast to the brilliant red and green surrounding him. On one unforgettable, soft Sunday morning, mourning doves cooing to us from the edge of the field, he joined Mary and me in our blackberry patch: as we slowly filled our baskets, we offered him a small clump of berries. He sniffed them, and with elegant ease, nibbled them from our hands. He made a discovery: he *liked* blackberries! He was our faithful companion for the rest of our berry-picking morning. These were quiet, timeless moments—made all the more exquisite by the presence of his solid frame, outer tips of his fur stirring in the soft breezes.

We will not see the likes of Ol' Floppy Paws again. He allowed us to hug him and stroke that extraordinary fur. He loved us, to be sure; but he was a companion more to Tag. He couldn't have had a better friend through life. I couldn't feel too bad. Mary and I would be happy enough to slip through the passage from this life as well, and in as good a company, as did our Ruffy-bear.

Chapter 24
Travelin' On

    We all did our best to fill in for Ruffin to keep Tag company in the months that followed. Crouched behind a deck chair, I made my best Ruffy-move to try to spice up the circle game as Tag whipped by. Mostly he just zipped past without effort. I was awkward and slow. What was I going to do, anyway? Zap out in front of him and mess him up? Then what was he going to do? Bite his owner on the nose? It just wasn't the same. Windi, on the other hand, filled in more time than ever with her brother, constantly snapping bees and chasing hummers. She and I joined in Tag's couch circle runs more frequently to liven up Tag's inside game.
    Unfortunately, the Dynamic Duo began extending their forays through the woods and across the dead-end road into neighbors' corn fields. With Chelsea older and content to do her own thing in and around our field, and Scamp dependably in or around the house, the Borders seemed to feel more free to expand their domain. This was unnerving to us, for we had learned what some of the folks in the area did to wandering dogs. And if that wasn't bad enough, we had seen the tell-tale cloud of dust billowing up behind the mail carrier driving at breakneck speed along the road bordering our land—first to take the mail to the last house on our dead-end road, and then to make the return trip back out past our property. As fast as the postal person sped down that road, it would have been too easy for our guys to get tumbled, or worse. We tried keeping a closer watch on them, but it was an ongoing battle: these were willful animals, and their determination only strengthened with age.
    Though more frequently spending time with Tag, Windi also found extra time for herself. She was the first of the pack to discover the siren song of the one deep, clear pool in the back creek. Though most refreshing on the hottest days, the allure was irresistible for her year-round. So sensuously did she literally immerse herself in the pleasures of the fur-flesh, that it felt sinful

watching her. She turned her languid moments in the deep pool into an art form. No crashing the glassy surface for this girl, no. She stepped lightly, one leg at a time, into the still water, then lowered herself, slowly allowing the cool wetness to filter its way through her long fur and thick undercoat. When the cool water finally reached her tummy, she closed her eyes, allowing herself to be saturated underneath, in a half-standing, half-floating ecstasy. At last, she opened her eyes, now glazed over with rapture. She was one with the planet. I stood a short ways away, transfixed by her simple, overwhelming enjoyment of nature, privileged to witness a very private side of our Windi girl.

At some point, Windi slowed down, rather dramatically. She smothered the air-conditioning floor vents more frequently, and for longer periods of time. Her sleeps there grew deeper; stirring her took a little more effort. Her hearing seemed to come and go, and walking looked awkward. We took her in for an exam. Lesions showed up on X-rays, and the diagnosis was cancer, although it was more of a guess. There was nothing specific about the alignment of these problem areas, so there was nothing recommended by the docs to do except keep an eye on her for signs of increased discomfort. Whatever was sapping her energy was probably also responsible for her fur not growing back completely after the last summer cut. Tag's had recovered as usual, but Windi's long hair returned only in staggered clumps. More than that, her fur had lost its luster; she looked ragged.

Walking more stiffly after a while, and lying down only after making studied preliminary moves to decide which one would cause her the least pain, Windi's condition was not responding to the only medications the veterinarian could think to prescribe. We began to discuss lightly the unthinkable—but inevitable. We tested her zest for life by tossing a ball; she gave it a bit of a go, but her body was not in the game anymore. She ate with little interest, then not at all. We spent one last weekend fully attentive to her. Late that February Sunday afternoon we sat on the floor next to the kitchen table—the scene of countless ball toss games and sofa-circle runs with Tag—and asked Windi what we should do. Windi hurt. She edged with difficulty toward Mary, and ever so gently pushed her muzzle straight into Mary's tummy, and held it there.

"Her bags are packed, honey," I said at last, as kindly as I could. "She's ready to go. She needs us to help her get there; she can't do it on her own."

Mary wept. We both did.

I couldn't let that moment go without something more to honor who we were suddenly discovering was the heart of our home. So I left them on the kitchen floor near the table Windi always felt safe under, walked to the desk, and wrote Windi a letter. My words were heavy in my heart, but they flowed easily through the pen, and it was only minutes later that I lay down under the table alongside our girl. It was from there that, with pride and joy, she had kept a constant watch on her beloved Mary while we ate our meals, discussed human business and other life events, and spent endless hours gazing out over the field through the glass patio doors. There, on the hard tile, I read my letter to her, while Mary listened:

My friend and I have known the same Earth for a long time briefly.

We could look at each other and know at the same moment what feeling was being felt—what wonder and happiness was being enjoyed, what sadness endured, what anxiety feared, what relief welcomed.

We have played games with life, with each other, with others around us, freely and without any worry of seeming silly or misunderstood.

We were always honest with ourselves, and trusted everyone else until given a reason not to.

We were at our best when we were needed to be by others, and were strong and brave in the face of anything that might be daunting to others.

My friend has given me moments of inspiration, reasons to laugh out loud, and was always ready to be at my side, no matter what.

We have talked without conversation, for we held each other's admiration; **we know each other's hearts**, for we have shared living space in them.

A part of me talks with her still, but my heart aches for her presence now, because I am left to tend to unfinished affairs of my life while my friend has ventured on with the same courage she has always shown.

I do not fear the next journey, because she has gone on before me, and will have prepared a safe place where we can once again share fully the wonderful meaning of life in whatever form it is made available to gentle spirits.

My missing your physical form, my friend, will dull somewhat in time, but will never leave me. Such is the pain of awareness in loving. But it is a pain that I gladly endure, for to feel otherwise would have been to have missed the immeasurable, boundless joy that you have brought me.

I hope and pray that our Creator will make certain that you know the true depth and completeness of my appreciation and love for you.

Thank you, **Windi...I love you always.**

The next morning, we stroked Windi's head and side with love in our hands, and comfort in our words, as the doctor helped her through life's most mysterious door. Her pain finally easing, her face softened—and finally relaxed. *God, this was hard.* It never gets any easier. We had prepared for it as best we could: we brought a few photo books with us, so that when we drove on into Reidsville to our special place, we could look through them there in honor and memory of our special girl. It had rained all that morning, which I found particularly appropriate. Dark clouds hung heavy overhead as we drove to Short Sugar's, but they parted when we sat down in the booth and opened the first album. A ray of sunlight burst through the restaurant window and onto the pages where Windi's likeness looked back at us, grinning as always, full of fire and fun. They let us sit in that booth as long as we wanted that morning; they knew what we were there for, and their touch on our arms spoke from the heart.

Having left Tag and Chelsea home, not sure what to do next, we drove a little ways around before turning onto our road and up our driveway. It was time to love those we still had, and we would do that the rest of this day—a work day—away from the office. This was a day to remember and grieve—to honor and celebrate an exemplary life lived by an extraordinary spirit.

Six years later, we would move to our mountain home. The letter to Windi hangs on our bedroom wall to greet us whenever we enter there. In the nook where our upper and lower driveways to the house converge, an old-fashioned lamp post stands next to a hemlock tree we re-planted out of harm's way when the bulldozer forged the driveways in preparation for construction of the house. It is a serene place, where we can sit on a small, curved concrete bench, and drink in a breathtaking view of three mountains. Just behind the bench, hanging from the lamp post, is a handmade wooden sign. In my dad's lettering, above Psalm 121:1, appear the words that call us home, "Windi Cove."

Chapter 25
Tag's Last Job

All our dogs had known times when one of their number was missing for a while, usually to be treated by a veterinarian in overnight stays at the animal hospital. So Tag didn't appear frantic with worry when Windi didn't come home with us from the vet the day we sorrowfully told her, "Goodbye." He probably picked up on our feelings the rest of that afternoon and evening, and while we made a conscious effort not to show any more sadness than we could help for that reason, we couldn't completely hide our feelings, either. This was life stuff, and like it or not, all of us had to deal with it in our own way, in our own time—and deal with it *together,* we would.

Losing Windi took the heart out of our little group. We turned toward each other more closely than before, feeling more vulnerable to life on a tough planet, trying to gain strength to face going on. Loss of a loved one makes you that much more poignantly aware of the essence, as well as the inevitability, of change. Accepting change requires motivation. And discipline. And courage.

I watched Mary become more withdrawn; she put up her usual brave front, but Windi had been her special ally and confidante, as she had been for Windi. The two of them were inseparable around the house. It was Mary's lap that Windi sought, and if that was not available, lying at Mary's feet would have to do. I was *okay* to play with, but Mary took the time to give long, lingering scratches and rubs, murmuring soft conversation the whole time. As much as my wife was giving to that dog, she was unconsciously getting that much more in return. Now there was a huge void in Mary, of a type that I had not witnessed since we lost Ratches, some ten years earlier. The only remedy then had been to suck in our breath, and meet life head-on as best we could by beginning again with new furry beings who would start out, at least, as strangers to us. Could we possibly do that again, after the countless ways Windi had stitched herself into our hearts?

One evening a few months later, I sat down with Mary, and asked her a question I had rehearsed in my mind for several days at the office: "If we're ever going to have other dogs, wouldn't it be better to get them started by the best teacher while we still have him?"

She looked at me, and said, "Yes."

Neither of us was really ready for this—it was too soon after losing the core member of our pack.

("Funny how you never know which one turned out to be the heart of us until he or she is gone, isn't it?" Mary had thought out loud while we were agonizing what to do about Windi's condition.

"Yes," I had answered. "She is the center of us.")

"But, you're right—if we are going to have more dogs, we should do it while they can learn from Tag," Mary said, wiping away a tear, looking out on the field, seeing...nothing.

The next day was Friday. At the table in my office, half-eaten sandwich to one side, I worked through the pet ads in the newspaper, and found a couple of possibilities. I circled them, and after a quick supper at home, we took off to look. Just before dark, we had made our way to a rural town an hour-and-a-half away from Reidsville to find a young family (and another daughter fretting the impending loss of puppies) with a healthy-looking litter of female black-and-whites. After not much discussion, we agreed we wanted smart puppies, who would learn the ropes fast from Tag. So Border collies seemed to be the best way to go: we still had the field and woods—plenty of space for working dogs to grow up in.

The first choice among the tumbling furmeisters was obvious: two of them were adorably snoofling and wagging their way into and over stuff, but the third one was full-bore into the toys! Stumbling and banging around, a clown and full of the devil, she explored and shook everything not nailed down: this one, which we would name Charley, was pure entertainment. Deciding between one of the other two, we ended up choosing the one slightly more shy—the one whose more narrow head favored her mother; she, as it turned out (in true doggy fashion), lived up to her name, "Skye." Initially named for a noted Scottish island, she soon demonstrated a vertical leap in ball-toss games any NBA team would covet.

A word about the pup's mom. While Mary was studying the antics of the pups, their mother was anything *but* shy: all over me, she leaned up against my side, licked my cheeks, shoved her head under my arm, wriggled closer each time I tried to get a glance around or over her to see her pups for a second. *Quit looking at them, fella*—I *need some attention, too, you know. Pet* me. *Pleeeeeze!* She was so sweet, but it was getting ridiculous, even drawing Mary's attention.

"Gee whiz, Skip, she's not letting you go home without her, is she?" observed Mary, tickled.

I began to think that was going to have to be the deal—take mom, too, or nothing. After running the dog-mom and human-daughter gauntlet, we handed human mom $300 for the pair of pups.

"You're...taking...*two* of them?" she blurted, surprised, and more than a little unsure about that.

"Yup. To keep each other company, you know." It turns out lots of folks *don't* know. I felt like I was raiding the national treasury. These folks were not expecting to release the bulk of their bunch at one time; but they did. (I wrote them Christmas cards for the next couple of years, complete with pictures of the growing, happy pair, showing off their antics at Meadowbrook, in the vain hope that daughter would forgive our raid on them. I probably needn't have worried; she was probably into friends or video games by that time, with our pups long forgotten. But you never know. In any case, I never heard back from them. Life just rolls right along.)

The pups slept through the long drive home in the dark. Charley never moved from her spot in the laundry basket on Mary's lap, but early on, Skye climbed her way up and out to snuggle against Mary's chest—claiming her as Windi had. Not wanting to stir things up when we rolled in late that evening, we by-passed Tag and Chelsea and slipped our cargo quietly into the house. The next morning, Skye was the one still in the basket: Charley was...somewhere else. I finally spotted her curled up in one of my yard shoes on the laundry room shelf. They hadn't done anything all night, so we set them out on the grass, where they promptly, in a choreographed move, fell over...and lay there, stunned.

Mary and I looked at each other.

"We've killed them," Mary finally said, "haven't we?"

We were going to need some special help with this pair.

****

Tag had literally raised all the dogs at Meadowbrook, except, of course, for already-grown Freckles. Looking back, he did this in incredibly professional fashion: parenting books should model their admonishments after him. He put up with no nonsense, carefully meting out discipline in proportion to the offense (and, admittedly, taking into account also the size of the offender—apparently you don't administer a mere slap on the wrist to a pup already your size or bigger). Mostly, discipline took the form of showing "wolf teeth" squarely in the face of the delinquent: that look froze Mary and me many a time, and we were looking at it only from the side. No wonder 300-pound rams back down from a Border collie a fifth their size.

Tag put up with a lot from me: my unawareness of things important in a dog's world, poor judgment, poor manners, undue emotionalism, careless inattention, selfishness—the list is endless. But one thing he did not tolerate well was my trying to inject myself into his business—especially the task assigned to him of raising the pack. When Scamp, as a new arrival, was showing her willful, irritating self, trying to escape the cardboard box she was in one evening in our kitchen, Tag was no doubt wondering when the infusion of newbies was ever going to stop. *Easy for them to drop another fur ball into the household: they can go off to work the next day and leave the mess for me to deal with.* He was already tired of the incessant resisting of authority that young Scamper was apparently going to be about, so he walked on over to the box, poked his head over the top, and growled *hard* at the little sh__. (That, by the way, became our customary reference to Scamp over the years. It was one we tried to remember not to use around company, but it slipped out once in a while. Lord knows she earned it often enough.)

I forgot myself, feeling that this poor orphaned girl-puppy had already been cursed with a tough start to life, and that she didn't need another snarling menace in her face right off the bat. So, knight to her rescue, I quickly started to reprimand Tag, the Bully.

"Tag, you leave her be. Be nice to her. She's part of the pack, too!"

Tag's head snapped up, and instead of looking wounded like he usually did when I scolded him, he looked bewildered—and then miffed: *What are you thinking? This is my job—let me do it. Geez!*

He might just as well have held up a stop sign: I got his message loud and clear, and backed off—for good. He was right. It was a good lesson, and I learned it right then. I was not always exactly sure *why* Tag disciplined one of the pack, but I never again questioned it overtly. Tag's steady paw at the helm made all the others know when and where they were to do their business, what to chase and how far, and mostly importantly, how to regard each other with respect so they could all get along and have fun doing it. This was our first experience having a pack of dogs. We had heard that in a pack, there will always be a pack leader. Tag taught us that having a *good* pack leader is critical.

****

Tag went right to work with the new recruits. It was what we hoped for: it seemed to give him something to do while he waited for a return of Windi he would not get. We have a photo of Charley (who would prove to be the next leader) lying in rapt attention, carefully scrutinizing every move Tag was making: snapping bees, warding off hummingbirds, running protective circles around the house. Tag showed them the boundaries of our property, when it was bedtime, how to patiently keep an eye on the field and house to protect against invaders. He showed them that you don't have to be noisy to be strong, or rough to be effective. And that if you're going to be a leader, you are always on duty. *Always*.

Tag didn't vary his basic routines just because Windi wasn't there. He went to bed at the usual time. I found him doing one thing differently, though, especially as the days turned into weeks after Windi's departure. Instead of trotting straight from our back door to the dog yard before we closed up shop for the night, he took to walking around to the front of the house, looking off into the distance in the direction where the driveway dropped down and away toward the road and listening. At first I waited a few seconds, then called him, but I quickly realized by his squint and slight lean forward that I was interrupting something important, so I learned to let him be at those times. "Those times" became almost nightly after a while. When nothing came to him from the driveway direction, he turned to look away from the house altogether, straight out into the darkest of our woods…listening.

Windi, where are *you?*

It was haunting, and so very sad. Or maybe she was reaching him in a way that she did in life—no sounds needed, just whispering to his mind and heart.

I'll never know for sure, I suppose, but I'm satisfied in hindsight that because this ritual intensified during the final weeks of Tag's life, something wonderfully mystical had been going on in those late night, quiet moments when Tag was somewhere else, with his sister.

After a day of instruction for the new black-and-whites, Tag was content to lie out on the living room floor under the desk and let the day wind down. Then one night Mary got him to do something that blew our minds: she coaxed him over to the sofa, encouraged him to raise his front legs up onto her lap, then pull his back legs up there, too. And if that wasn't enough, he actually, slowly, *very* slowly gave in to her gentle stroking of his back, and fell asleep. For the first time in his life (at least in our presence), his rock-hard muscles relaxed, all over, completely.

It was amazing—Mary dared not breathe to interrupt it. She whispered over to me, and finally got my attention: "Skip, look. He's asleep. Our Taggie has finally relaxed." For Tag to give himself over to a moment not on duty when in our presence, that was *something*. To witness the strong leader—the iron, constant will of our household—fully rest for the first time in our company and care, was a little disquieting, but genuinely sweet. *Well, earned, Captain; well earned*.

That interlude didn't last long, but it was repeated a few times thereafter on different evenings. Tag's breath was becoming more labored when he ran the house and dog yard circles, and I no longer pushed him with excited, "Wheees."

At some point he lost his appetite, and nothing the veterinarian prescribed seemed to help. His body was starving itself, and at this rate, his would be a quick end. Christmas was looming, and the thought of losing Tag then was unthinkable. I hoped so much for a miracle. He managed to hang on, but ate little—sometimes nothing at all—during the week before Christmas. Given his weakening condition, I wanted him to be inside with us at night, but persuading him to abandon his yard and house, even on the coldest nights, was difficult. *Ever the pack leader.* Occasionally I just gave in to what he wanted: it was his life, after all, and he had never given me any reason to believe he didn't know his own mind. Thankfully though, on the really raw nights, he allowed me to coax him back up the steps and into the laundry room, where he bedded down in Freckles' old spot.

I was desperate for some way to put weight back on him. In the wee hours one night just a couple days before Christmas, I padded out into the kitchen. I couldn't sleep, Tag on my mind all the time. He surprised me by walking out into the kitchen to greet me. A tentative wag.

"How about a cookie?" I whispered to him. My parents, staying with us for the holidays, were asleep in the nearby guest bedroom; I had left Mary sleeping upstairs. "Want to try one?" I asked again, in a hushed voice. "Sounds like a good Christmas snack, doesn't it?"

I fished around in the glass jar and came up with one of his favorite dog treats. Having sniffed but rejected everything of late, he could have knocked me over with a feather when he took it, and chomped it down! *Yeah!*

Barely controlling my happy vibes, I asked him, "That was pretty great, wasn't it, Taggie? How about another one?"

Another one fished out of the jar, and another one chomped down. Several more found their way down the hatch, until Tag was satisfied. I petted him a while, and then returned to bed, eager for the morning light so I could tell Mary what had just happened. I had prayed for a Christmas miracle, and got one.

Tag did begin to eat better after that night, and for a few months did okay. I thought whatever it was that had afflicted him might be going away, or even gone. His awful *Yowr!* of pain as he tried to run up the back stairs at bedtime one night two months later came as a crushing blow.

There are some screams of pain that animals make that you instantly recognize as needing immediate action. This was one of them. I raced to the back door landing to find Tag sprawled out halfway up the stairs, chest hard on the straight edge of one step, his back legs pressed hard and awkwardly on the next several steps down, his front legs through the opening on the back of the steps, his chin slammed down on the highest step he had reached before collapsing. The sight was wrenching. "Oh, sweetie!" was all I could say. I carefully gathered him up, as he screamed in pain again. I hurriedly laid him down on the laundry room floor, then tried to put soft blankets under him, but with each movement of his body, he exhaled a grating sound of pain. I had never heard such a terrible sound, and I hope I never will again.

I had called the emergency veterinary service number, thinking that we would take Tag to the animal hospital immediately. After answering a few questions from the doctor, I was advised that from the symptoms I described, Tag would likely make it through the night okay, but I should try to squirt a little water around his mouth at least, and unless things changed dramatically for the worse, bringing him in the next morning would be just as good as a late-night meeting.

I slept little that night. I stayed downstairs, and several times went into the laundry room to try to get him to drink water. He couldn't move—at all. I tried to get a drop or two of water into his mouth with a basting syringe. The drops just dribbled off his gums and down onto his bed. He looked away from me, in obvious discomfort, and I think, embarrassment. A very proud animal, this debilitation must have been extraordinarily hard for him to accept—especially in my presence. He labored when he breathed. The vet had said Tag would probably sleep. He didn't. And it was killing me. "Oh, Tag—you don't deserve this. You don't deserve this," I kept repeating. "Shhh," I whispered as I tried to gently stroke his body, but wherever I touched him, he cried in pain. I could do nothing but wait. I sat beside him for a few hours until sleep overtook me at last.

A few hours later, Mary drove my car to the animal hospital, while I lay beside Tag in the back. By this time, he was able to let me pet him gently, and I talked to him upbeat all the way. His eyes were soft and round, and several times he glanced ahead up at Mary, who looked around while she drove to offer her own comforting words to him. Later, she told me that he had looked so happy "to have his guy right beside him." A hard knot forms in my chest whenever I re-live that ride.

The doctor kept him overnight for tests and evaluation. When it came, the prognosis confirmed what I feared most: his heart had suffered damage, and he would not get well. Even if they could stabilize him, he would likely suffer a repeat of this incident, and the time in between would not be kind to him. Given his age and condition, we were given the suggestion I knew was coming. We put him to sleep, and a part of me died with him.

If there is a heaven, Tag rejoined Windi right then. Leave it to her to make the preparations—to bust down that door to make it easier for her pack leader to follow through. God, I loved those two. They were worthy successors to Ratches.

We didn't go to work that day, either. We honored Tag. We were lost. We came home to find a place without its leader. Mary always referred to me as Tag's pack leader. He could have done better. She said he adored me: his looks at me often seemed to confirm that. I hope I didn't disappoint him too often.

He was so earnest and insistent for my immediate attention, that sometimes it got on my nerves when I was trying to read, watch TV, whatever. I wish I could do all those moments over, but we never get them back.

"Taggie legs"—leg muscles of twisted steel, as we called them—are part of our active vocabulary. Mary and I try to keep ourselves in condition, which is easier now that we are walking up and down the inclines of our acreage at Windi Cove. As Tag aged and took on more and more members of his pack, I promoted him from sergeant to Cap'n Tag. Always just "Taggie" to Mary, he was "Boss Tags" to me. I miss our leader. He completed his last job of raising the new Borders with his usual excellence, and then his body gave out, as all of ours ultimately must. *Tag, I sure hope to rub your fuzzy muzzle again. Until then, Ratches and Windi, take good, good care of him.*

(top) First night, Charley over Skye
(middle) Chelsea pursued by Skye and Charley
(bottom) Scamp inspects Skye

(top) Leadership Training: Charley studying Tag;
(middle) New Gang: (back to front) Scamp, Skye, Chelsea, Tag, Charley;
(bottom) Same ball field, new players (Skye and Charley)

Chapter 26
Chelsea Stays Home

Tag and Chelsea had been companionable, but not all that close. Once established as an adult member of the pack, Chelsea became a forager of the field, and except for those moments when Scamp or Freckles would find whatever she was uncovering to be worth a romp over to investigate, she strolled and hunted the Meadowbrook field alone, content in her own world of sunshine and mice. Despite her independence, life for Chelsea did not go on seamlessly without Tag: it was left to her to be the role model for the two new charges. Scamp, after all, never gave up her couch-potato mission for long, preferring to be inside with us most of the time.

Being Border collies, Charley and Skye were outdoor pups—eager to see and conquer the world. Like it or not, Chelsea, by default, was the one they looked to for adventure. And Border collie puppies are all about adventure. Non-stop adventure. There's puppy energy, and then there's Border collie energy. *Come on, Chels—what do we do next, huh?* They badgered her mercilessly—followed her like twin shadows. Chelsea tried everything to once again avoid the motherhood role she had escaped with Scamp, only this time nothing worked. These two were relentless.

Their persistence paid off: at Frisbee time, she finally gave in and joined the fray. This worked out all right for a while, as her stride was longer to get her to the toss before the pair of youngsters could run it down. But before long, growing legs and genetic talent won out, and she was left out. Try as I might, I could not get the Borders to share the tosses with her. Turns out, that was okay with Chelsea, anyway: she just reverted back to mouse hunts on her own, while the new kids scrambled all over each other and through the weeds of the field to be first to the Frisbee. Life at Meadowbrook, though slightly different with new characters, was coming around full circle. Mary and I silently wondered how that was going to feel.

Two months later, the dreaded premonition of years before—that our original Meadowbrook "gang of four" would reach their life expectancies at about the same time—was confirmed: Chelsea died. We had lost our original pack of four wonderful furries in ten months. The way it happened was actually one of the most touching passages from this life I can imagine.

Her breathing more labored of late, she stopped more frequently on walks and up inclines to catch her breath. Chelsea's heart and lungs were struggling against the advancing erosion of time. "Old dog lungs," the vet called it. The tissues that make up our working parts are wonderfully created, and while healthy, are marvelously capable of giving us the means to fully explore the wonders of this planet. Sight, smell, touch, and hearing bring to all animals, in varying ways and to different degrees, the ability to drink in the gifts of nature. Chelsea fully used her body's senses to live a simple, rich life.

Name your dogs carefully: they will live in accordance with what you call them. "Tag" double-front-pawed me all his life. "Windi" flew like the wind to catch game-winning passes on our playing field. "Ruffy" bowled Chelsea over every time we began a pack-walk around the field, through the woods, or down our driveway. And "Scamp" took great delight (her grin gave her away every time) in, well, *being* one. "Miss Sunshine," named by Mary for Chelsea Gardens in London, where rays of sunshine grace a small patch of green and flowers in the midst of a city thick with concrete, asphalt and steel, showed us all how to live in glorious appreciation of the natural beauty all around us.

Not letting something as incidental to a dog as deteriorating health get in her way, Chelsea padded through her last days with dignity and fun, just like before—she just did it slower.

One day Mary called me at the office to tell me to meet her at the veterinary hospital. "Chelsea is gone," she tearfully whispered over the line.

Time stopped.

"I'll be right there. Don't you want me to come home first and help you get her there?"

"No," she said. "Dad came up and did that. I called him, and…"

I didn't let her finish. "Why didn't you call *me*?" I was hurt, and confused. *This dog was* our *dog,* my *lifelong friend, too. I appreciated Dad helping, sure, but why not call* me? This was not the nicest thing to be doing to her, but I was—upset. *Very upset.*

"You told me the judge had been on you for not being there enough with your employees lately, and I knew you would leave everything and come right away…so…"

Again, I didn't let her finish. "Honey," I began, "I can take care of my job. This is *important*. I wanted to be there with you when…and…." I couldn't finish. This wasn't getting us anywhere. What was done was done. Besides, Mary was obviously upset as much as me—maybe more. And Dad had dropped everything to help when asked. At that moment, something closed in my heart and it locked in a message to the rest of me: *Your work is keeping you away from life, and as soon as you can, change that. There are things more important than any job; and this…I can't do this anymore.*

I drove straight to Reidsville, and found Dad and Mary in the parking lot. I thanked Dad, and must have somehow connected with him that as much as I genuinely appreciated his having helped with a difficult chore, I wanted to be alone with Mary and my dog. He left, understanding. I saw in the bed of the truck the black fur that once was a doggy version of "sunshine in life," and I crawled in, tie and all, to lie alongside her. My palm stroked her side: it felt stiff, unyielding. My fingers searched for that wonderful, warm, Lab softness at the top of her head, but her fur felt…ordinary. I wanted to go back in time a few hours to be with her when she was alive. It is a universal longing, never satisfied. My tears came in sudden, racking sobs, as I buried my face into her chest and clutched her whole body in the agony of wanting to say goodbye, knowing she was already gone. I didn't care how long I might be there, but I was not the only one grieving, so I backed out of the truck bed, and hugged Mary. We both cried, and hugged each other more tightly. In less than a year, we had lost all four of our first Meadowbrook partners and friends. Our insides were ragged; we were drained. A mule could have kicked us repeatedly, and we wouldn't have felt it. This was what numb felt like. There just wasn't anything left. The world was becoming more brutal than we could deal with.

We went inside, somehow made the arrangements, and on the way back out to the truck, neither of us could finish the steps to it. There was no way we were going to get back inside that vehicle and resume our lives. Not aware of the world around us, or not caring if we were, we stopped and hugged each other as a tidal wave of pain tore through the core of our beings. This was unbearable. A few minutes later I felt a hand on my shoulder: one of the receptionists had come out to cry with us. Strange how I remember her exact words: "I just couldn't stand to see you two hurting that much." She embraced us together, just enough to help us want to breathe again. It was so sweet of her, and it helped. We thanked her, made our way finally to the truck, and drove home in silence.

Earlier, on the phone, Mary had told me what had happened, but I asked her to tell me all of it again and again, sparing no details. Since I hadn't been there, I wanted to know everything. I had lost a dear friend, and I wanted to know everything about her last hours. By the time she finished, I felt a little better...

April at Meadowbrook was usually warm enough to be comfortable outside, and the early afternoon this day brought a soft, slightly moist breeze down the field toward the towering Cyprus tree where Mary sat on a small lawn chair, Chelsea lying down beside her. While Mary looked at the budding trees surrounding the field, Chelsea sifted through the variety of fragrances filling the currents of air stirring the branches of flowering bushes around her. This was the very best of Chelsea's world: sunshine, warm breezes, birds calling from all sides, mice scurrying around their burrows out among the grasses and weeds. In the midst of these scintillating sounds and smells, she breathed with sudden difficulty, turning into spasms. Mary had just heard me say that the previous week at work, the chief judge was offering a critique that I should be "more of a presence" in the clerks' office, and that I wasn't sure how I was going to assimilate his suggestion into my management approach. She felt this would be a poor time to interrupt and probably terminate my day at the office, so she called my dad and asked him to drive the half-hour from Greensboro to help her load Chelsea into the truck to take her to the veterinary hospital. While Mary waited for him to arrive, Chelsea's breathing grew even more labored and erratic; it must have been scary to her, and painful. When Dad arrived and was helping Mary place her into the back of the truck, Chelsea resisted, raised up with a last effort, and expired. Her last breath audibly escaped from her, and her spirit eased out into the field she loved with all her being.

"She wouldn't leave her favorite place," Mary said at last, in the sweetest tone I have ever heard.

Again I lamented, "I wish I had been there with her."

"I don't think she would have let herself go if you *had* been there," she answered. "If you *had* been there, she would have tried harder to hang on and stay with us, and it was so hard on her to do that as it was."

I don't know where Mary found those words of comfort, but I will be eternally grateful to her for them. It was the only thing she could have said that would have helped me through that time and since.

I finally told her, "I *am* happy for Chelsea, that she could have been with you at the last. She couldn't have had a better person to be with to help her move on to the next life. And she was in the elements that made her happiest right to the end. I wouldn't want to selfishly change that."

Our desire for others we love to have lives that are healthier and happier than they might have been is normal and good; the pain we feel in losing loved ones is purely selfish. Chelsea lived the epitome of a dog's life—one tested by the sometimes harsh conditions of field and woods, but also rich with fun and creature comforts. Even her slip from the mortal bounds of Earth was made in a setting perfect for her. She deserved no less, and I can manage thanks—and at least a little smile—when I remember that.

Chapter 27
Farewell, Meadowbrook

That April, 2000 was probably beautiful at our country home, everything usually nudged into full bloom by then by gentle rains and warming days. I don't remember. The devastating losses we had suffered blocked my spirit's interest in anything of real value. I turned my full attention to the business of my office as my only way to get through the days. I enjoyed the new pups and Scamp, sure, and loved Mary as always, but my heart had been dealt too many blows to allow me to feel life for a while.

On my mind, too, was knowing that we were going to have to decide whether to commit to relocating to the North Carolina mountains on 24 acres we had purchased there two years earlier. A colleague of mine, retired in Alabama, had telephoned me one day at the office a while back to let me know how retirement life was going for him, and to question me about my having told him that we were thinking of moving away from our present country home.

"You know, from what you've described of your life where you are now, you just might already have found your retirement place," he said in his usual deliberate, deep southern tone.

There are moments when something someone says strikes a chord you can't deny, and that haunts you thereafter.

"You may be right, Jim," I said. "We have been wrestling with that."

"You give it some thought, Skip. The pictures you sent of your home are beautiful, and all the things you have there to do…'course, it's not for me to say. You know more about it than I do, but it might be something to think about."

I assured him I would. And we did. But every night at our supper table, when we looked out onto our field, we saw only the past: *Tag racing around the house; Windi alert, but on her tummy on one side of the patio landing; Chelsea leaning against the post on the other side of the landing, looking to see if deer dared to show themselves on* her *field; Ruffy lying upright on the patio at the base of the stairs, showing us his magnificent profile while he checked out Tag and speculated as to when would be a good time to "get in the circle race game."* Deer that been growing bolder as we began to lose our furry friends, now stood just thirty feet from the patio, munching fallen apples, knowing that the new pups were in the house with Scamp for suppertime, knowing that the days of testing the speed and desire of the pack were gone. The hummingbirds flew to and from the feeder hanging under our bedroom bay window without fanfare; bees zipped around the canna beside the patio undisturbed.

Our whole life there had been forged and fashioned in a million intricate ways by a pack of dogs—dogs expected and left by us to be dogs, but friends as well. They permitted us to be modified members of their pack, but retained their distinctly doggy ways of life, and allowed us to not only observe them, but to actually participate in some of them. Remarkable. What they gave us was an exceptional awareness of how different perspectives on living can give purpose to each other's lives and enrich them all the while. True to a dog's nature untainted by man, this lesson was given freely, over time, with love. Their character indelibly imprinted on us as their lives intertwined with ours. Our routines and theirs had merged to the point where we hardly knew where one left off and the other began. And there was one more dimension present that we had not known with Ratches in a city environment: here, in the sometimes tough and scary world of the country, we all depended on each other every day. Because of that we formed bonds that ran deeper and that connected us not only to each other but to this land as well, *for as long as we all were there.*

More than with our lives, though, the spirits of the dogs who had fully lived there but had passed on to the next adventure—Tag, Windi, Chelsea, Ruffin, and Freckles—were inseparably interwoven into the fabric of that land…that place. Meadowbrook was theirs more than it was ours. It didn't matter that they were the dogs, and we were the humans. Our guys had made this tiny part of the planet theirs in every sense that mattered, and with them gone, we felt like trespassers on it. We knew it would be too cruel to us to try to live our retirement years there in the emptiness that they left behind. Sure, there were things about the house and driveway that we weren't all that crazy about, but we were close to things and places we liked and could have explored with the time that retirement would offer. Facing the ordeal of building a new house again, especially in an area largely unfamiliar to us, was an unpleasant prospect. And we would never find the privacy of Meadowbrook again, anywhere; that worried us more about leaving than anything. We discussed the financial implications of both scenarios, along with everything else, until we were weary of all of it. Those after-work supper discussions at our kitchen table droned on, night after night.

Mary went to Texas to visit her brother and his family, as much to clear her head as anything. I stayed behind to tend to the new pups and Scamp—and to re-stain the deck and screened porch, just in case we decided to move forward with selling our home of thirteen years. By the time she returned, we both knew what we were going to do. Meadowbrook was a time in our lives that lost its appeal without the characters that made it a place we wanted to live in. The magic was no longer there, and the pain of realizing that was undeniable and intolerable. We *had* to move. Leaving that wonderfully private sanctuary of beauty and peace would be sad; staying there would be...impossible.

Through a series of coincidences of timing and fortuitous errors by all players, our house sold midway through the next year. We stumbled upon an adequate rental house with a fenced backyard in Greensboro, and found ourselves alone on the last day of the move in a house emptied of everything. Our footsteps echoed on the tile floors. *I know every inch of this house on the darkest nights*, I thought to myself. *So much living some of life's happiest and most stressful moments we have done here. How can we leave?* I walked over to the patio glass doors; Mary silently followed, and stood beside me as we looked out over the backyard and field through a growing mist.

"That's fitting," I said, nodding to the worsening weather.

"Yeah."

Freckles would have had to have been left with the place; she could not have been contained in a city yard—fenced or otherwise. *If she was somehow out there with Chelsea now, at least she didn't have to worry about coming in for suppertime, or getting rounded up for her annual exam and shots, or....* My heart was breaking.

Thoughts and moments like this between us had been all too common the previous twelve months. It was time to go.

Epilogue

Life flows as a river around one bend, then another, and another...it has no discernible beginning, and no point where it marks a new stage. Some underground stream emerges from under a rock or tree, and we call that the "headwaters," not the "start" of a river. Standing at any point on a river of any size, you can look to the horizon in either direction of the river's flow, and think you see the beginning or the end of it; but if you move to that far-off spot, it was only another midway point in the water's endless continuation. The river of life carries with it at every point parts that joined with it earlier to make it what it has become at that moment in time. Because of this, it is not static: its composition—its character—keeps changing.

Human beings are a complicated lot, made so by our own choosing. It is a human tendency to want to draw a line of demarcation at different times in life. From this inclination come phrases like "Turn the page" "Begin anew," "Don't look back," "Let it go." This desire to box the river of life into separate, manageable parts stems from a deep-seated need to more easily focus on whatever new has entered our lives, or escape the pain of remembering what (good or bad thing) is no longer in them. The latter keeps psychiatrists in business; their job is to help us drag out all the things that are harming us from the mental closet we have tried to keep them locked up in, and to deal with them in the only environment that the human psyche has to live healthfully in—reality. In the movie "Who is Harry Kellerman, and Why Is He Saying All Those Terrible Things About Me?" the central character having a nervous breakdown is constantly urged by his psychiatrist to "embrace reality."

Why should I embrace reality?" the patient responds to the doc, musing in a moment of dark wisdom. "Reality never did anything for me."

When we closed the front door that misty afternoon, turning our backs to the most magical place we would likely ever see, let alone live in, we did not leave our home there behind. The greater portion of our minutes, hours, days, weeks, months, and years there had been devoted, with laughter and tears, contentment and anxiety, joy and pain, to the dogs who completed our family that was Meadowbrook. Our hearts had filled with all of that—the stuff of life, and there was no breaking that apart or stopping it suddenly to start a new river of life. It would have been foolhardy to try, but we had no wish to forget and start our lives over. Loving begins with the heart, and stays there forever whether or not the object of that love has moved on ahead of you. We loved our lives that had become enriched at Meadowbrook beyond what we would have believed possible, and we had our special furry friends to thank for that. They—and the place they created—would remain with us always, wherever we went. And where we went was the city, and then the mountains, where we are now. Therein lies the final story of Meadowbrook.

****

We still had an original member of the Meadowbrook pack with us. Scamp sat for hours in the middle of our urban back yard, and watched the only house next door that wasn't blocked by a hedge. Looking in that direction, she could see two houses in a row: the nearest one featured two black labs (foundlings from the plant where the owner worked), the farthest a boxer that was hungry for attention and barked loudly trying to get it. The two labs became the object of watchful herding by Charley, one of several missions she appointed for herself there. (The other principal object of her attention was the lady on the other side of us, whose frequent lawn care and gardening activity fascinated Charley for hours on end. Instead of being unnerved by that, our neighbor got tickled to look up and see Charley sometimes lying with her muzzle full on the ground between low bushes at the fence—sometimes standing on a brick wall behind our garage, front legs up on the top of the fence—black eyes following every move she made with hoe or clippers. A quick, but short, wag of the tail was our clue that the two of them had made eye contact.)

Just as you know when someone is seeing something far beyond what they're looking at, Scamp's watchful gaze went beyond the neighbors' dogs and yards. At the end of one of those episodes, she dropped her head to the side, and, visibly startled to realize where she was, she looked around and side-to-side, finally back over her shoulder at our house, sighed, slowly got up, and ambled to our back door. One after another, this one-time orphan had lost her mothers and pals—beings she had become so thoroughly attached to that when they left and didn't return, she grieved openly longer than any of the others. Dogs grieve like people do: they sniff the beds where their friends had slept, lie down in spots that were their friends' favorites, but hardest of all to bear, they come up to you at the oddest moments, and in a way reserved only for this particular message, they look deeply into your eyes, and seem to ask, *Where did they go?* After more or less recovering from having had her world torn away from her repeatedly during that one terrible year, she had suffered yet another blow—this one probably the toughest of all: we had uprooted her from the only place she had ever known. Older people have withdrawn permanently after experiencing that: some shrivel and die. Life has to be desired to continue; too many folks forget that.

This would be the hardest test for Scamp. However much of a role that played in her health, I don't know, but the digestive disorder that afflicted Scamp earlier at Meadowbrook returned with a vengeance, complete with wracking her now-older body at both ends. Cleaning up blood, bile, excrement, and undigested food after a violent episode was a frightening experience to us, but watching it happen to our otherwise tough little couch dog was devastating. Time and again we rushed her to the 24-hour emergency veterinary clinic, mercifully only a two-minute drive from our house. Each time, they kept her alive through the night, until our regular vet could begin ministrations of glucose and other stabilizers that would slowly render her able to return home. Even then, her diet had to be cooked chicken or hamburger with rice—a bland diet that the masters of animal medicine have as their only recommendation for bad conditions they cannot fix. Through a series of these increasingly worse outbreaks, we watched the toll they and the medical treatments that followed were taking on our increasingly fragile girl. This was torment beyond tolerance.

The day we made the decision to put her out of this misery, she walked out to meet us in the tiny medical room, following another harrowing episode which had nearly killed her. She had a little prance to her step, looking beautiful as always, but thin. Her tail still bushy and golden, only her face—pinched from too many narrow escapes that would have ended the lives of lesser dogs—gave away the gravity of her condition. Seeing her looking too healthy to put to sleep, I lost it, hating myself every second for not having the courage Scamp had displayed all her life. She needed better than that from me, and I couldn't seem to deliver, try as I might.

"She acts so healthy, Doc! Look at her beautiful tail, how she moves—are we *sure* this is the right thing to do *now*?" I pleaded, begged for some kind of understanding of a world that I thought I controlled, but had now gone completely insane.

"They always act like that when they see their owners, Skip," he answered matter of factly. "That's what they *do* when they're glad to see you. They wag. They'll do that when they can't eat. It's what they *do*," he repeated, trying to make me understand something that the vision of Scamper before me contradicted.

"Are you *sure*?" I was frantic with despair that we were making the wrong call here—one we could not take back once done.

"Yes," emphatic now.

Silence. I worked hard to regain control of myself. Mary seemed so stalwart, but inside.... I nodded, the doctor went to gather what he needed, and the all-too-familiar litany droned on into oblivion. And so began the final part of the Meadowbrook story.

That night, after a hideous afternoon of yet another soul-wrenching round of grief, self-doubt, and an effort to swallow a tasteless supper, we said good night to the two new Borders and Fretzel, closed and locked the child (dog)-proof gate at the kitchen door separating the tile floor from the carpeted areas of the house (our concession to the landlord), and went to bed...

****

Fretzel could not be introduced earlier, because he never was a resident of Meadowbrook. He came to us by a peculiar set of circumstances a few months earlier, when in mid-December, on a 22-degree day in a landscape of ice and snow in the mountains where we were spending a weekend at our newly constructed house, dreaming of the time we could finally move to live there full-time, we happened upon a page in the local paper advertising puppies at the county animal shelter. We already had three, with Scamp, and didn't need any more dogs at this stage of our lives, especially living in a rented house where the owner was amazingly tolerant of our request to have *any* dogs—let alone three. Four would be ridiculous to consider for that reason alone; four would be financial idiocy. All we wanted to do was see what the animal shelter looked like—you know, part of getting to know your local community. That's what we told ourselves, anyway. Afterwards, each of us gave full credit to the other for this particular fork in our road.

We drove down a long, lonely road that the map said would bring us to the county animal shelter (the pound), but what we found at the end of it instead was the county landfill and one tiny concrete building, which I figured had to be the landfill office. Nope—it was the animal shelter, along with a collection of chain-link fences behind it, complete with "lost" dogs. Their metal buckets were filled with frozen water. Meager spreadings of straw barely helped cushion dog pads from sharp gravel. Plastic houses did little to keep out the stinging winds of the December mountain nights.

This was too much for Mary, who in her kindest but firmest voice asked the attendant, "Their water buckets are frozen; how can they get water?"

The young man's face was earnest—he moved the way people do who feel overworked. "I'm just getting to that," he hurriedly replied. I'll be switching that out in just a few minutes. Go ahead and look around." In other words, *Please let me get on with my chores, here; there's always too much to do, and I can't keep up.*

"Those buckets were probably frozen over early last night in this cold," Mary somberly noted to me as we walked closer to the cages. I'm sure she was right.

We walked slowly past one anxious muzzle after another, each pressing for our attention, for their escape to a better place. I was several cages ahead of Mary when I heard her softly say, "Somebody's working on you."

Without turning around toward her, I smiled to myself and replied, "Yeah, I know. I already saw him…he was doing that to me when I went by him." We were not there to get a puppy. I walked on a bit.

"He's really making a plea," she continued in the same quiet tone.

Geez. Sigh. I knew right then what the future held. Right then. But I turned around, anyway. I walked carefully (like *that* would help) back over to where Mary stood facing this little black, long-haired pup, sitting squarely on his hindquarters, chest and head erect, enduring a bunch of chow pups crawling all over him, trying to look dignified. The contradiction in that cracked me up. His eyes held mine in a steady gaze: none of that pound-dog-frantic-eye-movement stuff you usually see when reviewing the troops locked up in animal-shelter quarters. No, not for this little guy.

He was all about confidence. *I'm special. I have quality. I am right for you, and* you know it.

"Well, let's hold him just a second before we go, Mary."

"No, we do that, and we'll end up getting him."

"No, we won't; and anyway, it wouldn't hurt to see how it feels holding him; you can tell a lot by that you can't tell any other way," I countered, bringing all my wisdom to the fore.

Neither of us believed that nonsense, but she let it go, and a moment later Mary's neck was being nuzzled, her face licked, her heart stolen.

That was Saturday. We needed time to think about whether we were going to leap into the abyss. It was Christmastime. My parents were grappling with my mother's health, planning to spend several days at our mountain house for what I worried might be her last Christmas. We had a regularly sick Scamp, whose condition would erupt with only hours' notice. We had two Border collies only midway through their third year of life, just now finding themselves and trying to figure out why they lived in two different places, neither of which was either their original home nor the big field and woods we had initially transplanted them to.

This was *not* a good idea. But that look through the fence, chow puppies' legs splaying all over the little guy's face, he had withstood it all, looking dignified, intelligent. You can't let that be thrown away. The image of the massive landfill awaiting the unlucky ones not adopted—at Christmastime, no less—was too much. Monday morning we went back. Mary was coming down with a nasty, old-fashioned cold virus, but she braved the cold to hold that rascal again, confirmed she liked him (he indisputably confirmed likewise), and we left—all three of us. I dropped Mary off at our mountain house so she could go to bed and begin the arduous process of trying to get well, and the youngster and I began a long drive to a veterinary clinic in Boone for an exam and a week's boarding until the next weekend.

Filling out the initial papers, the young receptionist asked me the question Mary and I had unsuccessfully tried to prepare for. "Name?"

It came into focus for the first time: "Fretzel—like 'pretzel' only beginning with an F instead of a P." She didn't flinch, but there was a hint of a smile.

"Okay," she said simply, never looking up. Another, slightly wider smile.

"I don't know what 'Fretzel' means, but he's going to show us," I added, anticipating the inevitable question.

"I'm sure he will," she said, looking up at last, now sporting a full grin. "Let's have him," she said, dropping her pen, standing up and reaching out with both hands.

I handed him to her over the counter. Like a magnet, three other attendants—all women—cruised over en masse to get a look and feel of this guy.

Wow, whatever he has, guys everywhere would kill for, I thought.

"He is *adorable*," they cooed.

I watched him: he took all this adoration in stride, giving them love but not over the top. He was an instant hit. I didn't worry about leaving him there. I worried about getting him *back*.

****

Now still a puppy, having adjusted well to the routines of life at our rented house and fenced back yard, learning the ropes from Charley and Skye outside, and from Scamp inside, Fretzel was accustomed to sleeping on the small sofa out in the den, alongside Scamp. That ended earlier that day, but since Scamp had been left so many times overnight at the veterinary clinic—usually for several consecutive nights, none of the dogs seemed to think much about her sudden absence. She'd be back. Life was more or less normal.

We turned out our bedroom light, and fell asleep, tears on both our pillows, our hearts heavy—again.

Deep into the night, I was awakened by a lick. A soft, slow lick on the ends of my fingers, my arm hanging off the bed. *Scamp,* I groggily thought to myself, *you're here.* I jolted, fully conscious now. I saw a dark figure moving around to the end of our bed. The room was black.

"Jesus, Mary—there's a dog in here!" I cried out. "Turn a light on!"

Mary fumbled with the table lamp on her side of the bed, and when it finally came on, there was this furry face staring right at me from the end of the bed. With the room suddenly lit, two paws popped up onto the footboard, and in an instinctive, knee-jerk reaction, I yelled out, "*Aaah!*" and poor Fretzel fell over backwards, more scared than I was. *Klump!*

"Oh, sweetie—I didn't know it was you," I said, now a little more alert. "Oh, darlin', come here, Fretzel—come here." I patted the side of the mattress, and he walked, stunned, over to my hand, flumped down and let me pet his side for a few moments. Usually full of licks and non-stop head movements when we petted him, he sat motionless, staring at the doorway of our bedroom, out into the hallway.

How did he get in here? I wondered. *I know I locked the kitchen gate; he's too little to jump over it. I must have forgotten to close it.*

I stopped petting him, and still he stared out the bedroom doorway, unmoving. It was the stare of someone not conscious of where he is, or of what is going on—an unblinking gaze.

I whispered to him, "Do you want to go to bed?" As I carefully lifted my legs over and around him to get out of bed, he slowly raised himself, and padded ahead of me toward the hall. He looked straight ahead the whole time, slowing as we got to the kitchen gate. It was closed. And locked. When I opened it, he padded through with that same slow stride—like sleepwalking. He never looked back—just kept walking through the kitchen into the den, hopped up onto Scamp's end of the sofa, made the usual half-turn Scamp always had, and collapsed, instantly asleep. This behavior in every detail I recognized, as I had seen it a hundred times—from Scamp.

I returned to the bedroom, not quite sure what to think.

"Was the gate closed?" Mary wondered.

"Yeah."

"How did he get in here, then?"

"I don't know. I'm not sure it *was* him. I mean, it was *him*, but I think he might have had help. He might have been a messenger. I'll tell you what I think in the morning; I've got to get some sleep. I have to go to work tomorrow." *Always work tomorrow.*

The next morning, before I left our bed, I told Mary that the lick on my fingers was a lick I recognized from a lifetime of them from Scamp. Each dog has a distinct way of doing everything: way of licking you, way of holding the head to match exactly what is wanted (treat, go outside, play, reassurance)—everything. I was awakened by my fingers being licked as only Scamp had done. I told her all the things that struck me as odd about how Fretzel had acted from the moment I realized he was in the room with us—that he seemed to be in a trance the whole time, and when he moved, it was Scamper's patented movements, not his.

"I think she came to say goodbye and let me know it was all right, what happened yesterday," I said.

"I don't doubt it, knowing Scamp," said Mary. That was that; I dressed, and went to work. I thought that was the end of it.

The thing was, this wasn't the first time I felt visited by a spirit in the late hours while I slept. My maternal grandfather and I had a close relationship, though he was a thousand miles away in a Wisconsin Veterans Home for quite a while. While Mary and I focused on our new careers in Northern Virginia, Grandpa was losing ground to a failing heart. In the middle of the night in the bedroom of our tiny first house, I was awakened to hear the footsteps I remembered so well as those of Grandpa. They were distinctive; I was not startled, as I knew they were his, and that he must have died to be there right then. The footsteps came down the hall but stopped outside our closed bedroom door. *Just like him,* I thought, *to be that discreet and courteous not to intrude on our bedroom privacy.* After a few moments, the footsteps moved back the way they had come. Then the house was silent. He was gone.

Very early the next morning, the telephone woke me. It was on my side of the bed. When I managed to get it to my ear, still waking up, I heard my mother's voice: "Hi, honey—I need to tell you something." *I already knew what it was.* "Grandpa died last night."

"I know."

I knew she didn't hear or understand that. She went on to tell me it was congestive heart failure, and that he didn't suffer, and.... I smiled that ironic sort of smile you do when the world has dealt you a blow. I would cry later—hard, at the office, when I wrote and sent a telegram to be placed in his casket. But for this moment, I knew he had found a way to come to say goodbye to me. That meant everything. It was—good. I loved him, and it was mutual. The bond of love can transcend anything, it seemed. And *that* was especially good.

Now Scamp had made a visit from a place the living are not permitted to know. It was accomplished by love, whose ties are stronger than any of us can possibly imagine. *Wow,* I thought.

"Wow!" doesn't exactly cover Scamp's next move, which, as Paul Harvey's radio program would say, is "the *rest* of the story."

One of the women in the court where I worked told me something plainly one day; having had many dogs over the years, I knew the wisdom of it: "Dogs ain't worth a damn until they're two years old!" Then she laughed, looked at me, and asked, "Isn't that right?"

"You bet," I answered, nodding.

She and I then shared many accounts of the nonsense that growing dogs pull as they struggle to find their identities and purpose in life, and the way they are going to live with their human companions. Then, suddenly, somewhere in their twos, they begin to look you in the eye, study you, and begin thereafter to be aware of what you're thinking, how you're feeling, how they can interact with you on conscious and sub-conscious levels, and in all respects become your partner—your friend—for life. That transformation can have as much influence and impact on your life as you have room in your heart and schedule to allow; and like all such relationships, it can lead you in directions and to places you cannot predict. Life based on love cannot be controlled: it can only be lived.

Fretzel turned two in fall of 2005. It wasn't long thereafter that he began to do startling things. He was already deep into the habit of curling up on an ottoman alongside my legs during family TV-viewing time. Out of nowhere one evening, he raised up, lowered his ears, tilted his head, opened his muzzle, let his tongue slip out just a little, and held that pose for a long moment, looking up at me in a new way the whole time. That was never before in his repertoire, but it was most certainly a classic Scamp posture—I knew it from all the years we had her. Then he licked me—not in any of his usual variety of ways, but in a way absolutely *identical* to how Scamper did it.

I kept that first instance to myself. It wasn't too long after that, though, that Mary noticed the same kind of thing from Fretzel. "Doesn't that remind of you of Scamp?" she finally blurted out to me one night.

"Uh, huh."

"Where's he getting that from?" she pressed.

Darned if I knew. "I think she might be in there with him." With my hand I guided Fretzel's head to look me in the eye. "Are you in there with him, Scamp?" I asked him. That can make you feel strange—talking to a dog like that. But the weird stuff was just getting cranked up.

Mary said nothing. But she continued to look at Fretzel, not at me.

During house construction, Scamp's very favorite spot was alongside the long edge of the outer portion of the second level deck, at least twelve feet off the ground. She would lie there in the cold days of mid-winter, squinting into the wind as gusts blew back parts of her fur, perched right at the very edge of that deck—a deck that as yet had no rails or supports above deck level. There was nothing to stop her from free-falling over the side a long way down. Apparently oblivious to that, she slept. During the winter midway through Fretzel's third year, he began to bark at the deck door to go outside. Regardless of the temperature, he padded on over to Scamp's spot, lay down, squinted into the wind as it ruffled his fur, then turned onto his side and went to sleep in a perfect Scamper pose. Where did *that* come from?

In the *Star Trek* episode "Return to Tomorrow," one of the visiting characters temporarily "shares the consciousness" of one of the Star Trek crew, thereby hiding in that crew member to avoid being captured by another of the visitors—a more villainous character. Scamp had a distinctive tickity, tickity, tickity stride on hard floors when she chose to walk at that particular pace. Mary and I weren't the only ones to notice it: my parents on occasion were treated to it, usually when we were playing cards, and Scamp wandered over to see if she could corral a dog snack out of us or just nap at our feet. Fretzel began working on that, and was getting close. If he ever gets that down pat, and begins nosing around in our indoor trash cans to chew used facial tissues, the matter will be settled: Scamp and Fretzel will definitely be sharing consciousness. Well, I guess if it doesn't hurt Fretzel, I don't really care. I told Fretzel once, "It's okay if you're in there, Scamp—just don't hurt him." Talk about feeling like an idiot.

Your dogs can and do modify your outlook on life, and your behavior. Fretzel's most bizarre departure from what had been his normal routines once again copied Scamp to the letter. When we first bought the mountain property, we took all the dogs with us to our mobile home there to spend occasional weekends and dream of our future permanent home. Scamp continued a habit she had picked up at Meadowbrook of taking off at bedtime and being gone for hours, waking me to bring her inside when she was finally through roaming the night woods. I knew each time she was about to pull this stunt: she lifted her nose to sniff, then (probably only *pretending* to smell something) ears back (totally ignoring my irate calls of, "Get back here!"), tore off into the darkness. Geez, that was irritating. In rain, sleet or snow as often as in pleasant weather, she heeded some siren song of the wild that all our other dogs managed to ignore, if they heard it at all. The bad part, of course, was that I knew I would be waked up in the wee hours by that sharp, pretentious little bark of hers, which she would keep up until I got up and let Her Highness in. My goal of a good night's sleep was doomed at that point, and it always made me mad.

Fretzel, at age 2½, one night departed from his usual bedtime routine. Instead of sharing the usual short run around the house with the Border collies, and squirting on one of Mary's favorite flowers, he stood a short ways from me for a while, finally lifted his head, sniffed, laid his ears back, and charged off into the darkness. *Oh, no*, I thought. *You have* got *to be kidding*. Just as quickly and quietly as had Scamp before him, he was gone. Like Scamp, he would bark from some distance not that far from me or the house some time later, before I was asleep. But when I got out of my warm, cozy bed, stalked outside (muttering all the way) and called him, he, *à la Scamp* merely used my voice to re-charge his batteries, and off he blasted in yet another direction, invisible in the blackness. Then, back in bed and having been asleep again for a little while, I was awakened by that sharp little "Bark!" which he kept up until I got up and let His Royal Fretzelship in. I thought (hoped) this might be just an aberration, but no, like Scamp before him, young Fretzel had quickly made this a new bedtime routine. So, no longer trusting that he was responsibly in charge of himself at a late hour, I began putting him on a leash to do his business at bedtime.

Trying to make some logical sense out of this, I have speculated that he was just emerging from puppyhood to try to establish his place in the ongoing job of protecting the realm: whereas Charley did that during the daytime, perhaps Fretzel was assigning himself that job at night. I think that's a good theory; but it's the exact mannerisms that he employs that suggest something else is at work here.

****

The river of life flows on. Fueled by love—the strongest of ties, that flow can take many forms. If we allow ourselves to be attentive to it, life has more magic in it than reason would have us believe. Through years of everyday encounters, we learned that from the dogs of Meadowbrook.

Printed in the United States
131922LV00003B/197/P